Making Freedom *is a beautifully crafted five-volume sourcebook for classroom use. In its presentation of primary sources and learning strategies it has no rival in the area of African American history. This handsome, thought-provoking series belongs on the desk of every middle and high school United States history teacher who knows that without African American history there is only a partial and unbalanced United States history.*

GARY B. NASH
*Director, National Center for History in the Schools*
*University of California, Los Angeles*

*The* Making Freedom *Sourcebooks and CDs are a treasure trove of documents, analysis, and resources guaranteed to inspire lively classroom discussion and thoughtful student research. This original collaboration between teachers and scholars offers extraordinary access to the historical and continuing role of African Americans in the shaping of our nation.*

MARILYN RICHARDSON
*Former Curator, Museum of Afro-American History and*
*the African Meeting House, Boston, Massachusetts*

Making Freedom *offers teachers of American history a powerful and compelling teaching tool to help broaden their focus curriculum. The lessons are well crafted and provide students an opportunity to sharpen historical and critical thinking skills in a dynamic, meaningful, and relevant fashion. In the hands of teachers,* Making Freedom *will make a difference.*

JIM PERCOCO
*Author,* Divided We Stand: Teaching
About Conflict in U.S. History

*Developed through a skillful collaboration between scholars and experienced social studies teachers and curriculum specialists—and covering a span of time from medieval Jenne-Jeno to 1970—this excellent five-volume set is built around firsthand evidence (mostly written documents but also many visual materials). Undoubtedly it will be a valuable classroom resource for students and teachers alike.*

ROBERT L. HALL
*Department of African-American Studies*
*Northeastern University, Boston, Massachusetts*

*For many students, the fact that the past was made up of real people who made real decisions about issues that are not far different from ones that we face today rarely comes through in the textbooks that they use. Primary Source's* Making Freedom *helps open the history classroom to the lives of many different types of people. The range of documents and the tips on how to use them creatively give a real opportunity for teachers to help their students understand the past and its relevance to today.*

STEVEN D. COHEN
*Education Department, Tufts University*

*The curricula within these sourcebooks was developed by some of the most creative educators I have ever met. We are truly excited about sharing them with you.*

Rachel Zucker wrote "Paul Robeson" and "The Black Press" in Sourcebook 5

*I have found as both an educator and an administrator that I have learned more of my own history by being involved in this historical project. For teachers of color, it will be most helpful in the classroom where we can share the true stories of African American culture and help to correct some misinformation of the past. After all, African American history IS American history.*

Deborah Ward contributed to "The Exodusters—Ho for Kansas!" in Sourcebook 4

*I use primary sources in my curriculum because the students become more engaged in the process of discovering history for themselves. They are fascinated by reading and deciphering the art, documents, letters, diary entries, and law codes written in centuries past. I feel these exercises encourage students to empathize with people of the past and to better understand complex aspects of history. History comes alive!*

Laurel Starks wrote "The Slave Experience: Their Words and Others" and "Slavery and Resistance" in Sourcebook 3

*I recall deciding in the fourth grade that history was not for me or about me. It definitely did not make me feel connected to anything. The lessons I wrote in the Primary Source Black Yankees Seminar (subsequently a part of the series) gave me an exciting rebirth experience that forged a connection for me and turned on my search for historical truth. The* Making Freedom *series empowers teachers to make history come alive for students of all ages.*

Deborah Gray wrote "Slave Literacy" and contributed to "Schooling of Free Blacks—The Roots of 'Separate But Equal'" in Sourcebook 3

*I found that using these primary source materials with my students helped them understand more thoroughly the issues and complexities of the time periods being studied. Students and I use the key questions and organizing ideas to focus and guide our thinking through the many activities and assessments provided by the Sourcebooks. Students are engaged in the work and seek additional information to increase their knowledge of history.*

Leslie Kramer wrote a number of lessons in Sourcebook 1, including "Sugar and Slaves," "Riverine Craft—Bringing the Skills Over," and "Resistance and Rebellions"

*Writing lessons for the* Making Freedom *series represented the ideal scholarly endeavor: I could use my research and analytic skills to get to the heart of the topic and then draw on my teaching experience to present the material in a meaningful way to students. I appreciate being able to give students this opportunity to immerse themselves in the richness and subtlety of history.*

Mark Meier wrote "Urban Disturbances" and "Many Roads to Freedom" in Sourcebook 5

# Making Freedom

## African Americans in U.S. History

### SOURCEBOOK 1

# True to Our Native Land

## Beginnings to 1770

Making Freedom

African Americans in U.S. History

SOURCEBOOK 1

# True to Our Native Land

Beginnings to 1770

COMPILED AND EDITED BY
THE CURRICULUM SPECIALISTS AT
PRIMARY SOURCE, INC.

FOREWORD BY
JAMES OLIVER HORTON

HEINEMANN
PORTSMOUTH, NH

**Heinemann**

A division of Reed Elsevier Inc.

361 Hanover Street

Portsmouth, NH 03801–3912

www.heinemann.com

*Offices and agents throughout the world*

Acknowledgments for borrowed material can be found beginning on p. 208.

**Library of Congress Cataloging-in-Publication Data**

Making freedom : African Americans in U.S. history / compiled and edited by the curriculum specialists at Primary Source, Inc. ; foreword by James Oliver Horton.

   p.  cm.

  Includes bibliographical references.

  ISBN 0-325-00515-X (v. 1 : acid-free paper) — ISBN 0-325-00516-8 (v. 2 : acid-free paper) — ISBN 0-325-00517-6 (v. 3 : acid-free paper) —

  ISBN 0-325-00518-4 (v. 4 : acid-free paper) — ISBN 0-325-00519-2 (v. 5: acid-free paper)

  1. African Americans—History—Study and teaching.  2. African Americans—History—Sources.  I. Primary Source, Inc.

E184.7.M34 2004

973'.0496073'0071—dc22                          2003024628

*Editor for Heinemann:* Danny Miller

*Editor for Primary Source:* Liz Nelson

*Production service:* Lisa Garboski, bookworks

*Production coordinator:* Vicki Kasabian

*CD production:* Marla Berry and Nicole Guay

*Interior and cover design:* Catherine Hawkes, Cat & Mouse

*Typesetter:* TechBooks

*Manufacturing:* Steve Bernier

Printed in the United States of America on acid-free paper

08 07 06 05 04 VP 1 2 3 4 5

The Making Freedom *series is dedicated to the memory of*

## Clara Hicks,

*a former school principal in Newton, Massachusetts,*
*and a colleague at Primary Source.*
*She served briefly as a Project Administrator for this series*
*and has left us a legacy of wisdom and joy.*

*Primary Source has created the* Making Freedom *Sourcebooks*
*thanks to the generosity of these contributors:*

*National Endowment for the Humanities*
*Germeshausen Foundation*
*LEF Foundation*
*Massachusetts Foundation for the Humanities*
*Wellspring Foundation*
*and many individual donors*

# Lift Ev'ry Voice and Sing

JAMES WELDON JOHNSON

Lift ev'ry voice and sing,
Till earth and heaven ring,
Ring with the harmonies of Liberty;
Let our rejoicing rise
High as the list'ning skies,
Let it resound loud as the rolling sea.
Sing a song full of the faith that the dark past has taught us,
Sing a song full of the hope that the present has brought us;
Facing the rising sun of our new day begun,
Let us march on till victory is won.

Stony the road we trod,
Bitter the chast'ning rod,
Felt in the days when hope unborn had died;
Yet with a steady beat,
Have not our weary feet
Come to the place for which our fathers sighed?
We have come over a way that with tears has been watered,
We have come, treading our path through the blood of the slaughtered,
Out from the gloomy past,
Till now we stand at last
Where the white gleam of our bright star is cast.

God of our weary years,
God of our silent tears,
Thou who hast brought us thus far on the way;
Thou who hast by Thy might,
Led us into the light,
Keep us forever in the path, we pray.
Lest our feet stray from the places, our God, where we met Thee,
Lest our hearts, drunk with the wine of the world, we forget Thee;
Shadowed beneath Thy hand,
May we forever stand,
True to our God,
True to our native land.

# Contents

## Part I  ✣  Geographic, Historical, and Cultural Contexts

*How can maps and mapping activities be used to set geographical, historical, and cultural contexts? What defines the transatlantic slave trade? What trading patterns existed in Africa before Europeans arrived? How did the transtlantic slave trade develop? How did Europeans' demand for slaves affect Africans?*

## Part II  ✣  Personal Narratives

*How can first-person stories help us rediscover and investigate important dimensions of history? How do the personal narratives of Olaudah Equiano, Ayuba Suliman Diallo, and Venture Smith broaden our understanding of Africans in early*

*Colonial America? What did they have in common? What was unique to each man's experience? How does hearing these voices change our perspective on the past?*

## Part III ✳ Slavery: Changes Over Time

*How did slavery begin in Colonial America? What were the economic, social, and legal parameters of slavery in the seventeenth century? How and why did the institution change over time? How and why did it vary from region to region? What were the economic benefits of slavery to white people and to the development of the colonies? What can we learn about the skills and individuality of enslaved peoples in the colonies?*

## Part IV ✳ Preserving African Cultural Elements

*How can we learn about cultures from artifacts, speech, and music? In what ways did Africans preserve their cultures in America? What are appropriate ways to interpret the historical evidence: religious beliefs and practices; food and cooking; oral traditions such as singing, praying, and storytelling; tools and technologies; and creative expressions? To what extent did Native Americans, Africans, and Europeans exchange skills, knowledge, and traditions?*

## Part V ✳ Individual and Group Agency

*In what ways did African Americans advocate for their freedom? How did they organize, support, and express the demand for freedom? What were the life stories of free people of color in later Colonial America, such as Lucy Terry Prince and Amos Fortune? What developments shaped acts of resistance, such as the 1739 Stono Rebellion and the New York City slave riots of 1741? What gains toward freedom were made during the Colonial period?*

# Foreword

JAMES OLIVER HORTON

GEORGE WASHINGTON UNIVERSITY

The most exciting thing about history is the likelihood of discovery. Documents from the past—official papers, letters, diaries, newspapers, and maps—are windows into the public and private worlds of those who came before us, those who prepared the society that has shaped our lives.

The documents, lessons, and context essays in this book focus on the lives and experiences of African American people in the history of the United States. They make clear the importance of race in the formation of American culture and society. Through these documents and the interpretive essays that place them in historical context, *Making Freedom* illustrates a more inclusive American history, revealing the interracial, multicultural historical experience that Americans lived. It makes the critical point that African American history is American history made by Americans in America.

Every American has been—and continues to be—shaped by African and African American cultural heritage and its interaction with the multitude of other cultural heritages that have combined to form American culture. These documents help us to see the world of the past through the eyes of those who lived in that world and to understand the events of their time as they did. They enable us to appreciate the role of race in shaping American assumptions and expectations and understand the interconnection between the meaning of American freedom and the limitations Americans imposed on that freedom. If we are ever to have a successful conversation on race in today's society, it is essential that we come to terms with these issues.

Historical documents can bring history to life at a time when America needs a historical context for its contemporary concerns. Unfortunately, Americans are undereducated about their past, and our public school system has not successfully addressed this problem. If, as Thomas Jefferson believed, an educated citizenry is essential for the maintenance of democracy, America is in trouble.

Recent surveys make clear the critical need for better history education. The U.S. Department of Education reports that 60 percent of the nation's high school seniors cannot demonstrate even a fundamental knowledge of U.S. history. This ignorance is especially glaring on the subject of race. More than half of the students could not identify Africa as the continent from which people were brought to be enslaved in the Western Hemisphere. Almost two-thirds could not correctly identify the term "Jim Crow" as the set of laws that enforced racial segregation, and less than one quarter could explain the purpose of the Fifteenth Amendment as a Constitutional protection against discrimination in voting, even when the wording of the amendment was provided to them.

If there was ever a time to enhance history education, that time is now. The documents in this book do just that, and the accompanying lesson plans suggest effective teaching strategies. From first-hand accounts of the Atlantic slave trade, to descriptions of black seafaring communities after the Revolution, to the wartime experiences of black Civil War soldiers, to the emergence of the Harlem Renaissance, *Making Freedom* presents a compelling and dramatic American story. It introduces the major concerns and events of the African American experience and the significance of race in America. These documents transport students back in time and allow them to discover the past in its own words and on its own terms.

Standard history textbooks provide information about the past that is important, but too often less than engaging. These documents and lessons are as lively and interesting as the human struggles they portray. Whereas textbooks frequently separate African Americans from the general American experience, *Making Freedom* places African American history at the center of the broad sweep of national history.

Most important, it helps us to evaluate America's past through a reading of direct historical evidence. Students will come to understand history through their personal investigation. This critical component of learning can add excitement and meaning to the educational experience. Students become more than simply consumers of historical information. They move closer to being historians and begin to understand the excitement of historical discovery.

Most of us who have become professional historians remember the moment when history became something more than a list of names and events, when it became an adventurous search for meaning. At the moment when facts become not simply significant in themselves but inspiring bits of evidence to be used in building a case for historical interpretation, we started to feel like real historians, detectives on the trail of history.

When students feel like historical detectives they will have less trouble remembering the significant fundamentals of history and they will appreciate the importance of the past.

Those who understand how exciting history is and understand its meaning for the present and the future never find it boring. Instead, they become lifelong learners of history. The documents in *Making Freedom* open a new and exciting world of the past and provide a greater appreciation of the full range of American history and of the lives of the people who made it.

‑‑✳‑‑

# Project Staff

## Primary Source Staff

Anna Roelofs, Project Director
Kathy Bell, Librarian
Renee Covalucci, Picture Research
Abby Detweiler, Program Associate
Jim Diskant, Curriculum Specialist
Kathleen M. Ennis, Executive Director
Betty Hillmon, Kodaly Music Consultant
Eve Lehmann, Permissions Editor
Roberta Logan, Education Director
Rachel Margolis, Program Associate
Brande Martin, Program Associate
Charles Rathbone, Board of Directors
Jesse Ruskin, Music Researcher
Kelly Scott, Program Associate
Martha Shethar, Photo Researcher
Ann Vick-Westgate, Editor

## Interns

Lucia Carballo
Kendra Carpenter
Jessica Kyle Ellis
Mike Fearon
Tracey Graham, Mellon Fellow
Imani Hope
Meredith Katter
Nina Miller
Sam Schwartz

Special thanks to James Jones of Northeastern University for his musical expertise, to Marvin Karp, Benjamin Kendall, Jill Minot-Seabrook, and Anthony Parker for their advice, to The Lovejoy Society, DeKalb, Illinois; and to Pam Matz, librarian at Harvard University.

## Advising Scholars

Frances Smith Foster, Emory University
V. P. Franklin, Columbia University Teachers' College (Evaluator)
Paul Gagnon, Emeritus, Boston University
Gerald Gill, Tufts University
Robert Hall, Northeastern University
Emmett Price, Northeastern University
Heather Cox Richardson, Suffolk University
John Ross, National Center of Afro-American Artists, Boston

## Contributing Scholars

Robert Allison, Suffolk University
Edmund Barry Gaither, Museum of the National Center for African American Artists, Boston
Robert Hayden, Independent Scholar
Betty Hillmon, Park School
James Oliver Horton, George Washington University
Lois Horton, George Mason University
Grey Osterud, Historian
Patrick Rael, Bowdoin College
Marilyn Richardson, Independent Scholar
Julie Richter, Independent Scholar

## Teacher-Authors

Wendell Bourne, Cambridge Public Schools
Phyllis Bretholtz, Teacher/Educational Consultant
Ilene Carver, Boston Public Schools
Monny Cochran, Weston Public Schools
Julie Craven, Cambridge Public Schools
Andrea Doremus Cuetara, Boston Public Schools
Inez Dover, Newton Public Schools
Kathleen Drew, Cambridge Public Schools
Sharon Fleming, Abington Public Schools
Linda Forman, Framingham Public Schools
Richard Berry Fulton, Boston Public Schools
Deborah Gray, Community Educator

Andrea Gross, Westwood Public Schools
Jennifer Hames, Boston Public Schools
Deborah Hood-Brown, Cambridge Public Schools
Leslie Kramer, Cambridge Public Schools
Roberta Logan, Boston Public Schools
Peter Lowber, Malden Public Schools
Mark Meier, University of Virginia
Nicole Miller, Westborough Public Schools
Martin Milne, Eaglebrook School, Deerfield
Edward Morrison, Winthrop Public Schools
Melisa Nasella, Lincoln-Sudbury Public Schools
Karl Netter, Boston Public Schools
Catherine O'Connor, Newton Country Day School
Alexandria Pearson, Metro Director, Natick High School
Gwynne Alexandra Sawtelle, Westborough Public Schools
Andrew Shen, Lincoln-Sudbury Public Schools
Laurel Starks, Milton Academy
Sandra Stuppard, Boston Public Schools
Deborah Ward, Wellesley Public Schools
Joseph Zellner, Concord Public Schools
Rachel Zucker, Burlington Public Schools

⤝⚔⤞

# Introduction

*Making Freedom: African Americans in U.S. History* grew out of the synergy and vision of a group of Boston-area teachers, several scholars, and the program staff of Primary Source. Beginning in 1995 with a series of seminars on "Black Yankees" of the eighteenth and nineteenth centuries, the project grew and expanded to reach across the country and over time, up to the last quarter of the twentieth century.

Fortunately for all of us who see history as discovery, continuing scholarship is illuminating almost four centuries of African American thought, creativity, and activism in the social, political, and cultural development of our nation. Although work has been going on for years at the university level to understand the ways in which African American ideas and experiences influenced the development of our national culture and political ideology, little of this new thinking has yet become part of the standard school curriculum. The traditional historical narrative forming the basis of content for precollege students often relegates the study of African American history to separate units on slavery or to the struggle for civil rights. *Making Freedom* offers precollegiate teachers and their students exposure to exciting and informed scholarship on 400 years of history, thus strengthening the content and adjusting the lens through which African American history is viewed and understood.

The *Making Freedom* sourcebooks contain information and materials that demonstrate at least two important phenomena: the social agency and intellectual achievement shown throughout African American history from the colonial period forward and the inextricable relationship of African Americans to the collective history and cultural development of the United States. The primary sources contained in these sourcebooks reveal a diversity of perspectives and experiences among African Americans from their first arrival in British North America. In contemporary textbooks, slavery is often presented as a singular experience that shaped the character of all African Americans. *Making Freedom* intentionally illuminates the variety of the slave experience for African Americans, focusing both on individual ideas and actions and on collective efforts to hold America accountable to the ideals of freedom and equality.

Through the speeches and writings of scholars and activists, slave narratives, poetry, fiction, music, and fine arts, revealing agency in the face of repression,

*Making Freedom* illumines the ways in which Africans and African Americans have influenced American thought and cultural expression, as well as our traditions of freedom and democracy.

*Making Freedom:*

❖ provides teachers with multidisciplinary scholarship, primary source materials, and lesson plans concerning African American history from fourteenth-century Africa through the Civil Rights Movement of the 1970s

❖ presents this new material in ways that stimulate teachers and students to ask questions about how the intellectual history of African Americans relates to mainstream history and provokes a deeper understanding of the achievements and frustrations of African Americans in the pursuit of a lived freedom

❖ inspires teachers, who in turn inspire students, to become active learners, engaged in the process of historical research and community exploration, to tolerate both conflict and ambiguity in the historical narrative, and to learn more about themselves and others in an increasingly complex, pluralistic world

❖ addresses a variety of issues—scholarship, teaching strategies, and diverse student preparations for understanding history—and pulls them all together into a useful resource

❖ increases understanding and teaching capacity of both experienced and novice teachers for presenting the powerful and integral role of African American intellectual history in American history

The history of minorities *is* American history—to leave it out or mention it peripherally deprives students and teachers alike, giving an incomplete and often a false view of our past. Both majority and minority students gain from learning a more holistic story. Because mainstream history is often restricted to the story of one dominant group, complicating what is taught as history becomes a vital and legitimate goal for anyone seriously concerned with historical accuracy.

## How This Series Was Created

In the summer of 1998, with financial support from the National Endowment for the Humanities, an enthusiastic group of teachers and scholars met to imagine and then to begin to create a multipart series of curriculum sourcebooks. We formed into working groups, each with a scholar, teachers, and a curriculum specialist.

Since its inception, the project has been informed by emerging scholarship in African American history and the growing availability of primary source materials to the general public. History has been described as a funnel—lots of stories go in, but only a few emerge to be told. Our goal is to enlarge the mainstream narrative for teachers and students, offering an inclusive history that places African Americans among the founders and shapers of our culture. *Making Freedom* uncovers stories of African American agency and intellectual vision and demonstrates how this intellectual history catalyzed movements such as abolition and civil rights and contributed to new interpretations of the Constitution. Recognizing that some of the primary source testimony of African Americans is in nonliterary form, primary source documents may be in the form of original artworks and musical scores that illustrate African American contributions to the development of American art, folk culture, and religious traditions.

Although one major thrust of this curriculum initiative is related to content, there are pedagogical objectives as well. Teachers and students need tools and strategies to enable the process of discovery and to encourage investment in learning. By using these sourcebooks, teachers can help their students become active participants in history. Through reading firsthand, authentic accounts of moments in history, looking at an engraving or listening to a piece of music, students are moved to ask questions and learn to formulate their own opinions about a person, an issue, or an event.

As we designed *Making Freedom* and began to draft materials, we drew heavily upon James Banks' paradigm for transforming curriculum. Banks' model shifts the perspective away from a conventionally focused study to reveal a more inclusive and far more interesting array of interrelated content. Offering a variety of activities and nontextbook, original source material, this approach lays the groundwork for teachers to transform their teaching goals and methods.

## Who We Are

Primary Source, a teacher resource center in Watertown, Massachusetts, promotes education in the humanities that is historically accurate, culturally inclusive, and explicitly concerned with ethical issues such as racism and other forms of discrimination. Its services link university and school and combine scholarly research from original sources with practical knowledge of how adults and students learn. Through institutes, seminars, and conferences, Primary Source models an active, interdisciplinary approach to teaching. Primary Source offers educators intellectual enrichment and opportunities to participate in serious, professional dialogue with scholars and other classroom teachers.

Primary Source supports teachers' efforts to restructure their social studies teaching by serving as a conduit for primary source materials that reveal the voices of people from various ethnic, racial, and cultural groups within the United States and from countries around the world. Once these original source documents are brought to light and their intellectual and creative accomplishments are revealed, curriculum content is necessarily more inclusive of both genders and all racial and ethnic groups. Students may then see themselves in the curriculum and feel more connected to the educational process, to a cultural past, and to a civic future.

## Using Primary Sources

The organization Primary Source takes its name from the same term used by historians to distinguish original, uninterpreted material from secondary or third-hand accounts. Thus a photograph, a memoir, or a letter is a primary source; an essay interpreting the photograph or memoir is usually, though not always, a secondary source. A textbook, still further removed, is a tertiary source.

In some instances, the same document or other piece of evidence may be a primary source in one investigation and secondary in another. For example, Henry Wadsworth Longfellow's poem "Paul Revere's Ride" is a primary source when it is considered as a reflection of how nineteenth-century citizens romanticized the Revolutionary War. It is not, however, a primary source that provides information about the events of April 18–19, 1775. (Paul Revere never did arrive in Concord.)

*Making Freedom* utilizes a range of primary sources. Included are maps, travel journals, letters, illustrations, engravings and other kinds of art, business records, diaries, wills, autobiographies, contemporary biography, advertisements (including those for the sale or recapture of slaves), music (including folk songs), and photographs of artifacts.

Although it is imperative to read secondary sources in order to understand context and background, introducing students to "the real stuff" raises student interest and curiosity and offers opportunities for students to make discoveries on their own. The closer students get to real people's lives, the better chance they have to formulate real questions and to care about people and events from another time and place. In a March 2002 speech to members of the Boston Athenaeum, historian David McCullough advised, "To understand the people of a particular historical period, you have to read what they read, not just what they wrote. You have to listen to the music, look at the paintings . . . ."

When textbooks are used as the only source of information, it is much more difficult for students to take ownership, both of their own learning and of a particular body of knowledge. It is very difficult to remember other people's generalizations or conclusions. Original source material provides students with rich opportunities for inquiry, the chance to move from concrete to abstract thinking and back again.

## Teaching About Race

In the 1990s, a national dialogue about race was initiated by the Clinton administration. This endeavor was not widely covered in the media, and it is difficult to assess what was accomplished. The creators of this series believe that in order to bring about healing of a shameful national past, a dialogue about race needs to begin at the classroom level and be carried out into the world by students grounded in an honest study of history and committed to social justice.

### We Are All Involved

The seeds of ignorant, biased, and racist opinions and feelings are often sown in children as they grow up, through families, the media, friendships, and even schools and religious institutions. Although students are not to blame for bringing ignorant opinions into the classroom, we must all now be accountable for attitudes and actions we take into the future. Discussions of racism often focus on blacks and other people of color as victims, essentially making it a black problem. The question of racism's cost to white people is rarely raised. Yet racism presents a serious challenge to any individual's ability to reason, make sound judgments, and develop perspective.

## Individual Discovery

In studying the racial history of this country, we see that many painful things have happened in the past and continue to happen today in many communities. In general, students lack accurate information, ways to analyze this information as well as their own feelings and experiences, and an ability to articulate their analysis. Our job as teachers and students is to uncover the prejudices that exist in our institutions, our culture, and ourselves and to revisit our history in a careful, inclusive, and truthful manner. As a more accurate understanding of our complicated racial history is achieved, students can express their new knowledge in a variety of ways, as the activities in the lessons suggest. Finally, they can be encouraged to take action to address issues of unfairness in their schools and communities.

Depending on the composition of the class, there may be students who feel particularly vulnerable or targeted by the material discussed on a given day. Typically, students of color become angry and aggressive, while white students feel guilty and defensive. In addition, students who are of mixed race may feel conflicted. All students should be encouraged to express their thoughts and feelings; students learn a great deal from each other.

Giving students ample time to reflect in writing on what they have learned is a good outlet for feelings and is also a way to discover a student who may be having an especially difficult time. A piece of private reflective writing may reveal conflicts appropriate for the whole class to discuss or individual conflicts that need to be responsibly addressed by the teacher.

## Class Discussion

Students seldom have the opportunity to engage in critical, analytical discussions about race. Our role as educators is to provide them with the information and tools to do so constructively. Students can be engaged in setting class guidelines for discussion of controversial subjects. Some examples follow.

1. All opinions and expressions of feelings and emotions are accepted and respected in class, whether other students share them or not.

2. Opinions and feelings expressed on sensitive topics should be kept within the confines of the classroom, not discussed elsewhere.

3. Students should speak from their own experience, using "I-statements" as much as possible. This simply means that students should start with, "I think, I heard, I believe, I feel . . . " rather than "You're wrong because . . ." The former prompts reflection, whereas the latter can feel like a direct attack on another speaker.

4. Students should know also that it is fine to choose *not* to speak.

## How to Use This Book

*Making Freedom* is intended for use as a resource in all American history classes at the middle and high school levels. This series enables teachers to weave the African American story into and throughout the wider narrative. We have purposely emphasized individuals and events that are not often included in standard American history textbooks. Our purpose is to widen and deepen the narrative, not to repeat the few names and incidents already familiar to most teachers and students.

The five *Making Freedom* curriculum sourcebooks provide innovative, intellectually compelling curriculum materials that fit into the conventional scope and sequence. The sourcebooks specifically examine the African American intellectual tradition in the context of the following historical eras: (1) Colonial America; (2) Revolution and Forging the Nation; (3) Antebellum Reform; (4) Civil War and Reconstruction; and (5) The Gilded Age into the Twentieth Century. The five sourcebooks, with titles from "Lift Ev'ry Voice and Sing" by James Weldon Johnson, are:

> *True to Our Native Land:* Beginnings to 1770
>
> *A Song Full of Hope:* 1770–1830
>
> *Lift Ev'ry Voice:* 1830–1860
>
> *Our New Day Begun:* 1861–1877
>
> *March On Till Victory:* 1877–1970

**Each book contains the following:**

- ❖ a table of contents for the series
- ❖ one or two context essays written by scholars
- ❖ lesson plans, including primary sources
- ❖ a glossary

The accompanying CD-ROM includes all primary source materials, supplementary materials, and a time line and annotated bibliography for the entire series.

**Each lesson contains**

- ❖ Introduction
- ❖ Organizing Idea
- ❖ Student Objectives
- ❖ Key Questions
- ❖ Primary Source Materials
- ❖ Vocabulary
- ❖ Student Activities
- ❖ Further Student and Teacher Resources
- ❖ Contemporary Connections

Several lessons also include music selections.

Together, the **context essays** at the beginning of each book and the **introductions** to individual lessons provide background information necessary for understanding the primary sources and engaging in the activities. Teachers can use this introductory material in a variety of ways. For example, they can have the students read the introductions in their entirety, present the information in a brief lecture, create background information sheets with key points, or ask students working in groups to research the answers to questions that create a context for the lesson.

**Vocabulary lists** with topical words are included, and the words are defined in the **glossary**. In many instances, given the historical period of the documents, additional vocabulary lists are provided under supplementary materials to help students better understand what they read.

Each lesson includes a variety of teaching strategies designed to engage student interest. Suggested **activities** include study and analysis of primary sources, mapping, research and writing, debating, creating graphic displays, and role-plays that involve assumption of a particular perspective, sometimes an unpopular or (in the twenty-first century) an unacceptable one. This activity needs to be understood as an attempt to see things as they were in a particular time in the past. The challenge is to try not to view all events from the perspective and values of today. When an activity calls for speculation or analysis, it is important to have verifying information available close at hand—in the classroom, the school library, or online. A speculation exercise is not a standalone activity, but, together with research to clarify information and verify a theory, it gives students the opportunity to act as historians.

Because the context essays and lessons were written by a group of scholars and teachers, they offer a variety of writing and instructional approaches. Although the format for all the lessons is the same, we have respected the authors' voices and have not edited them to a uniform length or style. The lessons vary in length and level of detail and offer a choice of activities.

We would not expect teachers to use every activity in every lesson. Rather, they should choose those lessons—and, within the lessons, those activities—that dovetail best with their instructional plan and meet the needs and learning styles of their students. We have set out a buffet—we do not intend for all of it to be consumed by each teacher.

A list of **further resources** is provided with most lessons. Although every effort has been made to ensure that references to websites are current, they do change. Teachers may wish to check URLs before giving students assignments. Students should also be cautioned to evaluate information found in a website carefully, checking who is the author and who sponsors the site.

Each lesson includes a **contemporary connection**. Our intent is to demonstrate that the issues raised by studying the primary sources do not pertain only to the past. Some remain the same; others have been transmuted a little. This feature gives resources and often asks open-ended questions for further exploration.

Some of the **primary source materials** are difficult for students to read. They have been set in type, but no changes have been made to the original language. As a result, the documents contain syntax with which students may not be familiar, as well as vocabulary no longer in active use or for which meaning has shifted. Sometimes words are spelled differently. Each teacher knows best how to adapt a lesson to students' skill levels. The books include suggestions, such as having students work in pairs or small groups, reading the documents aloud to the class, and/or providing vocabulary definitions before students tackle the documents.

The lengthier documents have been abbreviated in the sourcebooks. All **primary source materials** appear in full on the accompanying CD-ROMs and can be printed out for classroom use.

This *Adinkra* symbol represents the Akan belief that we must look at and learn from the past in order to move with wisdom into the future. It teaches people to value and protect their cultural heritage.

# African to African American

EDMUND BARRY GAITHER

## Introduction

The story of how Africans, in successive waves over nearly five centuries, were molded into African Americans in the United States is above all a human story. It arises from the aggregation of millions of personal narratives shaped by powerful socioeconomic and political forces played out over time between Europe, Africa, and the Americas during the shaping of the modern, capitalist world. The result was the creation of a new people bound together within new social configurations forged in a crucible of horrific experiences and a dawning racial consciousness.

## The Situation in Africa

To understand and appreciate the complexity of this extraordinary drama requires careful study of the African sociocultural and physical environment before and during the period of transatlantic slavery, review of the economic and political forces that fueled European expansion and colonization, reconstruction of the conditions of the Middle Passage, examination of the various and varied circumstances in which Africans found themselves once they were on American soil and, finally, analysis of the myriad responses which they, by their own volition, made in adapting to their new settings. Additional challenge is presented by the fact that all these processes evolved over time and differed by degrees—and sometimes in kind—from region to region or colonial overlord to colonial overlord.

Prior to the late fifteenth century and the commencement of transatlantic slavery, the vast continent of Africa was theatre to numerous and shifting demographic groupings organized in an enormous variety of polities ranging from small clusters of related villages to vast  kingdoms with courts, royalty, and substantial wealth. Although situated on a single land mass, these peoples reckoned their distinctiveness along ethnic lines, because no compelling need had arisen to require that they define a continental identity. Operational social forces included kinship, religion, and shared cultural traditions. The notion of race did not exist, because here again, no compelling need required it. Africans from different ethnic groups generally lived in relative peace with each other as they met the ongoing demands of securing food, providing shelter, and maintaining their cultural integrity, but there were also wars and other conflicts over resources, wealth creation, expansion, and power. Such conflicts are ubiquitous in human experience. Occasionally, these conflicts were sustained and disruptive and wreaked havoc over large areas. Within Africa itself, these conflicts could lead to the enslavement of the vanquished, that is, work obligations might be imposed and freedoms circumscribed; however, the condition of slavery did not usually carry a permanent stigma, nor did it seek to dehumanize its victims. In these traits, African slavery was not unlike varieties of slavery widely found throughout the ancient world.

Slavery as a commercial, international enterprise flourished in the Byzantine Empire (395–1453) as Arab merchants developed markets throughout the Eastern Mediterranean and as far away as Turkey. Their endeavors also placed slaves in the caliphates of Spain. Other Africans—non-slaves—could be found in small numbers in other European countries, often, but not always, working in personal service. Thus, slavery was not new to Africans, but they could not have anticipated the full implications of its transatlantic manifestation when they began to facilitate it.

Following initial contacts between Europeans and coastal African kingdoms in the late fifteenth century, groundwork was laid for what was to become the sustained horror of slave trading across the Atlantic. Coastal kings, in exchange for goods ranging from guns to imported cloths and beads, permitted the construction of slave castles or forts along the Atlantic edge of Africa, and these forts became the holding pens for human cargo consisting largely of Africans captured in wars. Later, some of these captives proved to be unfortunates seized in raids primarily stimulated by the demand for labor in the Americas, for it seems clear that complicity in the African slave trade caused much internecine bloodshed and general social implosion. The provision of enslaved Africans by Africans accounts for only part of the draining of the continent, because in some regions, such as below the Bight of Benin, European slavers conducted raids directly, securing slaves without intermediaries.

Despite the apparent attractiveness of European goods and weaponry, many African groups refused to be seduced into the slave trade, and still others organized resistance to this encroachment. Of course, those whose lives were directly interrupted by slavers resisted heartily, fearing not only the loss of their freedom but also the chasm of the unknown and the rumors of the horrors that might befall someone taken in this voracious, new catastrophe.

Enslaved Africans awaiting the ships that would transport them to the Americas began the fusion that was to prove crucial to surviving the Middle Passage ordeal and that would, for a generation, provide the basis of a new fraternity. Whether from different, similar, or the same language groups, these men, women, and children were forced into a community of bondage. Later, aboard the crowded ships, they would be forced into an inescapable intimacy that virtually robbed them of the barest human dignity, stripping away minimum privacy and crushing volition to the maximum extent possible. In this context, suicide and revolt rivaled disease in shortening life. The horror of the Middle Passage, which could extend over months as ships sought to fill their holds before setting sail for the Americas, would etch itself on those later remembered as shipmates as indelibly as the brands burned into their bodies by the ship captains. Indeed, before captives left Africa for the crossing referred to as the Middle Passage, they had already begun to form new bonds of community which anticipated the process that would—in the end—make Africans in America into African Americans.

Research over the last few decades has clarified the regions from which enslaved men and women were brought to North America, allowing us to achieve relatively good agreement regarding ship routes, numbers transported, and even ethnic groups represented. Closer examination of records pertaining to the early presence of Africans in British North America has given us a richer understanding of differing situations in which blacks found themselves and of the strategies that they adopted in order to preserve their humanity. Still richer is our widening appreciation of the complexities of black situations as their numbers grew both before and following the American Revolution. Fresh light has been thrown on such previously underdiscussed topics as the relationship between African-born and American-born black people over the extended period when both were substantially represented in the demographic mix or how African ethnic identities were supplanted by an ascending consciousness of African Americans. Behind all these explorations are narratives of personal lives characterized, in the main, by longing for freedom and human dignity often translated as respect; autonomy (i.e., ability to secure an arena where individual volition or will could be exercised); belonging (i.e., the joy of family, and communal supports); creativity (i.e., the will to express the life of the imagination through artistic and cultural forms); and spirituality (i.e., the sense of relationship to forces that give meaning to life through ritual acts and symbolic exchanges).

The earliest presence of Africans in colonial America was a thin distribution of black people stretching from Virginia through the mid-Atlantic colonies to New England. Some of these black people were slaves, but many were indentured servants comparable in status to white indentured servants from Europe. They worked at assorted tasks, including domestic service, agriculture, and manufacturing, and frequently they lived within or nearby their master's household. In European American towns, individuals existed in cultural isolation, which doubtlessly eroded recollection of African cultural practices. Such losses must have been painful, because, as soon as numbers permitted, Africans sought each other's company and stamped their imprint on early American holidays such as Pinkster's Day, observed in upstate New York.

By the turn of the eighteenth century, the numbers of Africans introduced into the Carolinas, Chesapeake Bay, and the mid-Atlantic colonies was growing dramatically, and with such growth came a greatly changed social landscape. Despite the severe limitations imposed by the institution of slavery, enslaved African-born and American-born black people increasingly merged into a single elastic community eager to establish and maintain families, increase arenas of personal volition, and develop strategies for resisting the coercion that was their daily lot. Although small communities of free black people were always present throughout the colonies, they were subject to the racial prejudices that pervaded society. Whites tended to associate them with slaves and indentured servants, even when they asserted their autonomy.

## Plantation Life

By the turn of the eighteenth century, as large-scale plantations spread from the Chesapeake Bay southward, the objective condition of black life became more difficult. Race became a marker for enslavement, and white privilege became the norm. The plantation constituted the principal site where black people could be found, and its organization provided the framework for their lives. Despite the near total power that plantation owners held over their slaves, countervailing forces often restrained the most brutal excesses and rendered the plantation, as an enterprise, dependent upon a modicum of cooperation, or at least compliance, from the slaves. Slaves were able to exert negative pressures ranging from sabotage to slowdowns when they felt especially violated, and these actions could seriously depress productivity and, therefore, profitability, giving them a certain leverage in relation to their masters.

Large plantations, which often employed white overseers to enforce productivity and to assure control of slaves, generally gave wide latitude to these supervisors, who were free to whip or impose discipline on disobedient or recalcitrant black people. Many accounts document great cruelties inflected by drivers, yet it is also clear that many masters and drivers developed grudging respect for willful slaves and sometimes accommodated themselves to a level of productivity and privileges that slaves found acceptable. After all, if the plantation failed, everyone, slaves included, was adversely effected. In some cases, drivers were trusted black people whose experiences were almost certainly plagued with ambivalence: on one hand, they had risen in rank and demonstrated management skills, yet on the other hand, they were agents of the master even though they remained slaves. Perhaps they were better at mediating the divide between the big house and the slave quarters. Some coveted privileges, such as a wider range in which to exercise personal freedoms and judgments, that went with this heightened status. This latitude could be used to favor family and friends within the slave community.

The plantation was largely self-sufficient, meaning that it not only produced agricultural products and practiced animal husbandry but also manufactured many basic necessities, including furniture, tools, and textiles. No substantial work on the plantation was conducted without black workers. Slave blacksmiths made nails, plows, and numerous other implements, as needed. Slave carpenters' skills ranged from constructing houses and barns to cabinetmaking, that is, creating chairs, cupboards, bedsteads, and the like. Many were distinguished as potters, brickmakers, and masons working in brick or stone. In some extraordinary situations, as demonstrated by the African American potters who created the face vessels of Edgefield, South Carolina, works of quite different character seem to have been made for intragroup use, along with ordinary utilitarian ware. Such artisans and craftspeople sometimes were hired out to earn additional money for their master and themselves. They had reason to take pride in the quality of their work, even though the overall context of their productivity remained problematic and their just earnings were controlled by their masters, who generally allowed them to keep part of their wages.

Slaves engaged in artisan and craft endeavors sometimes had the opportunity to build upon skills that were valued in the world of their African ancestors. This was especially true on the rice plantations of South Carolina and Georgia, where the practice of growing rice as well as the related paraphernalia of fanner baskets and mortars and pestles were modeled on West African procedures. In these cases, the operation of the plantation was absolutely dependent upon knowledge that the slaves themselves had brought. Other skills and knowledge that Africans brought, ranging from how to cultivate tobacco to how to navigate swamps, were impressed into service in the South. Boatmen skilled in managing flatboats on swamps and rivers were extremely valuable, because they provided the means of transporting goods in much of the South before railroads were common. Black people predominated in this work. Those who did it not only enjoyed greater freedom compared to agricultural workers but also provided extremely important channels of communication between plantations as well as between plantations and cities.

Much has been made of the presumed breach between field hands and domestic servants, but this case has often been overstated. To be sure, domestic slaves were more finely dressed, performed less strenuous work, and enjoyed more privileges, but they were under the constant supervision of the master's family. This situation imposed its own psychological stresses. Nevertheless, domestic slaves also had a life within the slave community that was beyond the plantation owner's view. It was there that mates could be found and social support secured.

Plantations with many slaves generally provided housing, usually behind the master's house or at a little distance in clusterings referred to as slave quarters. The structures were grossly inferior, offering meager protection from the elements and very limited privacy. The chief virtue of slave quarters was that they were out of the master's view and thus allowed slaves a space where they could exercise control. Here they could speak to each other as they wished, find mates, exercise the prerogatives of family life, and socialize their children into the cultural forms that defined them as African American. Within the slave community itself, there were divisions. Recalling directly or via memories passed down from their parents, slaves who shared ethnic traditions could enjoy special relationships. The elderly, given the high regard accorded them in almost all African traditions, were rewarded with genuine respect. Persons believed to have access to ancient knowledge of medicine or magic were duly honored and sought out or feared. Tellers of stories, along with singers and dancers, found places of deep appreciation, because they both extended and reinvented African traditions of dance, music, and storytelling. It was within these dimly lighted nests that the essential elements of African cultural continuities were reinforced and transformed. It was also from within these quarters that African religious retention such as shout rings continued to flourish and evolve.

Not all plantations were large enough to have quarters, but even on smaller plantations where slaves lived closer to, and sometimes worked side by side with, their masters, black people maintained families and households as best they could. They also sought to sustain communication with other black people in their vicinity as well as with any whom they knew in towns or villages. They saw themselves as belonging to a community of black people larger than their own plantation.

Many dimensions of the plantation connected black and white people, and these often provided bridges for human sharing. Floods and droughts affected both, as did other natural calamities and epidemics. Because they were valuable property, the master had to care about the general health of his or her slaves. Moreover, white people were so dependent upon the services of the black people that if slaves were affected by contagion, the master's health and comfort were also endangered. For these reasons, a minimum level of medical attention was provided by the master. Childbirth and death were of much interest to masters and slaves, although for obviously different reasons.

Although plantations normally achieved a certain balance of expectations between masters and slaves, conflict was never far beneath the surface, and whites always harbored some fear of slave resistance and revolts. Slaves had come to understand that in general there were limits they were obliged to respect, but they knew that these limits were unjust and not permanently tolerable. Thus, they were forever devising strategies for subverting white control. Strategies were as abundant as slaves, because every slave asserting even the most trivial dimension of his or her right to freedom had to do so with a guise that would not bring immediate calamity upon his or her head. In the manner of a low-level war, slaves were truculent, uncooperative, insolent, and reluctant to whatever degree that they could muster without provoking dire consequences. Others feigned cooperation and devotion while at the same time undercutting their mistresses and masters. Still others won favors and enjoyed their masters' favor while in fact being involved in numerous duplicities. All these actions belong to a broader strategy of intransigence expressed as chronic underproduction. This design sought to undermine slavery by maximizing its inefficiencies and indirectly eroding masters' control over slaves.

## Slave Resistance and Rebellions

Slaves also resisted their situations directly, engaging in rebellious actions that are more commonly associated with the Caribbean islands and Brazil. For example, numerous documented cases report slaves escaping to Native American communities and there joining forces with resisters, particularly in the swampy lowlands of Georgia and Florida. These black runaways allied themselves with others who, like themselves, were seeking freedom and autonomy. Some black people also escaped to Spanish-controlled Florida and Mexico, where they were offered the promise of freedom. Perhaps the most remarkable resisters were those who sought to organize revolts against their masters, with the aim of taking control of the land and ending the involuntary servitude of their black brothers and sisters.

In South Carolina in the mid-eighteenth century, where black people formed a majority of the population, the Stono Rebellion marked an early effort at change by force. Early nineteenth-century insurrections, such as those planned in 1800 by Gabriel Prosser (1775?–1800) near Richmond, Virginia, and by Denmark Vesey (1767–1822) in Charleston, South Carolina, in 1822, as well as the partially executed revolt in 1831 led by Nat Turner (1800–1831) in Southampton County, Virginia, reveal the deep-seated and seething anger felt by blacks who refused to accept slavery as their natural condition. These men, often inspired by the Bible, the Constitution and Declaration of Independence, and the Haitian Revolution (1791–1802), dared to conceive of literally overthrowing the prevailing power of the slave states. Their ambitions show the power of ideas in hungry imaginations yearning for freedom. Emboldened by the success of the slaves of Saint Domingue in casting off France, a major European colonial overlord, men like Vesey anticipated a consciousness that only fully ripened in the twentieth century. Although unsuccessful, these revolutionaries helped create a narrative of heroic resistance that fueled later black struggle in the United States.

For the most part, revolts were organized from city bases and frequently involved free black people. The vast majority of free black people lived in only a half-dozen cities, such as Charleston, New Orleans, Richmond, and Baltimore. They were precariously placed in the slave-holding states. They sometimes maintained a separate society from slave black people, yet they were not accorded the same status as white people. Sometimes, especially within the creole order of New Orleans, they were educated, employed in trades and the professions, and held real estate, yet more typically, they were a little less grandly placed in the metropolitan centers of the upper and lower South. In these centers, the borders between free and enslaved black people were porous, and many in the former group saw their fate as inseparable from that of their less fortunate brothers and sisters. As part of the forging of African American identity, these groups realized that, in the eyes of the controlling white political and cultural order, they were all inferior.

## African Legacies

Over the centuries of the transatlantic slave trade, different ethnic, cultural, and religious groups were represented in shifting patterns in the cargoes unloaded at such major ports as Newport, Rhode Island; Charleston, New Orleans, and along the Chesapeake Bay. Various qualities were attributed to different groups according to reports current among buyers of slaves and those who ran the slave factories. Within colonial American and later the United States, these views influenced the distribution of slaves by ethnicity, because opinion had established ethnically specific expectations of behavior and skills. Some recent scholars have carefully examined the records in order to clarify the extent to which particular regions were influenced by the presence of large representations from specific ethnic groups. This promises to be a fruitful arena for exploration, because we know from witnesses (WPA interviews with elderly black people who remembered slavery and the immediate postslavery period) that, throughout the entire nineteenth century, many black people still knew others who were born in Africa or retained memories of African languages and cultural practices.

South Carolina and Georgia are extremely rewarding places for historical researchers, because the culture of the Sea Islands (Gullah culture) remained intact for a long period into the twentieth century. The tale of Ibo Landing, for example, not only builds on the Ibo ethnic group as lovers of Africa and of freedom but also underscores the central place of oral tradition in preserving important ideas and values. Specific relationships of language and basketry between the peoples of Sierra Leone and the Sea Islands have bridged the Atlantic and laid the foundation for a new dialogue between populations long lost to each other. Oral traditions and material links tell us that many Muslims were among those enslaved in that region, and this suggests more discussions such as Allen Austin's useful 1997 book, *African Muslims in Antebellum America: Transatlantic Stories and Spiritual Struggles* (New York: Routledge). Artistic documents such as the Harriet Power's "Bible Quilt" at the Museum of Fine Arts, Boston, strongly suggest the influence of the appliqué traditions of old Dahomey or the Akan cultures of Ghana. Likewise, the face vessels of Edgefield, South Carolina, offer vivid testimony to the power of Congo/Angola representations of Nkisi figures. Growing evidence supports the idea that we can bring extraordinary clarity to our understanding of African retentions within African American cultures. In so doing, we gain new depth in our understanding of how those who survived the Middle Passage and their descendants created a complex of cultures in rural and urban settings that, although informed by African elements, was nevertheless peculiarly American. These manifestations, which in their aggregate constitute African American culture, are both a black and an American commonwealth.

Although Africans who were brought to America came with fresh memories of their own ethnic heritages and although some found reinforcement of those traditions through discovering compatriots here, all sooner or later had to accommodate to their new situation and learn usable English and prevailing ways of doing things. Even though differences might have existed within slave communities regarding ethnic roots or in which colony their children were born, circumstances forced recognition of the need to make a common cause. Simple observation made clear that all the black people, whether African-born or not, whether "mixed" or "pure blooded," whether free or slave, were subject to the white people and perceived by white people as inferior to them. Self-worth told the slaves that this was not true and compelled them constantly to revolt in small and large ways in order to assert their volition and declare their humanity. So, despite their disparate origins and their varying intervening experiences, by the late nineteenth century, black people in the United Stated had acquired a consciousness of themselves as a people who, since the Middle Passage, had developed bonds forged by racial discrimination, prejudice, and economic injustice. The totality of these shared experiences has drawn black people into a group with considerable cultural distinctness and for whom Africa remains an ancestral symbolic legacy. Moreover, this specifically American consciousness has broadened itself into a global concept that identifies with all the black peoples of the world and, more generally, with colonized peoples everywhere.

# Slave Societies and Slave-Owning Societies

## Variations in the Institution of Slavery in Colonial America

JULIE RICHTER

## Introduction

The English people who came to the British North American colonies were familiar with the concept of lifetime servitude, but they did not have an established system of slavery to transport to the New World. However, because the colonists needed a cheap and ample supply of labor for their plantations and farms, slavery became legal in all the colonies during the seventeenth century. The institution of slavery in the Chesapeake differed from the slave systems that developed in the Low Country area of South Carolina and in the northern colonies by 1700. These differences reflected the fact that a distinctive way of life and work developed in each of the three regions. By the end of the seventeenth century, Virginia, Maryland, and South Carolina were slave societies—that is, societies in which slavery was the principal institution that shaped life. The Mid-Atlantic and New England colonies were slave-owning societies—societies in which individuals owned slaves, but slavery was not the main institution.

## The Chesapeake Colonies

The English colonists who arrived in Virginia in 1607 found that they had to adapt their way of life to the New World. Factors that made it difficult to recreate English institutions in Virginia included disease, conflicts with the Native Americans, the struggle to find a profitable commodity, and an acute shortage of labor. The colonists endured starvation and malaria and feared attacks by members of Powhatan's chiefdom during the colony's first decade. Their leaders turned to martial law to establish their authority and order in Virginia. They also wanted the colonists, whom they saw as lazy, to grow corn and catch fish, reducing their dependency on trade with the American Indians for food.

The fortunes and direction of the colony changed in 1614 when John Rolfe raised a strain of tobacco that sold in the English market. The men who grew rich from tobacco exploited the labor of others for their own profit. Those who labored in the tobacco plantations of the colony's prosperous residents included people from England, Europe, and Africa.

The first group of Africans—described in a letter written by John Rolfe as "20 and Odd Negroes"—arrived in Virginia in August 1619 on a Dutch ship. The Dutch had taken the Africans from a Portuguese vessel; the Portuguese had purchased them from slave traders in Africa. It is possible that the English also saw this group of Africans as slaves.

In the early years of the colony the English had not defined precise legal identities for English or African servants. The indenture process was informal and many people—white and black—faced indefinite terms as bound servants. English and Africans worked together in the tobacco fields and shared dwellings at night. There were opportunities for Anthony Johnson and other African men and women and their descendants to gain their freedom before Virginia's leaders firmly defined a system of slavery in 1662. Legislators declared that a child born to an enslaved woman would also be a slave for life.

Maryland followed Virginia and legalized slavery in 1663. The following year, Maryland added three restrictions on slaves. First, the legislators ruled that all Africans and Indians brought into the colony would serve for their entire lives unless a contract had been made before the individual's arrival. Next, they decided that Christian baptism had no effect on the legal status of slaves. Third, the lawmakers passed the first antimiscegenation law. Virginia added similar statutes in 1669, 1670, and 1691.

Virginia experienced a civil war in 1676. In the spring of that year, Nathaniel Bacon, a member of the English gentry who had recently arrived in Virginia, became the military leader of a band of Virginians who armed themselves against the Native Americans in defiance of Governor Berkeley. The governor responded by unsuccessfully dispatching men to confront Bacon and declared him a rebel. A number of Bacon's followers deserted him in early September 1676. He needed to increase the size of his army, so he proclaimed freedom for all servants and slaves who joined him. The rebel army that seized Jamestown in September of that year included white indentured servants, recently freed servants, and slaves. Bacon's decision to include servants, freedmen, and slaves in his army transformed the conflict from a war against Native Americans into a class struggle within the colony.

Bacon's sudden death on October 26, 1676, left his men without a leader, and the rebel movement lost strength. Indentured servants and slaves were among the last of Bacon's followers to surrender. Bacon's offer of freedom to servants and slaves helped to unite Virginia's successful planters, who feared the loss of their bound labor force. The colony's large planters consolidated their position in the colony and society after the defeat of the smallholders, freedmen, servants, and slaves in Nathaniel Bacon's army. During the last quarter of the seventeenth century, the legislators strengthened Virginia's slave code, made it more difficult for enslaved individuals to gain their freedom, enslaved the Native Americans who were captured during the rebellion, and placed new restrictions on free people of color.

As the supply of white indentured servants declined after 1680, the planters turned to a labor force of enslaved Africans and their descendants. Most of the slaves who arrived in Virginia and Maryland after 1680 were transported directly from Africa. By the end of the seventeenth century, both Virginia and Maryland were slave societies. Small groups of slaves tended fields of tobacco during the day under the watch of a white planter or overseer. At night, the enslaved workers slept in quarters that were separate from the dwelling of their white owner.

During the first half of the eighteenth century, Virginia legislators imposed harsher restrictions on enslaved laborers and took away many of the rights previously allowed to free blacks. Opportunities for black people to escape slavery all but disappeared, and some white people hoped to reduce those who were free to a lowly status equivalent to slavery. Slaveowners attempted to strip the more than 50,000 Africans transported to Virginia between 1700 and 1760 of their cultural identities and put most of the Africans to work at repetitious and backbreaking agricultural labor. Planters often used the newly arrived Africans' ignorance of English and their frequent passive and occasionally violent resistance to enslavement as excuses for imposing harsher discipline and more stringent work rules. Justices of the peace applied a separate criminal code to cases involving black people and handed down stiffer punishments. Informal plantation custom defined minimum levels of provisioning and work requirements.

As Chesapeake planters imported greater numbers of slaves from Africa, the majority of the region's enslaved population became African rather than West Indian or American-born. However, by the middle of the eighteenth century, the gentry did not have to import slaves in order to increase their labor force, as did their counterparts in South Carolina. The slave population grew through natural increase, and many planters encouraged their enslaved workers to form families. By the 1760s, Africans no longer made up the majority of the slave population in the Tidewater Virginia. Virginia-born slaves made some gains in their struggles with masters to limit work and to reclaim the rights held by slaves in the seventeenth century. Enslaved laborers also benefited from changes in Chesapeake society: the decreased productivity of tobacco fields in the Tidewater, the shift to grain production, and the growth of towns all ameliorated their conditions of life and labor. Planters reorganized work on their plantations as they decreased the proportions of their land devoted to tobacco. Wheat and other grains did not require the same labor-intensive work that tobacco did. Some slaves became artisans, and others worked as domestic servants for white residents of Virginia's and Maryland's towns and seaports—Williamsburg, Hampton, Norfolk, Baltimore, and Annapolis. Urban areas offered slaves the opportunity to hire themselves out—that is, to work for wages, pay their owners a set sum; and keep any surplus for themselves. Slaves who hired themselves out or who sold produce that they raised earned money and participated in the market economy.

A century after colonial lawmakers had passed statutes to legalize the institution of slavery, the Chesapeake economy was dependent on slave labor. Enslaved men, women, and children worked to produce the tobacco and grains that enabled the gentry to live in their plantation houses and to enjoy an elegant lifestyle. At the same time, native-born slaves created their own society based on both African and English cultures. These enslaved workers, like the first slaves in the region, knew the English language and negotiated with their masters to define limits on their work and to secure benefits for themselves and their families.

## The Low Country

In 1670, planters from the British Caribbean colony of Barbados relocated to the mainland area that became South Carolina. Many white plantation owners brought their slaves to the new colony. South Carolina began as a slave society. Between one-fourth and one-third of South Carolina's population was enslaved during its founding period. The colony's legislators enacted the first restriction on slaves in 1683 when they ruled that servants and slaves could not trade with each other. The law-makers passed a restrictive slave code in 1691.

South Carolina did not have a staple crop until the last decade of the seventeenth century. In the 1690s, planters found three products to export: naval stores such as tar and pitch, rice, and indigo (a plant that yielded blue dye). These commodities shaped the development of South Carolina's economy and society. Rice surpassed pitch and tar as the main export by the eighteenth century. Large planters purchased more land and greater numbers of slaves to grow rice. The cultivation of rice began on a small scale as slaveowners learned the complex process required for the large-scale commercial production of this crop. Enslaved Africans contributed crucial knowledge based on their experience with rice cultivation in Africa.

In the early eighteenth century, slaves made up the majority of the working class in the Low Country region of South Carolina, and Africans comprised the greater part of the enslaved population. Successful white South Carolinians also established plantations in Georgia and eastern Florida. Initially, the residents of the Low Country area of Georgia did not have slaves because the colony's trustees banned slavery in 1734. However, Parliament lifted the restriction in the middle of the century, and Georgia planters imported large numbers of Africans. As in South Carolina, the Low Country of Georgia had a black majority by the eve of the Revolution.

Most slaves in South Carolina labored in large groups. By 1720, three-quarters of the enslaved people in the colony resided on plantations with at least ten slaves. Thirty years later, in 1750, one-third of South Carolina's slaves lived with at least fifty other enslaved persons. Slaves worked under the close supervision of an overseer or driver. As planters saw their profits increase, they pushed their slaves to produce more and intensified their work.

Planters searched for another lucrative crop after profits from rice declined when overseas markets were lost during England's war with Spain. The 1739 Stono Rebellion also increased the colony's economic difficulties and intensified the fear felt by whites living among a black majority. Approximately sixty slaves, led by twenty slaves from Angola, tried to escape to Spanish Florida where they would be given their freedom. They encountered the militia at Stono, where the rebels killed twenty white people. In the aftermath of the rebellion, South Carolina's lawmakers imposed a high duty on imported slaves and tightened the slave code. Planters tried to become more self-sufficient, shifting some slaves to growing food, making clothes, and cobbling shoes. Other enslaved workers learned how to produce indigo.

The cultivation of indigo intensified the labor of slaves. The unhealthy environment of the Low Country and the demand of rice and indigo cultivation proved fatal to many Africans. Newly imported slaves were weak when they arrived because of the harsh conditions of the Middle Passage. The high death rate and predominance of males made it difficult for slaves to form families. Close to two-thirds of the imported Africans were men. The intense work schedule for rice and indigo made it hard for women to conceive and deliver healthy babies. By mid-eighteenth century, however, the mortality rate began to decline and the sex ratio became more balanced.

Planters relied on the task system: each slave had a set amount of work or a task to complete each day. After the task was finished, a slave could do his or her own work. Slaves gained some control over their labor, and the money they earned from the sale of goods they produced enabled them to participate in the market economy. A few slaves worked as slave drivers on plantations when planters realized that they could not control all aspects in the production of rice and indigo. On occasion, enslaved artisans were able to hire out some of their own time.

The life of an urban slave in South Carolina differed from that of his or her rural counterpart. Urban slaves lived in closer contact with their white owners than did slaves who tended the fields. Enslaved females worked as domestics and played an important role in the public markets. Enslaved men participated in all aspects of work in the port of Charleston. There were a substantial number of craftspeople who possessed a wide range of skills. Some owners hired out their slaves, and other owners allowed their enslaved men and women to hire out their own time. These opportunities in urban areas enabled slaves to earn money, acquire material goods and participate in the market economy.

The differences between urban and rural slavery in the Low Country can also be seen in the survival of African culture. Africans and African Americans struggled with white people over work and religion. At midcentury, urban slaves lived among a white majority in which European culture dominated. In contrast, plantation slaves lived apart from their owners. The physical separation of the slave quarters enabled slaves to incorporate elements of West African culture—language, appearance, dress, names, and religion—into their daily lives.

## New England and Mid-Atlantic Colonies

Three factors helped to shape the life of slaves in New England colonies (Massachusetts, Connecticut, and Rhode Island) and the Mid-Atlantic colonies (New York, New Jersey, Delaware, and Pennsylvania) in the seventeenth century: (1) the origins of the slaves, (2) the relatively small number of enslaved persons in the region, and (3) the way in which masters managed their labor force. Most of the Africans who labored in the northern colonies arrived from the Caribbean or the southern colonies rather than directly from Africa. A small number of slaves entered the northern colonies as prizes taken by pirates and privateers. New England merchants sent three ships to Africa to trade for gold and Africans in 1644, three years after Massachusetts became the first British mainland colony to legalize slavery. Connecticut's lawmakers legalized slavery in 1650.

The majority of the enslaved individuals in the northern colonies were familiar with European culture and languages. They formed connections to powerful men and institutions in their communities. In the city of New Amsterdam (later New York City), some slaves used their knowledge of the court system to improve their condition, to own property, to secure some rights, and to gain freedom. Africans found the latter difficult, even though New Netherland (later the colony of New York) did not have a system of legal slavery. Black people participated in all aspects of life in the Dutch colony by the middle of the seventeenth century.

The city of New Amsterdam was more dependent than the Chesapeake colonies on slave labor by the mid-seventeenth century because prosperity in the Netherlands and opportunities elsewhere in the Dutch Empire reduced the number of white people who wanted to journey to the colony. In 1664, slaves accounted for 20 percent of New Amsterdam's population and close to 5 percent of the entire colony's population (similar to the proportions in the Chesapeake). About one in five slaves had secured their freedom by the time the English gained control of the colony in 1664. British officials passed laws that legalized slavery soon after the Crown took possession of the Dutch colony. However, in spite of the new laws, slaves in New York continued to enjoy privileges such as property ownership and to be a part of public life into the first quarter of the eighteenth century.

Although a number of slaves lived and worked in northern cities—New York, Philadelphia, Newport, and Boston—the majority of slaves labored in the region's agricultural areas. In southern New England, the Hudson Valley, Long Island, and northern New Jersey, enslaved persons tended crops on farms along with their masters, white indentured servants, and hired workers. They did not work in gangs, as did slaves in the Low Country. Farms producing goods for the provisioning trade, rather than plantations, dotted the countryside in the New England and the Mid-Atlantic colonies. Africans and their descendants also worked in rural industries—tanneries, saltworks, lead and copper mines, iron furnaces—along with white laborers. Many northern slaves had one day a week to work for themselves and were able to hire themselves out. Most enslaved workers did not sleep in separate buildings as did their southern counterparts. Slaves in the New England and the Mid-Atlantic colonies usually slept in garrets, back rooms, closets, and cellars.

The fact that many slaveowners moved their enslaved workers back and forth between town and country meant that there was not a strong division between urban and rural slaves. The close living quarters made it possible for slaves to learn about the world of white people. The opportunities for interaction between slaves and indentured white laborers created a social division between free and unfree, not white and black.

At the end of the seventeenth century, more marked divisions between white and black people developed in the Mid-Atlantic and New England colonies. In 1699, less than twenty years after the first slaves arrived in Philadelphia, the city authorities allocated a separate area in the Strangers' Burial Ground for black people. The following year, Pennsylvania and Rhode Island established race-based slavery. Several northern colonies also passed laws to prohibit slaves from gathering, especially on Sunday.

In the eighteenth century, the character of slave life in the Mid-Atlantic and New England colonies changed, even though there was no "plantation revolution" as occurred in the Chesapeake and the Low Country. Between 1725 and 1775 a slow, uneven transformation took place across the northern colonies. The change had a greater impact on the Mid-Atlantic colonies than on New England, where the economy was based on family and wage labor. The transformation was also stronger in cities than in rural areas.

Slavery became more significant in the northern colonies as the region became more thoroughly incorporated into the Atlantic economy. The demand for labor increased in areas that underwent economic expansion. White city dwellers acquired additional slaves. In the eighteenth century, one-fifth to one-fourth of the slaves in the colony of New York lived in New York City. Portsmouth was home to one-third of the slaves in New Hampshire, Boston had a similar proportion of the enslaved residents of Massachusetts, and almost half of Rhode Island's slaves were in Newport. In 1750, 90 percent of Pennsylvania's population lived outside of Philadelphia, but 40 percent of colony's slaves lived in the city. In urban areas, female slaves worked as domestics, as did a few male slaves. Most enslaved men were wagoners, carters, stockmen in warehouses, sailors, or workers in ropewalks, shipyards, and sail factories. An increasing number of slaves became artisans.

The proportion of slaves grew in grain-producing areas of Pennsylvania, northern New Jersey, the Hudson Valley, and Long Island. Farmers in southern New England, especially around Narragansett Bay, also held more enslaved laborers by midcentury. However, most farmers in the Mid-Atlantic and New England colonies did not create plantations. Enslaved men still labored in small groups made up of indentured servants and wage laborers, black and white. Some enslaved women continued to work in the fields, while many became domestic workers.

In the eighteenth century, residents of the Mid-Atlantic and New England colonies began to purchase slaves imported directly from Africa to meet their growing need for labor. After 1741, 70 percent of the slaves imported into New York were from Africa, and 30 percent were from the Caribbean or other mainland colonies. These proportions had been the opposite before 1741.

The increasing importation of slaves from Africa affected the family life of the black people in the northern colonies. The mortality rate for Africans was high as they adapted to a new disease environment. The majority of imported slaves were males, so it was difficult for enslaved persons to find a partner. Some masters hindered their slaves from forming families, and enslaved husbands, wives, and children seldom lived together in either urban or rural areas.

As Africans began to predominate in the black population in the North, masters in this region adopted the practices developed by slaveowners in the Chesapeake and the Low Country. They imposed tighter discipline to control slaves who did not understand the English language and enforced harsher work requirements. Lawmakers placed restrictions on an owner's ability to free slaves and on the rights of free people of color. The proportion of free black people in the Mid-Atlantic and New England colonies declined. The free people of color in this region were less prosperous than their seventeenth-century counterparts had been. White people began to equate blackness with slavery.

Slaves imported directly from Africa revitalized African cultural elements in the northern colonies. American-born slaves heard new arrivals speak African languages and saw slaves with ritual scars and pierced ears. The influence of African-born slaves can be seen in the Negro Election Day in New England and Pinkster Day in New York and New Jersey. At these festivals, black men and women satirized white society as they dressed in fine clothes, marched in parades, and held elections. The inaugural festivities included dances, athletic events, cockfights, and games of chance. The officials—kings, governors, and judges—had symbolic power in the entire community and some real authority within the black community. Elected leaders took over the role of slaveowners and adjudicated small disputes. These festivals and role reversals gave slaves an opportunity to gather, express themselves, recognize the leaders of their community, and assert a measure of autonomy.

Many white residents of New York were concerned that slaves rejected Christianity in favor of African religions. An investigation of the 1712 insurrection in New York City found that "a free Negro who pretended to sorcery" and who gave the slaves "a powder to rub on their clothes to make them invulnerable" played a pivotal role in the revolt. African and Native American slaves set fire to a building in the town and then killed nine of the white men who arrived to put out the flames. A generation later, New York City again experienced unrest. In March and April 1741, there was a mysterious series of fires and thefts. White people believed that slaves set the fires and stole goods. The discovery of illicit meetings by black people at a tavern owned by a white man increased the fears of the city's white residents. Tensions in New York were already high because of economic depression and a harsh winter. Fears arose from white people's suspicion of strangers, dislike of people of a different ethnic or religious background, and concern over the growing number of black people in the city. There was also real discontent among the poor—both black and white.

By the middle of the eighteenth century, areas of the northern colonies began to resemble the slave societies in the Chesapeake and the Low Country. Urban centers in the Mid-Atlantic and New England colonies had larger slave populations than did the rural areas in these regions. A greater proportion of the enslaved people in the North arrived directly from Africa in the eighteenth century than in the previous century. Northern lawmakers increased restrictions on their slaves and on the rights of free people of color. However, the Mid-Atlantic and New England colonies did not complete the transformation from a society with slaves to a slave society. Slavery did not become central to the economy of the northern colonies as it was on the plantations in the southern colonies.

## Conclusion

On the eve of the American Revolution, slavery was legal in all thirteen colonies. Regional variations in the institution of slavery reflected the different ways in which owners managed the labor of slaves, the relative size of the enslaved population, and the role that slavery played in colonial social and economic organization. In spite of differences between the Chesapeake, the Low Country, and the northern colonies slavery in the British North American colonies had some common characteristics. Each colony passed statutes to legalize the practice of enslaving other human beings. In the eighteenth century, the increasing commitment of white colonists to the institution of slavery led to a rise in the importation of slaves directly from Africa. Lawmakers reacted to the presence of more Africans by passing laws that made slavery harsher. They also limited the rights that free black people had secured in the seventeenth century. In the worldview of white people, the white race became equated with freedom and the black race, including free people of color, became synonymous with slavery.

Slaves in all three regions shared a desire for freedom. From the time that the British enslaved Africans in their North American colonies in the seventeenth century, slaves resisted the institution of slavery in a myriad of ways. Enslaved men, women, and children might negotiate with their master, pretend to be sick, work slowly, break tools, or run away. In addition, some slaves decided to rebel against their masters and the slave system in order to gain their freedom. Virginia slaves seized an opportunity for freedom in 1676, enslaved laborers in South Carolina tried to escape to Spanish Florida for their freedom in 1739, and New York City slaves rebelled against the institution in 1712 and 1741. In the 1770s, slaves in the thirteen colonies heard their masters discuss the need to declare independence from Great Britain because they did not want to be enslaved to King George III. Fighting between British troops and the American colonies gave some slaves an opportunity to gain their freedom. Lord Dunmore, the last royal governor of Virginia, proclaimed that he would free all indentured servants and slaves who joined his forces to fight against the rebellious colonists. Dunmore and Patriot leaders were well aware that liberty was sweet to slaves everywhere in the colonies, from New England to the Low Country.

# Jenne-jeno

America, with its immigrants and indigenous peoples, offers a unique mix of world cultures discernible when the roots of the immigrants are examined along with their experiences as newcomers to America. However, not every American immigrated willingly. African immigration was for the most part a forced migration. Thus, Africans in America represent an American enigma. Their very *being* is an American paradox, a reminder of the chasm between American ideals and the American reality, between freedom and enslavement, and between opportunity and marginalization.

Who were these Africans? Where were they from? What was their cultural development? What were their worldviews, ideologies, and philosophies? How did they factor into the world economy of the fifteenth and sixteenth centuries?

The world economy, then as now, depended on trade, and the incentive for trade in these early centuries shaped the level of interaction among Africans and between Africans and Europeans. The geography of Africa, a land of stark contrasts, has long determined trading patterns. There are several ecological frontiers, areas where different environments exist side by side. The sahel, or desert edge, is one such area. The southern sahel borders the great savanna belt; further south, the savanna meets the tropical forest. The greatest incentive for trade existed along the frontiers and between different environments.

Thus, extensive trade occurred between desert nomads and sedentary farmers along the southern sahel. Specialized items such as salt, iron, copper, gold, and fish, plentiful in one area and scarce in another, offered inducements for early trade. The Dendi of southern Niger initially based their trade on salt deposits. The network became so extensive that Dendi became, and still is, the dominant trade language throughout much of Togo and Benin.

Despite the drying of the Sahara Desert about eight thousand years ago, which caused a mass migration south, and the fall of Egypt to foreign domination in 650 B.C.E., the economic needs of Africans south of the Sahara continued to be met by resources readily available *within* the continent. Extensive trade occurred, north to south and east to west.

The activities in this lesson focus on one example of the economic practices in West Africa (ranging roughly from present-day Senegal to the Republic of the Congo), before the beginning of trade with Europeans.

## Organizing Idea

Africa is the second-largest continent and a land of stark contrasts in topography, climate, and vegetation. Knowledge of the topographical features of the continent is essential to understanding the needs of the people living throughout the continent and the resources available to people in each region.

River systems were and are significant corridors of trade that unite vast areas of West Africa. In fact, Africans who later became sailors in the Americas came mainly from a 3,000-mile stretch of land in western Africa bounded by Senegambia and Angola. Merchants moved along trade routes that crisscrossed the continent in patterns of increasing complexity. The sahel, a semiarid area south of the Sahara desert, was a major trading area.

Jenne-jeno, an ancient city, became a center for sahel trade. Jenne-jeno is located in the inland delta region of the Republic of Mali, West Africa, where the Bani and Niger rivers meet. The city dates back to the third century B.C.E. The old city is located 1.86 miles from modern Jenne, where merchants still sell many of the same products sold in ancient Jenne-jeno.

## Student Objectives

Students will:

- ❖ learn about the physical diversity of the African continent
- ❖ consider how geography has shaped the economic activities of the continent
- ❖ understand that trade is an ancient practice, tying independent societies together and making them interdependent
- ❖ explore Jenne-jeno and understand the cosmopolitan nature of this ancient West African city

## Key Questions

- ❖ What are the major topographical features of the African continent? Which features encourage contact between peoples and which hinder travel?
- ❖ How do we know what we know about ancient civilizations? (Discuss and examine sources: oral; written; archaeological artifacts; fossils.)
- ❖ What is the significance of the discovery of Jenne-jeno?
- ❖ Why did Jenne-jeno become such an important city? What were the technological achievements of the inhabitants of Jenne-jeno?

## Primary Source Materials

DOCUMENT 1.1.1: "Finding West Africa's Oldest City" by Susan McIntosh and Roderick McIntosh, *National Geographic* (September 1982)

DOCUMENT 1.1.2: Photograph of excavation work at Jenne-jeno

DOCUMENT 1.1.3: Photograph of burial urns found at Jenne-jeno

DOCUMENT 1.1.4: Excerpt from *The Voyages and Travels of Captain Nathaniel Uring*, 1727

## Supplementary Materials

ITEM 1.1.A: Outline map of African continent

ITEM 1.1.B: Outline map of West Africa

ITEM 1.1.C: Map of West Africa and the Guinea Coast featuring Jenne

ITEM 1.1.D: Map of West African trade routes highlighting Jenne

## Supplies Needed

- ❖ map(s) of Africa's natural resources, geographic features, and major cities
- ❖ transparency acetate for copy machine
- ❖ large sheets of paper, such as butcher paper

## Vocabulary

| | | | |
|---|---|---|---|
| archaeology | equator | nomadic | savanna |
| artifact | evidence | pastoralists | tell |
| artisan | excavate | oasis | (archaeological |
| canoe | floodplain | radio-carbon | term) |
| commerce | fossil | dating | topography |
| delta | maritime | relative dating | tropical forest |
| desert | merchant | sahel | |

## Student Activities

Activity 1

### Mapping—African Continent

Students will create detailed maps, large and small, of the African continent using topographical and historical maps for reference. The term Big Map refers to an interdisciplinary teaching strategy that helps students place the stories of history in relationship to the lands and peoples whose lives and cultures they are studying. Students can embellish a base map with many different kinds of information from their discussions and readings as their study progresses.

To make a Big Map, place an outline map (Items 1.1.A and 1.1.B) on a copy machine and run a sheet of transparency acetate through the machine as if it were ordinary paper. The traced image will appear on the acetate exactly like a photocopy.

Tape a large piece of butcher paper onto a smooth wall. Using the overhead projector, focus the transparency on the paper, adjusting the projector until the map fills the entire space. Tape the transparency to the surface of the projector so that it will not inadvertently be moved once the students begin to trace the image onto the butcher paper. Ask two students at a time to begin tracing the outline map with the permanent marker. Do *not* trace the borders of the modern African nations, only the outline of the continent and offshore islands. Students then add features, such as rivers, names of places, natural resources, and transportation corridors, as they do additional research and learn about them, so that the story on the Big Map grows richer and more complete as the unit progresses.

Begin with Africa's natural resources. What are they, and where are they located? How are these resources used? Students should add natural resources in the appropriate areas. Maps should include places where the following are located: salt mines, copper mines, iron mines, gold mines, commercial fishing, and commercial agriculture. Natural features should be included: rivers, the Sahara, the sahel, mountains, highlands, etc.

Using the other maps included with this lesson (Items 1.1.C and 1.1.D), add the major cities of Africa and the established trade routes at the time transatlantic slavery began. Have students use acetate to create an overlay map showing the countries of modern Africa.

While the Big Map is being worked on, students should individually enter the same information on their own smaller versions of the map.

## Discussion and Analysis—Understanding Jenne-jeno

*Activity 2*

Begin with an introductory discussion of the kind of work done by archaeologists and how their discoveries shape our concept of history. The monuments and artifacts of Egypt, Greece, and Rome are familiar. Far less is known about civilizations other than Egypt on the continent of Africa.

Divide students into teams and have each team read one section in "Finding West Africa's Oldest City" (1.1.1) by Susan McIntosh and Roderick McIntosh in *National Geographic* and examine the photographs (1.1.2 and 1.1.3). The six sections are the introduction, "Soil Deposits Pose a Riddle," "Pottery Dates Advance New Ideas," "City Prospers on Trade," "Rains and Excavation Season," and "Thriving Jenne-jeno Abandoned." Each team should summarize for the class what they learned about ancient Africa, Jenne-jeno, and/or the work of archaeologists from studying their section of the article. Before their oral presentations, each team should prepare a one- to two-page summary of their findings.

## Reading and Discussion—River Commerce

*Activity 3*

Fishing and trading were major economic activities in Jenne-jeno. The vessels used in fishing and maritime trade were the canoe and the zopoli. Almadias, a Mandingo

## Music Connection

⸎

In *The Music of Black Americans* Eileen Southern writes about the music of West Africa: "For almost every activity in the life of the individual or the community there was an appropriate music." From agricultural ceremonies to religious rituals, from birth to betrothal, marriage, and death, music infused the lives of West African peoples in formal and informal ways.

The first two selections are a synthesis of traditional Ga Kpanlogo drumming and Dagarti xylophone music. Kpanlogo is a form of highlife, nontraditional, social music. Performed by members of the National Dance Ensemble of Ghana and David Locke, it was recorded by Paul Meyer in Ghana in April 1977. As you listen, pay attention to the role of the drum. How do the drums and xylophone weave together? How does the music make the listener feel? Can you join in with the rhythmic pattern?

The Ewe people of Ghana are known for their command of the complex techniques required to create the ancient percussive language known as Ewe drumming. "In Ewe drumming," writes Professor David Locke of Tufts University, "each instrument has a specific rhythm that it repeats over and over. Riding on this musical wave, so to speak, the lead drum sends musical signals that cue dancers when to do their different variations." These pieces were recorded by David Locke at the Wesleyan Recording Studio in Jananuary 1978.

vessel used along the Gambia River, is reported to have carried up to a ton of cargo. These vessels were best suited to negotiate the intercontinental waterways.

Read Captain Nathaniel Uring's 1727 account (1.1.4) testifying to Africans' seafaring skills and Europeans' reliance on African mariners and their experience with local waters. Think about the topography and physical characteristics of the African continent in general and of West Africa in particular. Why were seafaring skills valued by the Africans? By the Europeans?

## Further Student and Teacher Resources

Alagoa, E. J. "Long Distance Trade and States in the Niger Delta." *Journal of African History* 3, 1970, 319–29.

Bolster, W. Jeffrey. *Black Jacks: African American Seamen in the Age of Sail.* 2d ed. Cambridge, MA: Harvard University Press, 1998.

Bovill, Edward William. *The Golden Trade of the Moors: West African Kingdoms in the Fourteenth Century.* Princeton, NJ: Markus Wiener Publishers, 1995.

Curtin, Philip D. *Cross-Cultural Trade in World History.* Cambridge, UK: Cambridge University Press, 1984.

Degraft–Johnson, J. C. *African Glory: The Story of Vanished Negro Civilizations.* Baltimore: Black Classic Press, 1986.

Hull, Richard W. *African Cities and Towns before the European Conquest.* New York: W. W. Norton and Company, 1977.

Koslow, Philip. *The Kingdoms of Africa: Mali, Crossroads of Africa.* New York: Chelsea House Publishers, 1995.

Lang, Karen. "Djenne: West Africa's Eternal City." *National Geographic,* June 2001: 100–17.

Mann, Kenny. *Ghana, Mali, Songhay: The Western Sudan.* (*African Kingdoms of the Past*). Parsippany, NJ: Dillon Press, 1995.

———. *Kongo Ndongo: West Central Africa* (*African Kingdoms of the Past*). Parsippany, NJ: Dillon Press, 1996.

———. *African Kingdoms of the Past: Oyo Benin Ashanti, The Guinea Coast.* Parsippany, NJ: Dillon Press, 1996.

Thomas, Velma Maia. *Lest We Forget: The Passage from Africa to Slavery and Emancipation: A Three-Dimensional Interactive Book with Photographs and Documents from the Black Holocaust Exhibit.* New York: Crown Publishers, 1997.

## Website

http://geography.about.com/library/blank/blxindes.htm

## Contemporary Connection

⥅✳⥆

### Shift in Population

Between the seventeenth and twentieth centuries, the populations of Europe and Asia doubled and tripled, while the population of Africa remained static or declined as the slave trade increased. Most historians now agree that at least 12 million Africans were taken from the continent in slave ships. In the twentieth century, the decline was reversed. The population of West Africa increased from 45 million in 1930 to 87 million in 1960. It is estimated that the 1995 West African population of 220 million will grow to 430 million by 2020. The AIDS epidemic will be a factor in whether this growth occurs as predicted.

The proportion of the population living in towns and cities has grown from 4 percent in 1930 to 14 percent in 1960 and to 40 percent in 1990; it is estimated that by 2020 the figure will be 60 percent. Between 1960 and 1990 the number of urban centers with more than 100,000 inhabitants grew from twelve to ninety, and the number of towns with more than 5,000 inhabitants increased from 600 to 3,000 (http://www.oecd.org). Discuss the possible reasons for these changes and the implications of population shifts.

PRINCIPAL CITIES AND AGGLOMERATIONS OF WEST AFRICA
WITH A POPULATION OF MORE THAN ONE MILLION

| Rank | Name | Country | Population |
|------|------|---------|-----------|
| 12 | Lagos | Nigeria | 13,350,000 |
| 74 | Abidjan | Côte d'Ivoire | 3,750,000 |
| 107 | Luanda | Angola | 2,850,000 |
| 142 | Accra | Ghana | 2,300,000 |
| 197 | Ibadan | Nigeria | 1,725,000 |
| 218 | Douala | Cameroon | 1,575,000 |
| 237 | Yaoundé | Cameroon | 1,500,000 |
| 238 | Conakry | Guinea | 1,475,000 |
| 302 | Monrovia | Liberia | 1,225,000 |
| 351 | Ouagadougou | Burkina Faso | 1,100,000 |
| 378 | Freetown | Sierra Leone | 1,000,000 |

# Primary Source Materials for Lesson 1

## 1.1.1

### "Finding West Africa's Oldest City" by Susan McIntosh and Roderick McIntosh, *National Geographic*, (September 1982)

Two cities lie as neighbors on a stark river plain of West Africa. One stirs with the vigor of 10,000 inhabitants. The other, now lifeless, a thousand years ago held as many people, perhaps more. Three kilometers separate modern Jenne, busy with marketing and trade, from the ghost town Jenne-jeno—"ancient Jenne." Both sprawl across flats where the Bani and Niger Rivers weave braided courses in the Inland Delta region of the Republic of Mali.

In the scorched bleakness of the Sahel belt of West Africa, Jenne-jeno is a great wonder—and a paradox. From a start in the third century B.C., the city by A.D. 800 had grown to support many thousands. Mysteriously abandoned 600 years ago, Jenne-jeno lay forgotten for centuries. Today a few acacia trees and a clump or two of mangoes dot the barren ancient site, a vast teardrop-shaped mound that rises to a height of seven meters (23 feet)—beyond reach of annual floods—and measures two kilometers (1.2 miles) around its perimeter. Composed entirely of the debris of human occupation, this tell is a maze of eroded house walls, the surface littered with potsherds, glass beads, fragments of stone bracelets, and bits of corroded metal . . . .

. . . the radio-carbon dating from hearth charcoal [proved] that Jenne-jeno already had been occupied for 1,600 years when, about 1400, it was finally abandoned—not much after the time most scholars believe Jenne was founded.

Our discovery excited archaeologists and historians. It contradicted earlier assumptions that urbanism was introduced into West Africa only after North African Arabs penetrated the Sahara in the ninth century to control long distance trade. Catalyzed by expanded trade, cities grew, first in the southern Sahara, centuries later farther south. By this reasoning, Jenne-jeno should have developed in the

13th century. What then were we to make of our radiocarbon dates testifying that Jenne-jeno existed 1500 years earlier?

**Note: The full text of Document 1.1.1 is available on the CD-ROM.**

## 1.1.2

## Photograph of excavation work at Jenne-jeno

*As Susan and Roderick McIntosh and the team of archeologists worked on the site, many mud-brick foundations became visible.*

Dr. Roderick James McIntosh, Professor of Anthropology

### 1.1.3

## Photograph of burial urns found at Jenne-jeno

*About two dozen burial urns such as this one were excavated at Jenne-jeno.*

Dr. Roderick James McIntosh, Professor of Anthropology

### 1.1.4

## Excerpt from *The Voyages and Travels of Captain Nathaniel Uring*, 1727

*Nathaniel Uring was captain of a merchant ship during the reign of Queen Anne of England. His narrative describes his adventures and misadventures on the high seas. He was involved in the slave trade, along with many other ventures between the Old World and the New.*

We saw the Sea break so high, that we began to be afraid to venture, and were inclined to return," he wrote, "but the Canow [canoe] people encouraged and assured us there was no Danger. The Canow was large, and had Eight Men to paddle her . . . . When we came near the Breakers, they laid still and watched for a Smooth, and then push'd Forward with all their Force, paddling the Canow forward or backward as they saw Occasion, often lying between the Breakers, which was very terrible to see, roaring both before and behind us; when they saw a fair Opportunity, they paddled with all their Might toward the Shore and got safe thither.

# Using Maps to Learn
# About the Past

Maps of Africa created from the fourteenth through the eighteenth centuries are valuable primary sources for teaching and learning. Cartographers sponsored by royalty, the church, and private merchants created maps that include information such as the location of ports, castles, forts, rivers, deltas, navigation lines, and goods to be traded. Often they are also illustrated with sea monsters and historical figures such as Mansa Musa, ruler of the kingdom of Mali (1307–1332), holding out a nugget of gold to an approaching trader. Although the maps appear to us as works of art, these maps were, in fact, important repositories of information, vital to both European and African economic and political interests. Richly colored and intricate in detail, they reflect the large financial investment European kings and trading companies were willing to commit—to cartographers, to a sailing fleet with trained explorers and crew, and to gifts for foreign kings—in order to gain and maintain a monopoly over particular coastal trade routes and ports.

These maps can be used in a variety of ways. They are literally treasure maps because the knowledge they contain must be discovered through study and discussion. When students are asked key questions about the maps, they are better able to analyze the information each of these maps provides.

## Organizing Idea

Maps can introduce us to the complex connections between Africa's internal trading network and traders from the European world. Spanning three hundred years, the maps provided in this lesson represent the worldviews of different nations and reflect the mercantile interests of each.

## Student Objectives

Students will:

❖ use skills of observation and inquiry to learn about trading and navigational connections between Africa and Europe

❖ identify, describe, and compare information conveyed in the maps from different time periods and nations

❖ explain how maps may be used for political and economic purposes

❖ understand that primary source documents may contain or reveal unpopular or uncomfortable events or information that, nevertheless, must be studied to understand a complex story

## Key Questions

❖ What kinds of information can we learn from maps?

❖ How can we understand the perspective of a particular map?

❖ Maps tell stories. What were the political and economic purposes behind the creation of these maps?

## Primary Source Materials

DOCUMENT 1.2.1: Map with Mansa Musa, 1375

DOCUMENT 1.2.2: Atlas Map, ca. 1547, owned by Villard

DOCUMENT 1.2.3: Juan de la Cosa's 1502 Map, known as the "Portuguese Map of Africa"

## Vocabulary

| | | | |
|---|---|---|---|
| atlas | current | Kanem Bornu | navigation |
| Bight of Benin | equator | key | Niger River |
| Canary Islands | Gambia River | King Nzinga | Sao Tome |
| Cape Verde Islands | Gulf of Guinea | Kongo | Senegal River |
| Christian | indigenous | Mansa Musa | |
| Congo River | infidel | Muslim | |
| | Jula | nautical | |

## Student Activities

*General Suggestions*

❖ Post the historical maps of Africa in a visible, accessible place. Have at least one contemporary map of the continent for reference and comparison.

❖ Arrange students in pairs or small work groups to encourage greater participation by each member.

❖ Provide hand magnifying lenses for close examination; some of the text and details are tiny.

❖ Point out that the text on the maps is often in a language other than English.

## Supplies Needed

- ❖ multiple laminated copies of the maps for work groups
- ❖ one overhead copy of each map for class discussion
- ❖ charting paper for vocabulary and students' observations and questions
- ❖ art materials for students to create their own maps
- ❖ hand magnifying lenses

*Activity 1*

## Comparison and Contrast of Early Maps

Working in small groups, students study the same or different maps of fourteenth-to eighteenth-century Africa (1.2.1, 1.2.2, and 1.2.3). By using a copy of a map on an overhead projector, the teacher can enlarge detail and facilitate discussion of student findings. What do they see? What information does the map show? What is missing? Who would find this map useful? Why? How are color, size, illustration, scale, and language used to provide information?

Using specific examples from the maps, explain the similarities and differences between them. Which map is more informative and why?

*Activity 2*

## Analysis of a Mapmaker's Perspective

Have students place the historical maps in chronological order. What do they notice about the evolution of information? Which maps seem to take a more European perspective, and why might this be so? Which maps treat African kings and merchants as equals to the Europeans in trading relationships? Judging from the maps, what parts of Africa interested Europeans? What are the connections between the information provided on the natural resources map and the information—ports and illustrations—depicted on the European cartographers' maps?

*Activity 3*

## Discussion—What Should a Map Include?

Have students imagine they are the ruler of an African empire. What information would they choose to include on a map created by royal cartographers? How would this map be similar to and different from the European maps they've seen? Explain.

*Activity 4*

## Creative Extensions

Have students create a piece of work that demonstrates the depth and understanding of their response to what they have observed through this lesson. They may create:

1. an essay
2. an annotated map
3. a thoughtful, informed, detailed dramatic skit (for example, "A Day In the Life of Mapmaker Abraham Cresques," "How Navigator and Mapmaker

Juan de la Cosa Created a Masterpiece," "Mansa Musa's Reaction to His Portrait" (in the bottom right corner of 1.2.1)

4. a bulleted list of instructions for the mapmaker

Students should be prepared to explain their reasoning.

### Analysis and Discussion

*Activity 5*

Provide students with a map they have not seen before. Using the key questions, have them discuss and record their observations and provide evidence for what they see.

## Further Student and Teacher Resources

Bell, Neill. *The Book of Where: Or How to Be Naturally Geographic*. New York: Scott Foresman, 1982.

Black, Jeremy. *Maps and History*. New Haven: Yale University Press, 1997.

Demko, George J. *Why In the World: Adventures In Geography*. New York: Doubleday, 1992.

Greenhood, David. *Mapping*. Chicago: University of Chicago Press, 1964.

Knowlton, Jack. *Maps and Globes*. Reprint. New York: HarperTrophy, 1986.

La Pierre, Yvette. *Mapping A Changing World*. New York: Lickle Publishing, Inc., 1996.

"Meaning of Maps." *Faces: World Cultures for Readers Ages 9–14*. Cobblestone Publications, March 1990.

Monmonier, Mark. *How To Live With Maps*. Chicago: University of Chicago Press, 1991.

### Website

www.library.yale.edu/MapColl/

## Contemporary Connection

⟶❈⟵

### Mapmaking

The information recorded on maps has increased dramatically since World War II. Included on contemporary maps may be economic, social, and cultural data, topics such as health information, the spread of environmental pollution, and the GNP of various countries. Jeremy Black describes these maps as "information systems" that allow us to view a great deal of information all together in one place. Contemporary mapmakers face the challenge of how best to present so much data. As maps become part of the information revolution, it is interesting to contemplate how technology has altered the creation of maps (i.e., aerial photography and digitalization) and the advances that may be made in twenty-first-century mapmaking. Contemporary maps still tell stories. Consider how these stories differ from the stories told on maps from earlier centuries.

# Primary Source Materials
# for Lesson 2

## 1.2.1

### Map with Mansa Musa, 1375

*Mansa Musa, a powerful ruler of the medieval West African kingdom of Mali, traded extensively with Portuguese merchants. In this Catalan map, from a region that later became part of Spain, he is shown holding out a gold nugget to an Arab trader approaching on a camel.*

Bibliothèque Nationale de France

<u>1.2.2</u>

## Atlas Map, ca. 1547, owned by Vallard

*This map was probably made in Dieppe, France, and was owned by Nicholas Vallard, who likely used it for display. The cartographer is unknown, but scholars believe he was Portuguese. Note that the map is inverted. It was not unusual for medieval mapmakers not to put north at the top but to orient the map toward the east.*

The Huntington Library, San Marino, California

<u>1.2.3</u>

## Juan de la Cosa's 1502 Map, known as the "Portuguese Map of Africa"

*Although the map suggests extensive exploration by Europeans, especially in West Africa, notice the course of the Niger River.*

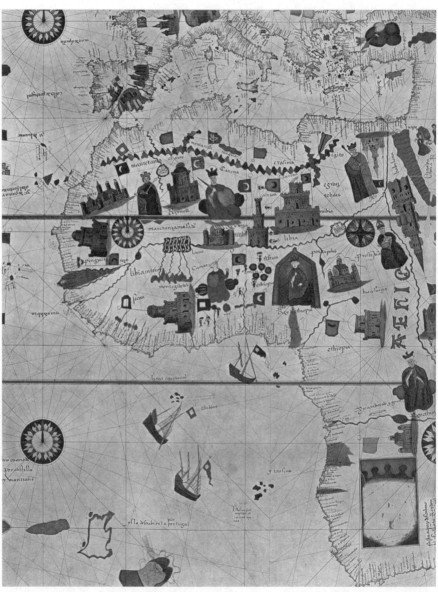

Museo Naval de Madrid

# Early Travelers, Traders, and Observers and the Role of Religion

Fourteenth-century visitors to West Africa from Europe and other parts of Africa traveled to these areas as traders, diplomats, or curious visitors. Their written observations provide detailed descriptions of West Africa on the eve of the transatlantic slave trade, as commerce between Europe and Africa was increasing.

Students should understand that the writings excerpted in this lesson represent a sample of observations over the centuries. They are not meant to be a complete account; instead they offer observations made by travelers and traders from a variety of nationalities and backgrounds. A number of the later accounts precede the trading company era by less than one hundred years, but Ibn Battuta's writings date from much earlier. The nations represented in this sample were in political and economic competition with each other. Documents such as papal bulls illustrate the ongoing struggles between Christian and Muslim mercantile and religious interests. (For more background on the European trading companies operating in Africa, see the introduction to Lesson 4, on the Royal African Company.)

Students must understand the religious, political, and social climate of Europe during the age of exploration. It is also important to be aware that trade, cultural, and intellectual connections had long existed between the African continent and Europe. The Mediterranean Sea served as a frequently used conduit, transporting goods and information in all directions. For example, gold, leather, salt, scientific and mathematical knowledge, and a relatively small number of slaves were sent from Africa to Europe, with metals and other goods being brought back to Africa. Trading with Africa entailed employing a network of middlemen, mostly North African Arabs, who were familiar with Saharan trading routes and centers, currencies, languages, and products. Black people were a common sight in southern Europe by the 1400s, and these individuals included black scholars and merchants as well as servants and slaves. Parts of the Iberian Peninsula formerly under Moorish control, such as the Muslim kingdom of Granada, maintained intellectual, religious, and economic connections with Muslim West Africa and other mercantile centers across southern Europe.

By the 1400s, the Portuguese began a series of expeditions, seeking a direct route to the sources of African gold, ivory, spices, and other goods and cutting out the middlemen, as well as competitors from other European powers. Portuguese involvement with African slavery began in 1441, when Captain Antao Goncalves sailed to Cabo Blanco, the extreme north of Mauritania, raided the marketplace, and kidnapped twelve Africans to bring back to Prince Henry. These people, referred to as "exhibits," were used to demonstrate how Portugal could successfully kidnap and enslave people from Africa without having to go through North African middlemen in the Mediterranean slave markets. Other Portuguese expeditions followed, along and around the African coastline as well as up various rivers, such as the Senegal (1444) and the Gambia (1445). By 1448, about one thousand black Africans had been transported to Portugal or the islands it had just acquired, the Azores and Madeira. Madeira's first sugar cane plantation was established in 1452, and this labor-intensive business would increase the demand for slave labor.

The Catholic Church, a strong and influential presence in Portugal and Spain, sanctioned and encouraged these slave-trading and slave-based activities through a series of papal bulls. According to *Webster's New International Dictionary*, "A papal letter [is] distinguished from other apostolic letters by being sealed with a bulla or with a red-ink imprint of the device on the bulla, by being written on parchment and in the third person, by opening with the pope's name and the formula 'Bishop, servant of the servants of God,' and by significance of subject matter."

In 1442, in his papal bull *Illius Qui*, Pope Eugenius approved Prince Henry's expeditions to Africa. This bull, issued without the Pope's ever having visited Africa or talked with any African rulers, granted Portugal exclusive rights over its African "discoveries." In 1452, in the papal bull *Dum Diversas*, Pope Nicholas V allowed the king of Portugal to "subdue pagans and other nonbelievers." The 1454 papal bull *Romanus Pontifex* allowed for the conversion of native populations to Christianity. This bull also granted Portugal a monopoly over all of Africa.

On October 7, 1462, Pope Pius II wrote to Bishop Puvo, the cleric charged with overseeing Portuguese Christians in West Africa. The Pope criticized and threatened severe punishment to those who would enslave African converts to Christianity because these new converts were considered vital to the entry of the church into Africa. Otherwise, the Catholic Church stayed out of the economic affairs of its most supportive countries, Portugal and Spain, each of which would soon bring enslaved Africans and a slave-based economy to the New World.

## Organizing Idea

The beginnings of European trade with Africa are documented in official and personal accounts by observers, traders, travelers, and diplomats from a number of European countries who visited West Africa. Evidence of trade between Portugal and the kingdom of Benin is revealed in a number of artifacts, including ivory salt cellars, brass plaques, and other objects used in part to document important events and people in a kingdom with no known written language. By studying a sample of these primary sources, students can develop a fuller picture of European-African trading connections and activities just before the onset of the transatlantic slave trade.

## Student Objectives

Students will:

- ❖ be able to describe some of the trading patterns and economic and religious tensions in West and Central Africa just before the beginning of the trans-atlantic slave trade
- ❖ study the impact of early European trading—especially that of the Portuguese and Spanish—on West Africa
- ❖ develop an understanding of the role of the Catholic Church and papal bulls in shaping European-African trading patterns during the fourteenth and fifteenth centuries

## Key Questions

- ❖ What are the benefits of using a *sampling* of documents to learn about a time period? What does the reader need to know to understand these texts?
- ❖ What information, if any, is common to most of or all the documents? What patterns can be detected in these excerpts? What kind of picture or pictures begin to emerge of West and Central Africa during the fourteenth through sixteenth centuries?
- ❖ What would a European merchant in this part of Africa need to know in order to be able to trade there?
- ❖ How might the papal bulls and Portuguese claims of sovereignty over Atlantic shipping lanes have affected trade between African and European merchants?

## Primary Source Materials

DOCUMENT 1.3.1: Ibn Battuta's account of his travels in Mali in 1352

DOCUMENT 1.3.2: Extracts from Leo Africanus' sixteenth-century description of the kingdoms of Western Africa

DOCUMENT 1.3.3: Ahmed Baba's views on slavery and Islam, from the sixteenth century

DOCUMENT 1.3.4: Excerpts from *The Golden Trade* by Richard Jobson, 1623

DOCUMENT 1.3.5: Selections from Papal Bull *Romanus Pontifex*, January 1454

DOCUMENT 1.3.6: Diago Cao's Padrao—a stone pillar with a cross brought from Lisbon and erected by the explorer at the mouth of the Congo River

DOCUMENT 1.3.7: Part I: Letter regarding the conversion of King Afonso to Catholicism, from Rui d'Aguiar, a Catholic priest in the Kongo, to the King of Portugal, 1516; Part II: Letter from King Afonso to the King of Portugal concerning the slave trade, 1526

DOCUMENT 1.3.8: Photograph of Afro-Portuguese saltcellar (Benin)

DOCUMENT 1.3.9: Brass plaque showing a Benin trader

DOCUMENT 1.3.10: Brass plaque of two Portuguese men above rows of manillas

## Vocabulary

| | | | |
|---|---|---|---|
| artifact | functionary | Kongo | Muslim |
| Benin | Gao | *manilla* (Benin) | Nzinga |
| Berber | Genoa | *marabout* | *padrao* |
| conversion | *infante* | medieval | saltcellar |
| cultural exchange | Islam | monopoly | Senegal |
| Diago Gomez | jula (djoula) | Moor | Sudan |
| diplomacy | Kano (a major | mulatto | Timbuktu |
| ducat | Hausa state) | (molatoe) | |

## Student Activities

The activities should be preceded by a discussion with students regarding the nature of sampling, its strengths as well as its limitation. Keep visible lists of vocabulary and student-generated questions.

*Activity 1*  **Analysis and Discussion of Readings**

Students work in partnerships or small groups to read, analyze, and discuss Documents 1.3.1, 1.3.2, 1.3.3, and 1.3.4. Consider the writer's nationality, his occupation, and the year he traveled. What did each man observe? What questions are left unanswered?

*Activity 2*  **Further Research on Leo Africanus**

Leo Africanus, born Al Hassan Ibn Muhammad Al Wazzan, continues to fascinate scholars. His detailed (1550) account of his travels, *The History and Description of Africa*, was for many years one of the key geographical reference works pertaining to Africa north of the sahel. Students can begin to learn about his life and accomplishments by checking *www.leoafricanus.com*, *www.trentu.ca/colleges/otonabee/leo/front.htm*, and *www.ucalgary.ca/applied_history/tutor/oldwrld/merchants/gao.html*.

*Activity 3*  **Writing to Extend**

Imagine walking thorugh the city of Gao or Walata with a tape recorder. What would you ask the people you encounter? And what would they reply? Write down the dialogue.

## Discussion—Documents Across Time

*Activity 4*

Have students arrange document excerpts in chronological order. What can be discovered about changes in African trading patterns? What seems to remain the same? What other events do students know about in world or European history at this time that might affect trade? As more European powers became involved in trade with West Africa, what effects did that have on African rulers and their subjects?

## Reading and Discussion of Papal Bulls

*Activity 5*

The papal bull (1.3.5) is challenging reading for students. Teachers may wish to read it aloud or assign short sections to students working in small groups. Students need to paraphrase and then summarize what each sentence in the document states. Share the summaries as a class and list the major points on the board. Examine how the Catholic Church viewed its authority. Consider the degree to which this document is concerned with economics, political power, religion, and/or salvation. Discuss how this and other papal bulls would have influenced merchants and explorers interacting with Africans. Can students think of a modern-day parallel to a papal bull?

## Research on Religion

*Activity 6*

Assign a mini–research project, including maps for students to learn about the history and nature of Islam and Catholicism. Where and when were the two religions in competition? Using the selection from the papal bull (1.3.5), have students consider the process of voluntary and forced conversion to Catholicism and/or Islam and the economic, political, and social issues and challenges kings faced during this time period.

## Debate

*Activity 7*

Arrange a student debate about whether economics or religion played a more important role in Europeans' trade with West Africa.

## A Study of Artifacts: Comparison and Connections

*Activity 8*

Students study Documents 1.3.8, 1.3.9, and 1.3.10, all objects created by Benin crafters and containing design elements from the cultures of both Benin and Portugal.

Additionally, the Portuguese supplied Benin with much of the brass used in objects such as plaques and statues. This brass was brought to Benin as *manillas* (horseshoe-shaped bracelets), a form of trading currency. Early inclusion of *manillas* and Portuguese faces in Benin designs indicate the importance of this trading link. What was each object made of, and what was each object's use? Was it a luxury item or one used in everyday life? Who might have been its intended user? What does the inclusion of design motifs with different origins say about the perspectives of the object's creator end/or its intended owner? What evidence do students have to support their opinions?

## Music Connection

⫲

"There is without doubt, no people on the earth more naturally affected to the sound of musicke than these people," wrote Richard Jobson in his 1623 account, *The Golden Trade*. He described the xylophone as the "principall instrument" in Gambia. About a foot high, it had "seventeene woodden keyes standing like the Organ, upon which hee that playes sitting upon the ground just against the middle of the instrument, strikes with a sticke in either hand, about a foote long, at the end whereof is made fast a round ball, covered with some soft stuffe, to avoyd the clattering noyse the bare stickes would make . . . . the sound that proceeds from this instrument is worth the observing, for we can heare it a good English mile, the making of this instrument being one of the most ingenious things amongst them: for to every one of these keyes there belongs a small Iron the bignesse of a quill, and is a foote long, the breadth of the instrument, upon which hangs two gourdes under the hollow, like bottles, who receives the sound, and returnes it againe with that extraordinary loudness."

The "High Life" piece (on the CD-ROM), recorded on location by Richard Hill, is representative of music of the Lobi and Dagarti peoples of northern Ghana and the Griots of Gambia and Senegal. It is played on an instrument very similar to the one Jobson described, except this one has fourteen keys rather than seventeen. Pay close attention to the rhythm. What is its role in the melody? Notice also how improvisation can be heard in the playing of the lead instrument. Both improvisation and the prominence of layered rhythmic patterns are music elements found in music of African Americans.

## Further Student and Teacher Resources

Davenport, Frances Gardiner. *European Treaties Bearing on the History of the United States and its Dependencies to 1648*. Baltimore: The Lord Baltimore Press, 1917.

Diouf, Sylvaine. *Servants of Allah: African Muslims Enslaved in the Americas*. New York, New York University Press, 1998.

Hopkins, J. F. P., and Nehemia Levtzion, Editors. *Corpus of Early Arabic Sources for West African History*. Cambridge, UK: Cambridge University Press, 1981.

Linden, H. Vander. "Alexander VI and the Demarcation of the Maritime and Colonial Domains of Spain and Portugal 1493–1494." *American Historical Review* 22:1 (October 1916): 1–20.

Thornton, John. *Africa and Africans in the Making of the Atlantic World*, 1400–1800. Cambridge, UK: Cambridge University Press, 1992.

### Websites

www.middlepassage.org/timeline.htm#DAYS
*Annotated time line of the history of the slave trade involving West Africa, European powers, and the Americas*

www.mariner.org/captivepassage/departure/dep001.html
*Information about the slave trade*

http://gropius.lib.virginia.edu/SlaveTrade
*Images (photographs and drawings) with accompanying explanations of significant West African sites and European interpretations (drawings, sketches, water colors, etc.) of West African peoples and scenes from the sixteenth century on*

www.millersv.edu/~columbus/data/art/SCHULTZ1.ART
*An important essay: "The Role of the Vatican in the Encounter," by Richard Schultz, includes descriptions of influential papal bulls and their effects on West African peoples*

www.hist.ucalgary.ca
*A graphics and text website explaining the roles and effects of religion and exploration on Europe and Africa*

www.faculty.de.gcsu.edu/~dvess/afart.htm
*Detailed sketches and descriptions of West African art*

http://educate.si.edu/resources/lessons/siyc/currency/essay5.html
*A website sponsored by the Smithsonian Institution describing Africans' trade with Europeans and currency used. According to this site, the Portuguese traded brass manillas (c-shaped bracelets for the hand) for Akan—West African—gold.*

---

## Contemporary Connection 1

✠

### Tourism

According to the World Tourism Organization, no West African countries are among the top sixty travel destinations in the world. Furthermore, of the top ten destinations in Africa, only one, Ghana, is located in West Africa. In 1993, West Africa had a 7.8 percent share of the global tourist market (1.4 million tourists). This contributed $809 million to the local economy. Forty percent of the tourists came from other African nations, while 33 percent came from Europe. American tourism to West Africa is a small but growing phenomenon. Most American tourists are interested in African art, seek adventure, or have some African ancestry. Explore the reasons for these statistics.

---

*Source:* World Tourism Organization, *Yearbook of Tourism Statistics*, 1995, WTO Commission for Africa and Regional Representative for Africa. See *www.umassd.edu/SpecialPrograms/caboverde/werlin.html.*

## Contemporary Connection 2 ✠

### Trade and Development

Sub-Saharan Africa is made up of some of the poorest nations in the world, with an average per capita gross national product (GNP) of $503, compared to Latin America with an average GNP of $3,706. In January 2003, the GNP in the United States was $9,549. For information on contemporary trade issues, search "African Trade News" on the Internet.

## Contemporary Connection 3 ✠

### Initiatives in Congress

In 2001, the U.S. Congress introduced legislation related to:

❖ human rights, famine relief, and oil in Sudan

❖ trade and development policies regarding the rights of African farmers

❖ support for the African Development Bank and Fund

❖ prohibiting importation of cotan and tantalum ore from Rwanda, Uganda, Burundi, and the Democratic Republic of Congo

❖ the development of strategies to reduce hunger and poverty and to promote free-market economies and democratic institutions in sub-Saharan Africa

Find out what happened to this legislation and what has been proposed since. See *www.congress.gov.*

# Primary Source Materials for Lesson 3

### 1.3.1

## Ibn Battuta's account of his travels in Mali, 1352

*Not all the accounts of the African kingdoms were this glowing. One of the most famous and extensive of them was composed by Ibn Battuta, a Berber scholar and theologian from Tangiera city on the northwest coast of Africa. Ibn Battuta crossed the Sahara in 1352 and spent about a year in the kingdom of Mali, which by this time had supplanted Ghana as the dominant force in the Sudan.*

I set out on the 1st Muharram of the year seven hundred and fifty-three [February 18, 1352] with a caravan including amongst others a number of the merchants of Sijilmasa [present day Morocco/Algeria frontier region]. After twenty-five days, we reached Taghaza, an unattractive village, with the curious feature that its houses and mosques are built of blocks of salt, roofed with camel skins. There are no trees there, nothing but sand. In the sand is a salt mine; they dig for the salt and find it in thick slabs, lying one on top of the other, as though they had been tool-squared and laid under the surface of the earth. . . .

Of all peoples, the Negroes are those who most abhor injustice. The Sultan pardons no one who is guilty of it. There is complete and general safety throughout the land. The traveler here has no more reason than the man who stays at home to fear brigands, thieves or ravishers . . . . The blacks do not confiscate the goods of any North Africans who may die in their country, not even when these consist of large treasures. On the contrary, they deposit these goods with a man of confidence . . . until those who have a right to the goods present themselves and take possession.

**The full text of Document 1.3.1 is available on the CD-ROM.**

## 1.3.2

## Extracts from Leo Africanus' sixteenth-century descriptions of the kingdoms of western Africa

*A Moorish traveler and scholar by the name of Al Hassan Ibn Muhammad All Wazzan recorded his travels to Mali. Muhammad, a Muslim who was nicknamed Leo Africanus by Italian scholars, went into great detail describing his trip to the capital of Mali in the six-teenth century. According to Africanus, the capital had approximately 6,000 dwellings and several mosques and Islamic schools. The majority of the workforce was composed of arti-sans and merchants working and dealing with a wide range of goods. Africanus was so impressed with the capital that he depicted its inhabitants as being superior to their neigh-bors in behavior, industry, and education. His major work,* The History and Descrip-tion of Africa, *contains this report of the opulent capital of Songhai:*

Gao is a very large city similar to Kabara, that is, without surrounding walls. The city is about 650 kilometers from Timbuktu to the southeast. Most of its houses are ugly; however, a few, in which live the king and his court, have a very fine aspect. Its inhabitants are rich merchants who travel constantly about the region with their wares. A great many Blacks come to the city bringing quantities of gold with which to purchase goods imported from the Berber country and from Europe, but they never find enough goods on which to spend all their gold and always take half or two-thirds of it home . . . .

**The full text of Document 1.3.2 is available on the CD-ROM.**

## 1.3.3

## Ahmed Baba's views on slavery and Islam, from the sixteenth century

*Ahmed Baba, a prolific scholar and jurist from sixteenth-century Timbuktu, wrote:*

Let it be known that infidelity, whether on the part of Christians, Jews, idolaters, Berbers, Arabs, or any other individual notoriously rebellious to Islam, is the only justification for slavery; there is no distinction to be made between miscreants, Sudanese [black] or not.

*People from Bornu, Kano, Songhai, and Mali were not to be enslaved, Baba main-tained, because they were recognized as Muslims.* As for the Djilfos [Wolof] they are Muslims according to what we have learnt, this has been proved; there are among them *tolba* and *fuqaha* [specialists in law] and people who know the Koran by heart. *The rule, then, was not to trade in people whose provenance was unknown, warned the scholar, who added,* this commerce is one of the calamities of our time.

*Concerning the treatment of slaves, Baba stressed that God commands they be treated with humanity, as stated in the Koran and the Hadith, and he concluded,* One must pity their sad fate and not treat them harshly because the fact of becoming the property of somebody else breaks the heart, because servitude is inseparable from the idea of vio-lence and domination, especially when it concerns a slave taken far from his country.

*Asked about the biblical "curse of Ham," which vows that Ham's descendants will be slaves of his brothers' progeny (Gen. 9:20–25), Ahmed Baba answered that there was no difference between the human races in the Koran, and that even if Ham was the father of the Sudanese, God was too merciful to make millions of men pay for the mistake of one.*

## 1.3.4

## Excerpts from *The Golden Trade* by Richard Jobson, 1623

*Richard Jobson was an English sea captain sent to Africa in 1620 to explore the Gambia River area and assess it for potential trade. He published an account of his observations in London three years later, including a description of slavery.*

### Excerpt from Part III

They call themselves, Portingales, and some few of them seeme the same; others of them are Molatoes, betweene blacke and white, buut the most part as blacke, as the naturall inhabitants: they are scattered, some two or three dwellers in a place, and all are married, or rather keepe with them the countrey black women, of whom they beget children, howbeit they have amongst them, neither Church, nor Frier, nor any other religious order. It doth manifestly appeare, that they are such, as have been banished, or fled away, from forth either of Portingall, or the Iles belonging unto that government, they doe generally imploy themselves in buying such commodities the countrey affords, wherein especially they covet the contry people, who are sold unto them, when they commit offences . . . .

**The full text of Document 1.3.4 is available on the CD-ROM.**

## 1.3.5

## Selections from Papal Bull *Romanus Pontifex*, January 1454

*Beginning in the early middle ages, when popes issued important mandates, scribes recorded them on parchment and sealed them with a lump of lead, called a bulla in Latin. The pope then "signed" the document by pressing his signet ring into the soft lead. The round seal had a representation of St. Peter and St. Paul on one side and, on the other, the name of the pope. These formal apostolic letters came to be known as papal bulls. Diane Childress, writing for Calliope (April 1998), explains that "because the pope was the spiritual leader of western Europe, papal bulls carried the weight of international law among Roman Catholic countries and could be used to arbitrate disputes between rulers. A ruler who disobeyed the pope's decree risked excommunication, or exclusion from the Christian community." On January 8, 1454, the pope was Nicholas V.*

We [therefore] weighing all . . . the premises with due meditation, and noting that since we had formerly by other letters of ours granted among other things free and ample faculty to the aforesaid King Alfonso—to invade, search out, capture, vanquish, and subdue all Saracens and pagans whatsoever, and other enemies of Christ wheresoever placed, and the kingdoms, dukedoms, principalities, dominions, possessions, and all movable and immovable goods whatsoever held and possessed by them and to reduce their persons to perpetual slavery, . . . in order that King Alfonso himself and his successors and the infante may be able the more zealously to pursue . . . this most pious and noble work, . . . the right of conquest which in the course of these letters we declare to be extended from the capes of Bojador and of Não, as far as through all Guinea, and beyond toward that southern shore, has belonged and pertained, and forever of right belongs and pertains, to the said King Alfonso, his successors, and the infante, and not to any others . . . .

**The full text of Document 1.3.5 is available on the CD-ROM.**

## 1.3.6

Diago Cao's Padrao—a stone pillar with a cross brought from Lisbon and erected by the explorer at the mouth of the Congo River

*Diago Cao was the first European to see the Congo River (also known as the Zaire River), which ran through the ancient kingdom of Kongo.*

"In the year . . . of 1482 since the birth of our Lord Jesus Christ, the most serene, most excellent, and potent prince, King D. Joao of Portugal, did order this land to be discovered and these *padraos* to be set up by D. Cão, an esquire of his household."

— Inscription on the padrao erected by Cão at the mouth of the Zaire River.

## 1.3.7

**Part I: Letter regarding the conversion of King Alfonso to Catholicism, from Rui d'Aguiar, a Catholic priest in the Kongo, to the King of Portugal, 1516**

May your Highness be informed that Alfonso's Christian life is such that he appears to me not as a man but as an angel . . . For I assure your Highness that it is he who instructs us; better than we, he knows the Prophets and the Gospel of Our Lord Jesus Christ and all the lives of the saints, I must say, Lord, that he does nothing but study and that many times he falls asleep over his books . . . When he gives audience or when he dispenses justice, his words are inspired by God . . . .

**Part II: Letter from King Alfonso to the King of Portugal concerning the slave trade, 1526**

We cannot estimate how great the damage is, because the merchants capture daily our own subjects, sons of our noblemen, vassals, and relatives . . . and cause them to be sold . . . . It is our will that in these kingdoms there should not be any trade in slaves or markets for slaves.

### 1.3.8

## Photograph of Afro-Portuguese saltcellar (Benin)

*This artifact, a container for salt, from the former kingdom of Benin, indicates cultural interchange between African crafters and Portuguese.*

© Copyright The British Museum

### 1.3.9

## Brass plaque showing a Benin trader

*It is probable that the Benin trader depicted here was appointed to deal with Europeans. He carries a staff of office in his right hand and a* manilla *(used as currency) in his left.*

© Copyright The British Museum

### 1.3.10

## Brass plaque of two Portuguese men above rows of *manillas*

Manillas *were horseshoe-shaped pieces of metal used as an early form of trade currency.*

The Metropolitan Museum of Art, Gift of Mr. and Mrs. Klaus G. Perls, 1991 (1991.17.13). Photograph, all rights reserved, The Metropolitan Museum of Art

# The Royal African Company, Independent Traders, and African Rulers in the Transatlantic Slave Trade

By the time Europeans became involved in the slave trade, West Africans and Arabs had been trading for centuries. Slaves were included in that trans-Saharan exchange, but it centered on goods such as guns, salt, gold, and ivory. The Portuguese, the first Europeans to arrive in Africa and participate in the slave trade, encountered a thriving West African economy. At first, the purchase of slaves was only part of a diverse commercial exchange. The relatively small number of slaves the Portuguese purchased was taken to Portugal and other parts of Europe, usually to work as domestic servants.

Europeans' demand for slaves increased as labor-intensive agriculture, especially the cultivation of sugar and tobacco, was established on colonial plantations on the Caribbean Islands and in North and South America. Although the Portuguese were probably the first Europeans to export enslaved Africans, the Spanish were the first Europeans to establish plantations based on slave labor in the Caribbean. Soon, other European countries entered into fierce competition to profit from the highly lucrative trade in slaves.

Europeans obtained a significant proportion of the slaves whom they exported indirectly, by trading with African rulers along the coast, rather than by sending parties into the interior to kidnap them directly. Initially, many Africans sold into American slavery were captured in wars between neighboring African rulers; later on, those wars were conducted largely for the sake of capturing people for sale. African rulers who attempted to slow down or stop the taking and export of captives faced military threats and economic competition from other rulers who benefited from selling slaves. In some cases, Europeans conspired with or bribed Africans to overthrow legitimate rulers who refused to trade in slaves. Many African rulers depended on European-made guns for the defense of their kingdoms, so they could not afford to stop trading captives for weapons. This vicious cycle of warfare and slave trading, which was initiated, armed, and perpetuated by Europeans, led to a significant loss of population and a profound disruption of African societies.

European traders negotiated agreements with African rulers to set up "factories" or forts along the West African coast. Initially, factories were "manufactories," places where raw materials such as salt and ivory were processed by hand (that is, manufactured) for export to Europe and other parts of Africa. Soon they were used as holding pens for captives until slave ships arrived to transport them overseas, so these places were fortified. One especially infamous fort is São Jorge da Mina at Elmina (in modern Ghana); built by the Portuguese in 1482 for gold trading, it was taken over by the Dutch in 1637 and devoted to the slave trade.

Competition among European powers intent upon establishing profitable colonial empires led to the rapid expansion of the transatlantic slave trade. British interest in the trade was a response to merchants' desire to seize opportunities in the commercial shipping of slaves to the Americas, as well as a response to the labor demands of British colonial planters in places such as Barbados. The English government chartered the Company of Royal Adventurers in 1660. The company's charter stated explicitly that its purpose was to participate in the slave trade and gave it exclusive rights—that is, no British merchants other than agents of the company could carry slaves from Africa to the colonies. This company collapsed in 1667, but its successor, the Royal African Company (RAC), was chartered and given a similar monopoly in 1672.

The Royal African Company maintained exclusive trading privileges until 1698, when Parliament, responding to pressure from independent merchants who sought a share in the profits, opened the transatlantic slave trade to all British subjects. The numbers of enslaved Africans carried on English ships rose rapidly, to an average of more than 20,000 people per year. Through relationships with African kings and traders and control over specific African coastal forts and castles, Britain was able to dominate the international slave trade from the late seventeenth century well into the eighteenth. By 1713, English ships were carrying slaves to the flourishing Spanish as well as English sugar plantations on the Caribbean Islands.

## Organizing Idea

The transatlantic slave trade expanded in the seventeenth century, when European powers established colonial plantations in the Americas and competed to control and profit from the lucrative trade in enslaved Africans. Britain became the dominant power in the transatlantic trade during the late seventeenth and early eighteenth centuries. The Royal African Company, independent traders, and African kings all played central roles in shaping this important element of the world economy.

## Student Objectives

Students will:

- describe the Royal African Company as a business whose charter granted it special privileges
- explain the competition between independent traders and the Royal African Company to profit from the growing demand for slave labor in the American colonies

❖ discover that both African rulers and European traders participated in the transatlantic slave trade

## Key Questions

❖ What were the rights and limits specified by the Royal African Company's charter, and how did the King of England benefit from granting it a charter?

❖ What were the similarities and differences between the operations of the RAC and those of independent traders?

❖ What arguments did each group use to appeal to Parliament to restructure the trade?

❖ What do the records reveal about how the RAC and independent traders interacted with African rulers in the slave trade?

## Primary Source Materials

DOCUMENT 1.4.1: The Trade of the Royal African Company, 1672

DOCUMENT 1.4.2: Excerpts from Capt. John Phillips' Journal, 1693–1694

DOCUMENT 1.4.3: Hetchcott and Gardener's letter protesting the actions of the Royal African Company and advocating free trade, 1694

DOCUMENT 1.4.4: Reports to the Board of Trade on Importation of Slaves to the Colonies, 1708–1709

DOCUMENT 1.4.5: Reports and Petitions to the House of Commons regarding the relationship with African kings, on African forts, and to support both RAC and free trade, 1709

DOCUMENT 1.4.6: São Jorge da Mina, the Castle at Elmina, an engraving by Theodor de Bry, 1604

DOCUMENT 1.4.7: Modern view out to sea from a window of the Castle at Elmina

## Vocabulary

| | | | |
|---|---|---|---|
| American plantation | Gambia River | "interloper" | Royal African Company |
| Bight of Benin | Governour | "Lycence to Trade" | shilling |
| castle | Gromettoes | petition | Sierra Leone River |
| charter | Guinea (various spellings) | pound sterling | River |
| factory | House of Commons | Province | |
| fort | | | |

## Student Activities

**Activity 1**

### Reading and Interpreting the Documents—RAC Agents, Independent Traders, and African Rulers

Students read the documents (1.4.1–1.4.5) and analyze the roles that Royal African Company (RAC) agents, independent traders, and African rulers played in the transatlantic slave trade. What else do students want to know in order to understand these documents? What evidence is there of conflicts among all three parties to the trade? What caused those conflicts, and how were they handled?

**Activity 2**

### Creative Extension

Students identify the constraints and opportunities facing RAC agents, independent traders, and African rulers, and then write and perform a role-play about the situation from the positions of all three groups. Next, students reflect on those whose voices and viewpoints are largely absent from these documents: the Africans who worked for wages at the factories and forts, the Africans who were held there awaiting shipment to the Americas, and the British soldiers who defended the fort from attack by other European powers and by Africans. Students should try to add their perspectives and actions to the role-play.

**Activity 3**

### Regulating the Slave Trade

The chartering of the Royal African Company was an effort to regulate Britain's trade with Africa so that the Crown, the nation, and its colonies would benefit economically and to guarantee that the trade would be conducted in an orderly and profitable manner. Merchants and artisans did not agree about whether an exclusive monopoly granted to the Royal African Company or free trade would be the best way of achieving those goals. Analyze Documents 1.4.3 and 1.4.5, paying special attention to the rather formulaic arguments made by parties on both sides. Then write an essay arguing one or the other position, giving both general considerations and specific reasons for that viewpoint.

**Activity 4**

### Debating the Transatlantic Slave Trade

Whose interests did the transatlantic slave trade serve? European rulers, merchants, and colonial planters? British sailors and artisans? African rulers? Who exercised the most power in the shaping of this trade? After the debate, students reflect on whether, in the long run, the slave trade served the best interests of any of the parties involved.

**Activity 5**

### Writing to Extend—The View of a Slave

Students examine the engraving from 1604 (1.4.6) and the modern photograph taken from a window of the Castle at Elmina (1.4.7). Then students imagine they have been captured and sold into slavery, torn from their family and village and transported hundreds of miles; now they await shipment across the Atlantic. Students write a first-person essay, journal entry, or poem expressing their thoughts and feelings. This written work may be read out loud, exchanged, or posted on the bulletin board in the classroom. Students with artistic talents might illustrate their pieces.

## Further Student and Teacher Resources

### Websites

www.fas.harvard.edu/~atlantic/abstr96.html
*1996 WP Abstracts*

www.middlepassage.org/timeline.htm#DAYS
*Annotated time line, comprehensive description of Middle Passage Foundation*

www.pbs.org/wgbh/aia/
*Africans in America/Part 1/David Blight*

www.pro.gov.uk
*The Royal African Company's online records*

http://gropius.lib.virginia.edu/SlaveTrade/
*A selection of descriptions and images of forts, castles, and factories*

---

## Contemporary Connection

✣

### Revisiting the Transatlantic Slave Trade

Today, some 200 million people of African descent live in North, Central, and South America and the Caribbean. Although many African Americans were cut off from their African roots with the passing of many generations, as well as the end of the international slave trade, some wish to explore the experiences their captured and enslaved ancestors underwent as they were shipped to the Americas, as well as to discover the peoples from which they are descended.

Recently, Americans—both black and white—have traveled to places like Elmina to see for themselves what remains from the past.

Facing such fraught subjects and imagining such horrific experiences is not easy. Participants in organized journeys have recorded and published their reflections on their experiences along the West African coast. African nations, too, have recently been turning these sites into historic monuments and museums. Search the Web for first-person accounts of these journeys of exploration and reflection. If any participants are local, ask them to come speak to the class.

---

# Primary Source Materials
## for Lesson 4

### 1.4.1

### The Trade of the Royal African Company, 1672

*Account of the Limits and Trade of the Royal African Company*

The company's limits under his Majesty's Charter begin at Sally in South Barbary new Tangier and end at Cabu Buen Esperanca where the East India Company's limits take place . . . . Next begins the North Coast of Guinea. On James Island in the River Gambia the companies have a fort where are kept 70 men, and a factory whence elephants' teeth, bees-wax, and cowhides are exported in very considerable quantities; the river is very large and runs up much higher than any discovery has been made, and the gold is supposed to come most from places at its head; in this river they have small factories at Rio Noones, Rispongo, and Calsamanca, and trade by sloops to Rio Grande and Catchao, for those commodities and negroes . . . .

**Note: The full text of Document 1.4.1 is available on the CD-ROM.**

### 1.4.2

### Excerpts from Capt. John Phillips' Journal, 1693–1694

*John Phillips was one of the captains sailing for the Royal African Company.*

When we had selected from the rest such as we liked, we agreed what goods to pay for them . . . how much of each sort of merchandise we were to give for man, woman, and child . . . Then we mark'd the slaves we had bought in the breast, or shoulder, with a hot iron having the letter of the ship's name on it, the place before nointed with a little palm oil, which caused but little pain, the mark being usually well in four or five days, appearing very plain and white after . . . .

We spent in our passage from St. Thomas to Barbadoes two months eleven days, from the 25th of August to the 4th of November following: in which time there happen'd much sickness and mortality among my poor men and negroes, that of the first we buried 14, and of the last 320, which was a great detriment to our voyage, the royal African company losing ten pounds by every slave that dies, and the owners of the ship ten pounds ten shillings, being the freight agreed on to be paid them by the charter-party for every negroe deliver'd alive ashore to the African company's agents at Barbadoes; whereby the loss in all amounted to near 6,650 pounds sterling . . . .

**The full text of Document 1.4.2 is available on the CD-ROM.**

## 1.4.3

## Hetchcott and Gardener's letter protesting the actions of the Royal African Company and advocating free trade, 1694

That wee are advised that at present there is noe Affrican Company in being for that the said Company stand Actually dissolved by an Act of this present Parliam't. That while they were a Company, they acted very Illegally and Oppressively.

1. By Stoping shipps outward bound and bringing them up from Gravesend when they were loaden and ready to Sail, and had paid all Duties and were cleared according to the Laws of the Land and deteining such Shipps until the Masters and owners had given Bonds on Great Penalties not to Trade on the Coast of Guiny to the great Damage of the Merchants and overthrow of many of their Voyages.

2. By seizing many Shipps with their Merchandizes in the open Sea and in ports in a Hostile manner, whereby severall lost their lives.

3. By setting up arbitrary Courts of Judicature in Foreigne parts and trying the validity of their Actions by their owne Agents . . . .

**The full text of Document 1.4.3 is available on the CD-ROM.**

## 1.4.4

## Reports to the Board of Trade on Importation of Slaves to the Colonies, 1708–1709

*Massach'ts.* To the Returne made to the Governour of the Massachus'ts Bay, he adds that there are in that Province 550 Negroes, of which number about 200 were

Imported from Barbadoes, Jamaica, or the Leeward Islands Since the 24th of June 1698, the rest were borne in that Province.

*New Hampshire.* In the Province of New Hampshire there are about Seventy Negroes and onely twenty thereof have been imported since the 24th June 1698.

## 1.4.5

## Reports and Petitions to the House of Commons regarding the relationship with African kings, on African forts, and to support both RAC and free trade, 1709

The Company further complain that the Natives grow insolent, and are encouraged by other Traders to insult the Companys Forts, and bring them out of Difficultys on purpose to obtain Bribes, to compose from their Factors, and particularly that one of the Separated Traders, having made a bargain for some Negroes carryed them to Barbadoes without paying for the same, but that the Company in order to secure the Peace and a friendly correspondence with the Negroe Kings, sent to Barbadoes and bought the said Negroes and returned them to the king from whome they were so taken . . . .

A Petition of the Shipwrights, Sail-makers, Rope-makers, and other Tradesmen, concerned in Shipping, inhabiting in and about London, was presented to the House, and read; setting forth, that the Petitioners and their Families, have been very much supported and maintained by the building, repairing, and fitting out, the Shipping, belonging to the Royal African Company in their Trade to Guinea, which is very much declined, but the great Difficulties and Discouragements, the Company has met with under their present Settlement, to the Prejudice of the Publick, and the Ruin of many of the Petitioners: And praying, that the said Company's Trade to Africa may be sercured, and encouraged, by such Means, and the House shall judge fit . . . .

**The full text of Document 1.4.5, including additional petitions, is available on the CD-ROM.**

1.4.6

## São Jorge da Mina, the Castle at Elmina, an engraving by Theodor de Bry, 1604

*São Jorge da Mina was built by the Portuguese in 1482 at Elmina, in present-day Ghana. In time, forts such as this one became known as castles. Here slaves captured inland awaited shipment across the Atlantic.*

Rare Book Division, New York Public Library

1.4.7

## Modern view out to sea from a window of the Castle at Elmina

Photograph by Roberta Logan

# Sugar and Slaves

Sugar, once a luxury product, had become an item in great demand among Europeans of all social classes by the fifteenth century. In the 1450s, following the method used by Genovese sugar plantation owners, Portuguese investors set up their own sugar plantations on the Atlantic island of Madeira and on the Canary Islands. Originally workers on these plantations were Muslims captured in wars, as well as people indigenous to these islands. The labor force soon included a mix of Africans, free and enslaved, some from Portugal and others brought directly from Africa.

Sao Tome, an island off the west coast of Africa, was claimed by the Portuguese in 1472. By 1520, it became the site for enormous sugar factories worked by enslaved Africans. Most were from Kongo. Kongo traders had sold them to plantation owners. These slaves were brought to the coast by *pombeiros*, people of mixed African-Portuguese descent who traveled far into the interior to buy these individuals from slave dealers. Sugar production, which included cultivating, harvesting, and processing sugar cane, was physically demanding and dangerous work; the life expectancy for slave laborers averaged five years. Thus, there was a constant demand to replenishing the labor force with West African slaves.

Sao Tome's sugar plantation system provided the model for the sugar industry in the West Indies. Sugar became more affordable as production increased, and it was considered a medicine as well as a tasty addition to the bland European diet. The quest for sugar exacerbated an already intense competition for raw materials among European powers. The Spanish set up the first sugar plantation in the New World on the island of Hispaniola (now Haiti and the Dominican Republic). At first the island's indigenous people were forced to work as slaves. When that labor force proved unworkable, Spanish growers brought over the first African slaves in 1502. The English set up their first West Indian sugar plantation on Barbados in 1627. Other European nations followed, claiming islands and gaining tremendous wealth from their exploitation of enslaved African labor.

## How Sugar Is Made

Sugar cane, which was planted and harvested continuously according to a set schedule, took up to eighteen months to mature. It had to be cut when it was ripe, ground as soon as it was cut, and boiled and refined by strong, skilled, and knowledgeable laborers. This commodity, dependent on time, strength, and skills, shaped the structure, schedule, and workforce of a successful sugar grower's plantation.

A plantation, a tremendous capital investment, was a combination of farm and factory. Both sugar and subsistence crops were grown, using mostly enslaved labor. According to Sidney Mintz in *Sweetness and Power*, this work entailed "specialization by skills and jobs, and the division of labor by age, gender, and condition into crews, shifts, and 'gangs'." Punctuality and discipline were stressed (p. 47).

The process of making sugar demanded continuing coordination among all workers. The juice pressed from sugar cane was transferred to the boiling house, where it was reduced by boiling at a certain temperature for a specific amount of time. Then it was clarified by careful skimming and crystallized by pouring, draining, and drying in molds. Molasses had to be drained, and rum was distilled as well. Sugar had to be stored for shipment to European markets. During harvest season, the boiling houses operated all day and part or all of the night, with skilled boilers operating furnaces, regulating the heat constantly to ensure uniform, high-quality results.

The increased demand for sugar by the English over the 100-year period covered by the following chart created an increased demand for enslaved labor. (This chart is adapted from information in Mintz, p. 39. A hogshead is a large cask of varying size; the standard measure is 63 gallons, or 238.5 liters.)

| Year | Imported into England | Exported from England |
|------|-----------------------|-----------------------|
| 1660 | 3000 hogsheads | 2000 hogsheads |
| 1700 | 50,000 hogsheads | 18,000 hogsheads |
| 1730 | 100,000 hogsheads | 18,000 hogsheads |
| 1753 | 110,000 hogsheads | 6,000 hogsheads |

Two tiny Caribbean islands that supplied the European market with sugar reflected the labor-hungry nature of sugar production. From 1701 to 1810, Barbados received 252,500 slaves; during the same time period, Jamaica received 662,400 slaves (Mintz 1985).

## Organizing Idea

Once sugar became known in Europe, an eager consumer market set an industry in motion. Capital was supplied by increasingly wealthy nations; technology was available in the form of skilled, seasoned, and experienced slave labor. In the view of Europeans, the tropical islands off the coast of Africa *and* in the Caribbean were theirs for the taking. The transatlantic slave trade arose from the European demand for labor to work the sugar plantations in the New World.

## Student Objectives

Students will:

- ❖ understand the increasing demand for sugar in Europe
- ❖ understand the labor-intensive nature of growing, harvesting, and processing this crop
- ❖ understand the movement of the plantation system of sugar cultivation and production with slave labor from islands off the coast of Africa to the Caribbean

## Key Questions

- ❖ How did the demand for sugar develop? Who was consuming sugar, and when?
- ❖ How did the increasing importation of sugar into Europe change the lives of Europeans? How expensive was it, and how did its price change over time?
- ❖ Why did sugar production create such an explosive rise in the need for slave labor?
- ❖ During the fifteenth century, where was sugar grown commercially and why was the plantation system moved to the Caribbean Islands?
- ❖ What place does sugar have in your life?

## Primary Source Materials

DOCUMENT 1.5.1: Tabernaemontanus (ca. 1515–1590), writing about the medicinal uses of sugar

DOCUMENT 1.5.2: Excerpts from W. Vaughan's *Natural and Artificial Directions for Health*, 1633

DOCUMENT 1.2.3: Juan de la Cosa's 1502 map, known as the "Portuguese Map of Africa" (See Lesson 2.)

DOCUMENT 1.5.3: Thomas Tryon's 1700 account from Barbados

DOCUMENT 1.5.4: Theodor de Bry's drawing of sugar production in Santo Domingo, 1565

DOCUMENT 1.5.5: Engraving of a sugar mill, 1681

## Supplementary Materials

ITEM 1.5.A: Translation of legend for sugar mill (for Document 1.5.5)
ITEM 1.5.B: Map of the Atlantic world

## Vocabulary

| bile | dropsy | Madeira | melancholia |
| Canary Islands | flux | medicinal | seasoned |

## Student Activities

### Reading and Discussion of Writings about Sugar

*Activity 1*

In pairs or small groups, students should read the scientific writings about sugar (1.5.1, 1.5.2), making sure that they understand the language and syntax of the documents. Have students explain how these documents help answer Key Question 1. Ask students to respond in a variety of written forms to the medical advice being given. Does it seem applicable today?

### Map Reading and Discussion

*Activity 2*

Ask students to carefully observe and record what they see on the Portuguese map (1.2.3). Ask them to explain how the cartographer revealed his purpose for creating the map. In what language are the words written? Do the royal figures look African? European? Who would find this map useful?

### Reading and Analysis

*Activity 3*

Students should study three documents, Tryon's account (1.5.3) and the two drawings (1.5.4, 1.5.5), as a thematic packet; alternatively, each primary source can be studied separately by a small group. Each source presents an important perspective on the part of its creator within a certain context of an enlightened, scientific era. It is important that students note that Tryon voiced complaints regarding profits, while at the same time he exploited his African slave labor.

### Translation from French

*Activity 4*

Students with some proficiency in French should translate the description of features on the sugar mill engraving (1.5.5) and share it with the class. (A translation is available on the CD-ROM in supplementary materials, Item 1.5.A.)

### Observation and Interpretation of Art

*Activity 5*

By studying the two engravings (1.5.4, 1.5.5), students gain a better appreciation of the physical demands of sugar production. Ask them to consider the planters' callous disregard for those who performed the real labor. Students study each engraving and, for each, compare and describe the setting, the people, the labor being performed, and the machinery being used. Ask students to identify any other pertinent details that inform us about what is happening in the picture.

Students need to consider the reasons for the physical misrepresentation of African slaves as well as inaccuracies in the engravings of the sugar industry. Who would be reading this written work and looking at these illustrations? How might the writings be interpreted if they were being illustrated with accurate drawings? What were Europeans given to understand about slavery through these drawings? Students need to identify and record the various steps in sugar production shown in the drawing. Students should compare the two drawings for mood, intent, audience, and accuracy.

## Activity 6     Writing

Students create a series of journal entries from the perspective of a slave. Imagine what a typical day would be like, given the harsh working conditions. What labor would have been performed?

## Activity 7     Research and Mapmaking

On a blank or a student-created map, students can trace, label, and annotate the movement of the sugar industry from its origins in the Eastern Mediterranean to the Canaries, Madeira, and Sao Tome, and then across the Atlantic to the Caribbean. They can identify and label the islands represented in the primary source documents they studied. (Item 1.5.B, a map of the Atlantic world, can be used.)

## Activity 8     Research

Students may use the Internet, travel brochures, or other sources to learn more about the plantation industry in the Caribbean Islands and Brazil today. Teachers could arrange for guest speakers to recount growing up in this setting. Does sugar still dominate the economy? What artifacts can the speaker share?

---

*Contemporary Connection* ⫘

**The Wreck of a Slaver**

In 1972 the treasure hunter Mel Fisher was sailing off the coast of Southern Florida when his crew alerted him that they had found the wreckage of a ship. Among the first things to be found in the wreckage were ivory tusks and a pair of rusty shackles. When the ship's cast bronze bell was brought up and cleaned, the inscription on it read: THE HENRIETTA MARIE 1699.

This ship had sunk on a return voyage in 1701 after taking an enslaved group of Igbos to Jamaica, more than likely to work on a sugar plantation. In 1992 the National Association of Black Scuba Divers placed an underwater plaque and monument at the wreck site. The plaque reads: HENRIETTA MARIE. In Memory and Recognition of the Courage, Pain and Suffering of Enslaved African People. "Speak Her Name and Gently Touch The Souls Of Our Ancestors." Dedicated November 15, 1992.

Learn more about this and other discoveries of shipwrecks related to the slave trade. See *www.historical-museum.org/exhibits/hm/sss.htm.*

## Further Student and Teacher Resources

Mann, Kenny. *Kongo Ndongo: West Central Africa (African Kingdoms of the Past)*. Parsippany, NJ: Dillon Press, 1996.

Mintz, Sidney. *Sweetness and Power, The Place of Sugar in Modern History*. New York: Penguin Books, 1985.

Nardo, Don, and Darlene Clark Hine. *Braving the New World 1619–1784, from the Arrival of the Enslaved Africans to the End of the American Revolution*. New York: Chelsea House Publishers, 1994.

### Websites

www.sugartech.co.za/news/

www.sugaronline.com/index.htm

# Primary Source Materials
## for Lesson 5

### 1.5.1

### Tabernaemontanus (ca. 1515–1590), writing on the medicinal uses of sugar

*Tabernaemontanus (ca. 1515–1590), known also as Jacob Theodor, was a professor of medicine and botany who specialized in herbal remedies. He is considered by some as the most important European physician and botanist of the sixteenth century. He gave sugar a generally positive assessment, even while identifying one of its disadvantages.*

Nice white sugar from Madeira or the Canaries, when taken moderately, cleans the blood, strengthens the body and mind, especially chest, lungs and throat, but is bad for hot and bilious people, for it easily turns into bile, also makes the teeth blunt and makes them decay. As a powder, it is good for the eyes, as a smoke it is good for the common cold, as flour sprinkled on wounds, it heals them. With milk and alum it serves to clear wine. Sugar water alone, also with cinnamon, pomegranate and quince juice, is good for a cough and fever. Sugar wine with cinnamon gives vigor to old people, especially sugar syrup with rose water which is recommended by Araldus Villanovanus. Sugar candy has all these powers to higher degrees.

### 1.5.2

### Excerpts from W. Vaughan's *Natural and Artificial Directions for Health*, 1633

Sugar is of a hot quality, and is quickly converted to Choler; for which cause I cannot approve use thereof in ordinary meates, except it bee in vinegar or sharpe liquor, specially to young men, or to them which are of hot complexions: for it is most certain that they which accustome themselves unto it, are commonly thirsty and dry, with their bloud burned, and their teeth blackened and corrupted. In medicine-wise, it may be taken either in water, for hot Feaves, or in syrups, for some kinde of diseases. In beer I approve it most wholesome.

**The full text for Document 1.5.2 is available on the CD-ROM.**

## 1.5.3

## Thomas Tyron's 1700 account from Barbados

*The Barbadian colonist Thomas Tyron—whose complaints must be viewed with some skepticism, because he was a planter himself—nonetheless conveys well the environment in this seventeenth-century mill:*

In short, 'tis to live in perpetual Noise and Hurry and the only way to render a person Angry, and Tyrannical, too; since the Climate is so hot, and the labor so constant, that the Servants [or slaves] night and day stand in great Boyling Houses, where there are Six or Seven large Coppers or Furnaces kept perpetually Boyling; and from which with heavy Ladles and Scummers they Skim off the excrementitious parts of the Canes, till it comes to its perfection and cleanness, while other as Stoakers, Broil as it were, alive, in managing the Fires; and one part is constantly at the Mill, to supply it with Canes, night and day, during the whole Season of making Sugar, which is about six Months of the year; so that what with these things, the number of the Family, and many other Losses and Disappointments of bad Crops, which often happens, Master Planter has no such easy life as some may imagine, nor Riches flow upon him with that insensibility, as it does upon many in England.

## 1.5.4

## Theodor de Bry's drawing of sugar production in Santo Domingo, 1565

*In* Sweetness and Power, *Sidney Mintz notes that in this "fanciful drawing . . . . the workers resemble Classical Greeks more than Africans or Indians, and the cane processing is confusingly presented: a 'mill' at the upper right shows only a sluice and a water wheel, while the device inside the shed is an edge-roller, long employed in Europe to crush olives and apples and in India and elsewhere to crush cane, but whose use is not documented for the New World."*

From *Sweetness and Power* by Sidney W. Mintz, Viking Penguin, 1985

1.5.5

## Engraving of a sugar mill, 1681

*According to Sidney Mintz, this type of sugar mill design was used for centuries.*

From *Sweetness and Power* by Sidney W. Mintz, Viking Penguin, 1985

# Olaudah Equiano

The autobiography of Olaudah Equiano is one of only a few first-person narratives written by enslaved Africans in the eighteenth century. The story was written by Equiano later in his life in the service of the abolitionist cause. It was published in England and endorsed by 321 subscribers, including the Prince of Wales and the Duke of York.

Equiano was a young boy living in what is now the province of Benin in Nigeria but was then the autonomous land of the Ibo people when he was kidnapped into slavery. After many transactions, in 1756 he was taken by British slave traders to Barbados, shipped on to Virginia, purchased by a British naval officer, taken to England, and renamed Gustavas Vassa (a Portuguese name). He served his owner by fighting in the British navy. At the end of the Seven Years War in 1763, Equiano hoped to acquire his freedom; instead he was returned to the West Indies for resale.

A Quaker merchant from Philadelphia purchased Equiano and put him to work on one of his sailing vessels. The captain of this ship helped Equiano earn enough money to buy his own freedom, and by 1766 he was free. Eventually he returned to England and worked for the abolition of the international slave trade and the institution of slavery.

In 1789, Olaudah Equiano (or Gustavas Vassa) published his memoir. This personal narrative is of great value to us as we study this period in history. Through the eyes of a native person, we learn about a specific region of West Africa as it was in the eighteenth century: the terrain, trade, foods, crops, and the culture of people living there. Equiano also describes his experiences as a young boy after capture, without English language skills and with little understanding of various strange customs and artifacts. We learn of the oppression to which slaves in the West Indies were subjected, and we learn of the masters who owned Equiano and the skills he learned. Finally, Equiano's writing offers a passionate and articulate call for the abolition of slavery.

## Organizing Idea

Equiano's story follows a path quite different from that of most young Africans stolen from their homeland. He was not put to work on a plantation; instead, he was able to develop skills as a sailor, and he eventually became a citizen of substance, free and living in England, campaigning there for the abolition of slavery. This story, examined with other extant narratives, expands our understanding of slavery and of the individuals who lived within this unnatural institution.

## Student Objectives

Students will:

❖ gain an understanding of Equiano's heritage, his enslavement, his observations and interactions with others, and his determination to bring an end to slavery

❖ understand that the experience of slavery varied over time and was experienced differently by individuals, depending on the circumstances of their capture and sale

❖ begin to understand something of what we mean by "the human condition;" that is, people in all times and places feeling joy, sadness, fear, and resolve

❖ be able to document the existence of black abolitionist activity as early as the eighteenth century and the role of African-born ex-slaves in that movement

## Key Questions

❖ What can we learn about the life of Equaino and about slavery from this narrative?

❖ How can we describe this West African culture after reading Equiano's description?

❖ What feelings and fears can we identify in common with Equiano as a young boy? What is different and why? Why is knowing this important?

❖ What were abolitionists trying to accomplish in the eighteenth and nineteenth centuries?

## Primary Source Materials

DOCUMENT 1.6.1: Excerpts from Equiano's autobiography, *The Interesting Narrative of the Life of Olaudah Equiano, or Gustavus Vassa*, 1789

DOCUMENT 1.6.2: Portrait of Olaudah Equiano or Gustavus Vassa, the African, 1791

## Vocabulary

| Bight of Benin | Edo | Guinea | Niger River |
|---|---|---|---|

## Student Activities

### Activity 1    Reading and Discussion of Excerpts from Autobiography

Ways of approaching this reading will vary, depending on the age and skill levels of the students. Please be aware that Equiano's descriptions of the slave ship are graphic. Skillful readers can engage with the entire narrative in the following way: Divide the class into groups. Each group reads one chapter, discusses the story among themselves and then, by turns, each group, beginning with Chapter 1, tells the story to the class. After hearing Equiano's story, encourage students to share ideas and questions, keeping in mind the Key Questions.

For younger or less skillful readers, use the selections included with this lesson. There are four sections: (I) a description of Equiano's Africa, (II) Equiano's experience of the Middle Passage, (III) Equiano's childhood experiences while enslaved, and (IV) his work on behalf of abolition. Each selection can be read aloud by the teacher, assigned for homework, or approached as a group reading as described above, with each group being responsible for only a small portion of the text. A pre-reading vocabulary lesson may prove useful. After reading, provide time for students to respond to what they have read, raising questions, sharing ideas and feelings, and responding to the key questions.

### Activity 2    Dramatization of Portions of Narrative

Working in small groups or as a class, students choose one portion of the narrative that especially interests them. Have students tell that part of Equiano's story; then ask them to make a list of the characters needed to tell the story. Together, they create a script for a play that dramatically presents a portion of Equiano's life. This play (or plays) can be performed for other students in the school.

### Activity 3    Writing to Extend

Students create a piece of writing (essay, poem, journal, fiction story, play) in response to what they have read and discussed. The writings should incorporate elements of Equiano's description of his country and its customs, the horror of the Middle Passage, his fears and adventures as a young enslaved African, and/or his efforts on behalf of other Africans who are still enslaved.

### Activity 4    Discussion of England's Abolitionist Movement

What can we learn about eighteenth-century efforts in England to abolish the international slave trade and the institution of slavery by a careful reading of Equiano's speech before a group of Quakers and his letter to Queen Charlotte? How can we find out what the Queen's attitude about abolition might have been? Who were the Quakers, or (as they called themselves) Friends? What do we know about this religious group both in the eighteenth century and today?

## Research on England's Abolitionist Movement

*Activity 5*

Many ex-slaves from the United States worked with abolitionists in England in the early nineteenth century. To learn what was happening during the previous century, students research abolitionist movements and activities in England in the late eighteenth century, at the time Equiano was speaking and writing against slavery throughout the country. These abolitionists were primarily motivated by their religious beliefs; many were Quakers as well as members of other dissenting denominations. The most available sources of information on this topic can be found on the Internet. Look for Granville Sharpe, especially on the website *www.spartacus. schoolnet.co.uk*, William Wilberforce, George Whitefield, John Newton (composer of "Amazing Grace"), John Wesley, and Thomas Clarkson.

## Analysis of Engraving

*Activity 6*

What can we learn by looking carefully at the engraving of Equiano (1.6.2)? Note his clothing and the book that he holds. How can we learn more about his life after he bought his freedom?

## Music Connection

⁑

Olaudah Equiano in his *Narrative* stressed that in Africa "every great event, such as a triumphant return from battle or other cause of public rejoicing, is celebrated in public dances, which are accompanied with songs and music suited to the occasion." Drums then, as now, were most frequently used in royal or religious occasions. They came in a range of sizes and shapes, from 1 foot to 10 feet long and in diameter 2 inches to several feet across. The drums were made from hollowed logs or by cutting gourds. Skin was stretched over both kinds, and Africans played the drums with their fingers, the palms of their hands, or crooked sticks.

"Atsiagbeko" (on the CD-ROM) was recorded by Richard Hill on location and represents ritual music in Ghana. Over time, the ritual war dance this music accompanied evolved into a narrative dance depicting past acts of bravery and the blessing of peace. You will hear five drums, a shaker, and a double bell. Pay particular attention to the various drum parts. What are the roles of the bell and the shaker? Listen to the piece several times and follow a different drum each time. Also, notice the "calling out" at the beginning of the piece and remember it when you listen to the music in Lesson 15.

"Music for a Cult Ceremony—The Finale" (on the CD-ROM) was also recorded by Richard Hill in Ghana. He explains that "the final hour or so of the ceremony is devoted to drumming and dancing." Listen to the call and response in the singing, the use of drums to provide rhythmic accompaniment, the improvisational nature of the singing, and the playing of the lead drummer.

## Further Student and Teacher Resources

Andrews, William L., and Henry Louis Gates, Jr., eds. *Slave Narratives*. New York: The Library of America, Penguin Putnam, 2000.

Bolster, Jeffery. *Black Jacks: African American Seaman in the Age of Sail*. Cambridge, MA: Harvard University Press, 1997.

Curtin, Philip D., ed. *Africa Remembered, Narratives by West Africans from the Era of the Slave Trade*. Madison: University of Wisconsin Press, 1967. (The book is out of print but can be found in many libraries and is available secondhand from Amazon.)

Equiano, Olaudah. *The Interesting Narrative of the Life of Olaudah Equiano, or Gustavus Vassa, the African, written by Himself*, ed. Werner Sollors. New York: Norton, 2001.

Feelings, Tom. *The Middle Passage: White Ships, Black Cargo*. New York: Dial Books, 1995.

Meltzer, Milton. *The Black Americans: A History in their Own Words*. New York: Harper Collins, 1984.

Steele, Ian K., and Nancy L. Rhoden, eds. *The Human Tradition in Colonial America*. Wilmington, Delaware: SR Books, 1999. (See especially the essay on Equiano by Robert Allison.)

Wood, Peter H., et al. *Strange New Land: Africans in Colonial America, 1516–1776. The Young Oxford History of African Americans*, vol. 2. New York: Oxford University Press, 1996.

### Videos

*Son of Africa: The Slave Narrative of Olaudah Equiano*, 1996. 28 minutes, available from California Newsreel, San Francisco, CA.

*Africans in America*, video 2, WGBH Educational Foundation, 1998.

### Websites

www.brycchancarey.com/equiano/index.htm

www.cocc.edu/cagatucci/classes/hum211/coursepack/Equiano.htm
*Extensive information about Equiano, including a map of his journeys*

www.pbs.org/wgbh/aia/part1/1p276.html
*Africans in America site, with many resources*

www.georgetown.edu/bassr/heath/syllabuild/iguide/vassa.html
*Directed at teachers, interesting ideas for writing and on comparative literature*

## Contemporary Connection 1 ⇥⌖⇤

**African Voices**

Discussion about colonial slavery has continued into the twentieth and twenty-first centuries on both sides of the Atlantic. This website includes the voices of living Africans: *www.bbc.co.uk/worldservice/africa/features/ storyofafrica/rams/9audio2.ram.*

## Contemporary Connection 2 ⇥⌖⇤

**Retelling the Slave Experience**

The slave narrative has had a pronounced effect on African American writers. The story line of many novels, including Toni Morrison's *Beloved* and Ismael Reed's *Flight to Canada*, centers on the retelling of the slave experience. Another literary link to slave narratives may be noted in the continuing dominant interest of African American writers in autobiography. Langston Hughes, Zora Neale Hurston, Richard Wright, Malcolm X, and Maya Angelou are twentieth-century writers whose books and poems serve to pass on these stories. Explore their writings.

# Primary Source Materials
# for Lesson 6

## 1.6.1

Excerpts from Equiano's autobiography, *The Interesting
Narrative of the Life of Oladah Equiano
or Gustavus Vassa*, 1789

**Selections from Chapter 1**

THE AUTHOR'S ACCOUNT OF HIS COUNTRY, AND THEIR MANNERS AND
CUSTOMS, ETC.

My father was one of those elders or chiefs I have spoken of, and was styled
Embrence; a term, as I remember, importing the highest distinction, and signifying
in our language a mark of grandeur. This mark is conferred on the person entitled to
it by cutting the skin across at the top of the forehead, and drawing it down to the
eye-brows; and while it is in this situation applying a warm hand, and rubbing it,
until it shrinks up into a thick weal across the lower part of the forehead . . . .

Our manner of living is entirely plain; for as yet the natives are unacquainted
with those refinements in cookery which debauch the taste: bullocks, goats, and
poultry, supply the greatest part of their food. These constitute likewise the principal wealth of the country, and the chief articles of its commerce. The flesh is usually
stewed in a pan; to make it savoury we sometimes use also pepper, and other spices,
and we have salt made of wood allies. Our vegetables are mostly plantains, eadas,
yams, beans, and Indian corn. The head of the family usually eats alone; his wives
and slaves have also their separate tables. Before we taste food we always wash our
hands: indeed our cleanliness on all occasions is extreme; but on this it is an indis-
pensable ceremony. After washing, libation is made, by pouring out a small portion
of the food, in a certain place, for the spirits of departed relations, which the natives
suppose to preside over their conduct and guard them from evil . . . .

## Selections from Chapter 2

*Equiano's story continues with a description of his capture, probably at age 11, by slave traders and his journey on a slave ship bound for Barbados. Of Barbados, he writes:*

The first object which saluted my eyes when I arrived on the coast was the sea, and a slaveship, which was then riding at anchor, and waiting for its cargo. These filled me with astonishment, which was soon converted into terror, which I am yet at a loss to describe, nor the then feelings of my mind. When I was carried on board I was immediately handled, and tossed up, to see if I were sound, by some of the crew; and I was now persuaded that I had got into a world of bad spirits, and that they were going to kill me . . . .

## Selections from Chapter 3

### THE AUTHOR IS CARRIED TO VIRGINIA . . . AND SETS OUT FOR ENGLAND

On the passage [from Barbados to North America] we were better treated than when we were coming from Africa, and we had plenty of rice and fat pork. We were landed up a river a good way from the sea, about Virginia county, where we saw few or none of our native Africans, and not one soul who could talk to me. I was a few weeks weeding grass, and gathering stones in a plantation; and at last all my companions were distributed different ways, and only myself was left. I was now exceedingly miserable, and thought myself worse off than any of the rest of my companions; for they could talk to each other, but I had no person to speak to that I could understand. In this state I was constantly grieving and pining, and wishing for death rather than anything else . . . .

## Selection from Chapter 12

### LETTER TO THE QUEEN

*To the* QUEEN's *most Excellent Majesty.*

MADAM,

YOUR Majesty's well known benevolence and humanity emboldens me to approach your royal presence, trusting that the obscurity of my situation will not prevent your Majesty from attending to the sufferings for which I plead.

Yet I do not solicit your royal pity for my own distress; my sufferings, although numerous, are in a measure forgotten. I supplicate your Majesty's compassion for millions of my African countrymen, who groan under the lash of tyranny in the West Indies.

The oppression and cruelty exercised to the unhappy negroes there, have at length reached the British legislature, and they are now deliberating on its redress; even several persons of property in slaves in the West Indies, have petitioned parliament against its continuance, sensible that it is as impolitic as it is unjust—and what is inhuman must ever be unwise.

Your Majesty's reign has been hitherto distinguished by private acts of benevolence and bounty; surely the more extended the misery is, the greater must be your Majesty's compassion, and the greater must be your Majesty's pleasure in administering to its relief.

I presume, therefore, gracious Queen, to implore your interposition with your royal consort, in favour of the wretched Africans . . . .

**The full text for Document 1.6.1 is available on CD-ROM.**

### 1.6.2

### Portrait of Olaudah Equiano or Gustavus Vassa the African, 1791

American Antiquarian Society

# Ayuba Suleiman Diallo

Ayuba Suleiman Diallo of Bondu, known to Europeans as Job Ben Solomon, was a Muslim merchant from the Senegambia region of West Africa. His story, written down by Thomas Bluett and published in 1734, describes him as the son of the high priest of Bondu and a member of a family of Fulbe Muslim clerics. People of the Senegambia region had been trading directly with Europeans since the fifteenth century for goods such as gum arabic, gold, ivory, hides, beeswax and, as a minor part of their trade, for slaves. The Senegal and Gambia rivers provided navigable trading routes for both Africans and Europeans.

Stiff competition arose between French and English traders, and Africans themselves acted as merchants and agents. According to his account, Diallo himself participated in trade. It was during one such exchange with an English ship stationed on the Gambia River in 1730 that Diallo, accompanied by two servants, planned to sell two "Negroes" and buy paper and other necessities (Curtin 1967, p. 39). Diallo instead was captured by English traders, who took him to Annapolis, Maryland, to work as a slave on a tobacco plantation. He was eventually discovered by Bluett, emancipated, presented at the British court, and finally returned home to Africa.

Very little is known about Thomas Bluett, who recorded Diallo's story and published it in 1734. He knew Diallo from the Gambia River, where Diallo's family traded. According to Springfield College professor Allan Austins, Bluett was a lawyer; why he was in West Africa is unknown.

## Organizing Idea

Ayuba Suleiman Diallo's account is the story of a prosperous West African Muslim merchant involved in the slave trade who himself become enslaved. Understanding his heritage and the events in his life helps to make more complex the picture of who might become enslaved; the role of Muslim merchants and their interactions with Europeans along the Gambia and Senegal rivers and the coast; and European attitudes regarding an educated and Muslim African.

## Student Objectives

Students will:

❖ learn to interpret the stylized writing of such eighteenth-century accounts and get beyond the unfamiliar form of the English language to find a compelling story

❖ use maps to follow Diallo's journey from his home and capture in the Senegambia area of West Africa, across the Atlantic to Maryland, then to England, and finally his return to Africa

❖ analyze Diallo's portrait as they gain an understanding of his life

❖ recognize that Diallo's emancipation and return to Africa was the exception, rather than the rule, to the fate of most enslaved Africans

## Key Questions

❖ Why do you think Thomas Bluett "at length resolved to communicate to the world" the story of Diallo's life? What might the English-speaking world of 1734 want to know about a former slave's life?

❖ What seems unique about Diallo's capture?

❖ Why would Diallo's Muslim beliefs bring him exceptional treatment as a slave in Maryland?

❖ How was Diallo received in England? What might be some reasons for this?

❖ What does the reader need to think about while reading the account of one person's life written down by another person? How accurate is such an account? Can we determine its accuracy?

❖ Cultures and attitudes change over time. What distinctive ideas from Bluett's time should we keep in mind when analyzing his account?

❖ What might be missing from this version of Diallo's story?

## Primary Source Materials

DOCUMENT 1.7.1: Excerpts from the story of Ayuba Suleiman Diallo, written down by Thomas Bluett and published in 1734

DOCUMENT 1.7.2: Ayuba's return to Africa, from the journal of Francis Moore, 1738

DOCUMENT 1.7.3: Portrait of Ayuba Suleiman Diallo, known to Europeans as Job Ben Soloman

DOCUMENT 1.7.4: Letter from Ayuba Suleiman Diallo, known to Europeans as Job Ben Solomon, to Jacob Smith, from "Yanimerow in the River Gambia," dated January 27, 1735/6

## Supplementary Materials

ITEM 1.5.B: Map of the Atlantic world

## Vocabulary

| | | | |
|---|---|---|---|
| benefactor | Gambia | gum arabic | Royal African |
| Bondu | River | Jollof | Company |
| Futah Jallon | gaol | Koran | Senegal River |

## Student Activities

### Reading and Discussion of Diallo's Story

*Activity 1*

Students read Bluett's account of Diallo's life (1.7.1). The reading can be divided among small groups, with each group being responsible for telling one part of the story. Or the story can be read aloud over a class period, stopping to ask the following questions:

- ❖ What was the sequence of events involving Diallo's capture and shipment to Maryland?

- ❖ What made his experience both typical and atypical for captured Africans?

- ❖ What did Diallo do that seemed to set him apart from other Africans?

- ❖ How were his daily routines and practices determined by his Muslim beliefs?

- ❖ Why do you think that, in the end, Diallo was treated so differently from other captured Africans?

### Creating Reference Materials

*Activity 2*

Have students create a time line to keep the events of Diallo's life in order and to use for further reference.

### Mapping Diallo's Journeys

*Activity 3*

Using the time line and the narrative (1.7.1 and 1.7.2), students trace on an outline map of the Atlantic world (Item 1.5.B) the events of Diallo's capture and movements in West Africa, his travels west across the Atlantic Ocean, in North America, over to England, and back to West Africa. A Big Map can also be created, as in Lesson 2, *Using Maps to Learn About the Past.*

### Writing to Answer Key Questions

*Activity 4*

Students select one of the Key Questions and, using information they have learned and their own ideas, write an essay addressing the chosen question. The essays may be shared with the class.

Activity 5          **Research**

Students research the nature of slavery within Africa, as well as the Koran's position on slavery. How did the practice of enslavement change when it became institutionalized in the Americas?

## Further Student and Teacher Resources

Austin, Allan. *African Muslims in Antebellum American: Transatlantic Stories and Spiritual Struggles.* New York: Routledge, 1997.

Blassingame, John W., ed. *Slave Testimony, Two Centuries of Letters, Speeches, Interviews and Autobiographies.* Baton Rouge: Louisiana State University Press, 1977.

Curtin, Philip D., ed. *Africa Remembered: Narratives by West Africans from the Era of the Slave Trade.* Madison: University of Wisconsin Press, 1967.

Diouf, Sylviane A. *Servants of Allah: African Muslims Enslaved in the Americas.* New York: New York University Press, 1998.

Gomez, Michael A. "Muslims in Early America," *Journal of Southern History*, LX (November 1994), 671–710.

### Website

http://vi.uh.edu/pages/mintz/2.htm
*An excerpt from Thomas Bluett's account*

## Contemporary Connection
⊁⊩⊰

### Islam in Africa

Today Islam has more adherents worldwide than any other religion except Christianity. In Africa, one-half of the population is Muslim. Islam entered the continent through Egypt around 640 C.E. and was spread through armed conquests, trading activity, and education. The expansion of this religion was aided by several factors. Islam was more inclusive and egalitarian in terms of race than Christianity was, so more attractive to Africans. In the face of colonial domination, Africans looked for a worldview other than the one imposed by Europeans. Anticolonial movements in Africa often accompanied conversion to Islam. The Islamic faith now permeates North Africa as well as much of sub-Saharan Africa. Today many African political systems, laws, language, literature, music, art, and culture show significant Islamic influence. For further information on the Muslim faith in Africa today, explore.

http://web-dubois.fas.harvard.edu/dubois/

http:/exploringafrica.matrix.msu.edu/curriculum/1m14/stu_actthree14.html

www.pbs.org/wgbh/pages/frontline/shows/muslims
Frontline *features stories of individual Muslims in Africa today.*

www.islamtz.org/articles/islam_in_africa.htm

www.mrdowling.com/605westr.html
*General information about the religion of Islam*

*Islam in Senegal:*

www.isim.nl/newsletter/1/regional/01AC11.html

www.geocities.com/jbenhill/religion.html

*Islam in Nigeria:*

www.op.org/nigeriaop/kenny/sist.htm

www.afrikaworld.net/afrel/islam-atr-nigeria.htm

www.palo.org/yoruba/islam.html

www.freedomhouse.org/religion/news/bn2002/bn-2002-03-27.htm

# Primary Source Materials for Lesson 7

Excerpts from the story of Ayuba Suleiman Diallo,
written down by Thomas Bluett
and published in 1734

**The Capture and Travels of Ayuba Suleiman Ibrahima [known to Europeans as Job Ben Solomon]**

INTRODUCTION

Having had occasion to inform myself of many considerable and curious circum-stances of the life of Job, the African priest, in a more exact and particular manner than the generality of his acquaintance in England could do; I was desired by him-self, a little before his departure, to draw up an account of him agreeable to the infor-mation he had given me at different times, and to the truth of the facts, which I had either been a witness to, or personally concerned in upon his account . . . .

SECTION II

[Upon landing] Job [was sold] to one Mr. Tolsey in Kent Island in Maryland, who put him to work in making tobacco; but he was soon convinced that Job had never been used to such labor. He every day showed more and more uneasiness under this exercise, and at last grew sick, being no way able to bear it; so that his master was obliged to find easier work for him, and therefore put him to tend the cattle. Job would often leave the cattle, and withdraw into the woods to pray; but a white boy frequently watched him, and whilst he was at his devotion would mock him and throw dirt in his face. This very much disturbed Job, and added considerably to his other misfortunes; all which were increased by his ignorance of the English language, which prevented his complaining, or telling his case to any person about him. Grown in some measure desperate, by reason of his present hardships, he resolved to travel at a venture; thinking he might possibly be taken up by some master, who would use him better, or otherwise meet with some lucky accident, to divert or abate his grief . . . .

**The full text of Document 1.7.1 is available on the CD-ROM.**

## 1.7.2

### Ayuba's return to Africa, from the journal of Francis Moore, 1738

**Ayuba's Return to Africa**

The next day [8 August 1734] about noon came up the *Dolphin* snow, which had saluted the fort with nine guns, and had the same number returned; after which came on shore the captain, four writers, one apprentice to the Company, and one Black man, by name Job Ben Solomon, a Pholey [Pulo] of Bundo in Foota, who in the year 1731, as he was travelling in Jagra [Jarra], and driving his herds of cattle across the countries, was robbed and carried to Joar, where he was sold to captain Pyke, commander of the ship *Arabella*, who was then trading there. By him he was carried to Maryland, and sold to a planter, with whom Job lived about a twelve month without being once beaten by his master; at the end of which time he had the good fortune to have a letter of his own writing in the Arabic tongue conveyed to England . . . .

**The full text of Document 1.7.2 is available on the CD-ROM.**

## 1.7.3

Portrait of Ayuba Suleiman Diallo, known to Europeans as Job Ben Solomon

1.7.4

## Letter from Ayuba Suleiman Diallo known to Europeans as Job Ben Solomon, to Jacob Smith from "Yanimerow in the River Gambia," dated January 27, 1735/6

YANIMEROW IN THE RIVER GAMBIA Jan: 27th: [1735/6]

*Sir*, this is to acquaint you of my safe arrival at and return here from Bonda being conducted safe and used with great civility all the way, which was owing to the respect and regard all the natives in every part have for the Company and by being conducted by one white man only which was the Governors nephew on the Companys behalf which made no little noise and was of much service to me, one of my wives had got another husband in my room and the other gave me over, my father died soon after my misfortune of being seized and sold as a slave, but my children are all well, my redemption was so remarkable and surprizing that my messengers and letters sent on my arrival here were not credited, but how elevated and amazed they were at my arrival, I must leave you to guess at, as being inexpressible as is likewise the raptures and pleasure I enjoy'd, floods of tears burst their way and some little time afterwards we recover'd so as to have some discourse and in time I acquainted them and all the country how I had been redeem'd and conducted by the Company from such distant parts as are beyond their capacity to conceive, from Maryland to England, from thence to Gambia Fort, and from thence conducted by them to my very house, the favours done me by the Queen, Duke of Montague and other generous persons, I likewise acquainted them of and all with me praised God for such his providence and goodness, and as a more publick acknowledgment thereof I kept from my arrival a months fast, I should think myself very happy in your company in these parts if your inclination continues to come in the companys service.

I am Sir, Your obliged and most humble servant<br>JOB THE SON OF SOLOMON<br>Of the nation (or tribe) of Jalot.

# Venture Smith

In 1735, Broteer, the six-year-old son of a West African prince, was captured by raiders from his village in Guinea and taken several hundred miles west to the Gold Coast, where he was sold and shipped as cargo to Connecticut. According to his autobiography, he was purchased by a crew member "for four gallons of rum and piece of calico, and called VENTURE on account of his having purchased me with his own private venture." For the next thirty years, Venture Smith worked as a slave in Connecticut and Long Island. After purchasing his freedom and that of his wife, daughter, two sons, and several others, Smith was in business for himself, cutting wood, farming, fishing, and shipping out on whaling vessels. Against great odds and through hard work, perseverance, and planning, Smith could be described as having lived the American dream, attaining personal independence and property ownership. He was a self-made man. He bought and sold land and other property and employed his own fleet of twenty sailing vessels to trade all around Long Island Sound. A newspaper advertisement for his autobiography described him as "a negro remarkable for size, strength, industry, fidelity, and frugality, and well known in the state of Rhode Island, on Long Island, and in Stonington, East Haddam, and several other parts of" Connecticut.

Smith's autobiographical narrative, A *Narrative of the Life and Adventures of VENTURE*, was published in 1798 in Connecticut when Smith was sixty-nine years old. Although perhaps subject to the exaggeration of things remembered, his narrative offers us information and insight into the lives of enslaved and free black people in New England in the late colonial and early national period. It offers a complex picture of the slave trade and slavery through the eyes of a man who, in many ways, represented American values but who nevertheless had a proud recollection of things African.

## Organizing Idea

Reading about the lives of individuals in their own words is a powerful way to learn about the past. Venture Smith's story offers us a window into life in New

England in the eighteenth century—the values, economy, power, and possibilities for blacks moving from slavery to freedom. It also allows us to make the acquaintance of a remarkable man.

## Student Objectives

Students will:

- ❖ hear the voice of a person living more than 200 years ago who helped to shape the country in which we now live
- ❖ see, through the use of biography, a model of individual initiative and of the possibilities for choice and control over one's life

## Key Questions

- ❖ How does Venture Smith describe his early years in Africa? What more do we as twenty-first-century Americans need to know to understand these experiences? How can we find the information we need?
- ❖ What do we learn about Venture Smith's character early in the story when he was still a young boy? Where might he have learned the values he displayed?
- ❖ What did Venture Smith do to buy his own freedom? Why do you think he wanted to do that?

## Primary Source Materials

DOCUMENT 1.8.1: A copy of an advertisement for the *Narrative* in the *New London Bee*, 1798.

DOCUMENT 1.8.2: Excerpts from Chapters 1, 2, and 3 of *A Narrative of the Life and Adventures of VENTURE, a Native of Africa: But resident above sixty years in the United States of America*, 1798.

## Supplementary Materials

ITEM 1.5.B: Map of the Atlantic world

ITEM 1.8.A: Outline of a human head, for use as a Historical Head

## Vocabulary

| | | | |
|---|---|---|---|
| Broteer | hillocks | pinioned | victuals |
| gaol | palliation | polygamy | |

## Student Activities

### Analysis of Advertisement

As a class, look together at the newspaper advertisement for *A Narrative* (1.8.1). What can we learn from this ad? How is Smith described? What is the irony in the four-line poem included in the ad?

### Reading and Discussion of *Narrative*

Introduce Chapters I and II of Venture Smith's *Narrative* (1.8.2). Chapter I describes details of Broteer's capture from his village in Guinea. Chapter II describes his arrival in Rhode Island. Venture (as he was now called) was very young, about 6 or 7. He describes the work he learned to do, the harsh treatment he received, his several owners, and his marriage. We also begin to see how strong and resilient he was and how he continued to work to purchase his freedom despite broken promises from the men who owned him. Either (1) do a read-aloud to the whole group, (2) do a group reading in which small groups each read a few pages and share, or (3) have the students, as individuals, read Chapters I and II of the *Narrative*. Then, as a group, take turns telling the story as recorded in Chapters I and II.

Ask the students: what parts of the story surprise you? What questions do you have? Does the story remind you of other reading you have done? Explain. In order to understand this person, what other kinds of information will you need?

### Mapping Smith's Journey

Students create a class map tracing Venture Smith's childhood journey to America. It begins in his village in Guinea, moves to the Gold Coast, crosses the Atlantic to Barbados, and ends in Rhode Island and Connecticut. Students should use an outline map of the Atlantic world (Item 1.5.B), the narrative, and an atlas. (*Note:* the Gold Coast is now the nation of Ghana.)

### Creative Extensions

Using the outline of a human head (Historical Head, Item 1.8.A), have each student, working alone or with a partner, begin to fill this head with images or symbols representing Venture Smith's thoughts, ideas, motivations, visions, and experiences. Number the images. Write a corresponding statement to identify each image. Post the works in progress so students can see each others' ideas.

### Reading and Discussion of *Narrative*, Continuing Work on Historical Heads

Read aloud Chapter 3 of the *Narrative* (1.8.2), which describes Smith's life as a free man, the liberation of his family, his acquisition of property, and his disappointment

## Contemporary Connection
⧫⧣⧫

### Life Is So Good

In May 2000, the *New York Times* ran the headline "At 102, a First Author Recalls Slave Relatives." The article begins: "In the annals of publishing, few people have had to wait as long as George Dawson to see their name on a book jacket. Mr. Dawson is 102. But then he didn't begin to read until he was 98." With help from a school teacher, Mr. Dawson wrote *Life Is So Good*, a story based on his experiences growing up in East Texas among relatives who had been slaves. As in the Venture Smith story, also written in his later years, readers learn about the life of one man in the context of the times in which he lived. *Life Is So Good* (published by Random House) reveals the history of a segment of black American life in the 1920s and 1930s, a dangerous era when the Ku Klux Klan was on the rise, lynchings were common, and it was unsafe even for a black baseball team to defeat a white team. Autobiographies provide a wonderful way to learn about the past.

in his children. After discussing Smith's work, his pride, and his successes and failures, have students add to their biographical head using additional knowledge gained from Chapter 3.

**Activity 6**  **Discussion**

How does Venture Smith's story give us insight into the lives of enslaved people?

**Activity 7**  **Writing to Extend**

Students create a piece of writing that demonstrates their knowledge of Venture Smith and his life and times. The writing can be in the form of a journal entry, an essay, a short story, a letter, or a children's book with illustrations.

## Further Student and Teacher Resources

Bontemps, Arna. *Five Black Lives; The Autobiographies of Venture Smith, James Mars, William Grimes, the Rev. G.W. Offley, [and] James L. Smith*. Middletown, CT: Wesleyan University Press, 1971.

Buckley, Susan, and Elspeth Leacock. *Journeys in Time: A New Atlas of American History*. Boston: Houghton Mifflin, 2001.

Hine, Darlene Clark, and Earnestine Jenkins, eds. *A Question of Manhood: A Reader in U.S. Black Men's History and Masculinity*. Bloomington: Indiana University Press, 1999.

Zagoren, Ruby. *Venture for Freedom; The True Story of an African Yankee*. Cleveland: World Publishing Co., 1969.

## Websites

http://coyrant.ctnow.com/projects/bhistory/vsmith.htm
*Connecticut website at burial spot of Venture Smith*

www.lihistory.com/vault/hs313avl.htm
*The narrative online*

http://teacher.scholastic.com/researchtools/articlearchives/honormlk/venture.htm
*Narrative edited for students*

www.pbs.org/wgbh/aia/part2/2p80.html
*From "Africans in America" series*

# Primary Source Materials for Lesson 8

## 1.8.1

A copy of an advertisement for the *Narrative* in the *New London Bee*, 1798

## 1.8.2

Excerpts from Chapters 1, 2, and 3 of
*A Narrative of the Life and Adventures of*
VENTURE, *A Native of Africa: But resident above sixty years in the United States of America*, 1798

**Chapter I Containing an account of his life, from his birth to the time of his leaving his native country**

I was born at Dukandarra, in Guinea, about the year 1729. My father's name was Saungm Furro, Prince of the tribe of Dukandarra. By his first wife he had three children. The eldest of them was myself, named by my father, Broteer . . . . I descended from a very large, tall and stout race of beings, much larger than the generality of people in other parts of the globe, being commonly considerable above six feet in height, and every way well proportioned . . . .

Word reached my father of . . . a numerous army from a nation not far distant, furnished with musical instruments, and all kinds of arms then in use, that they were instigated by some white nation who equipped and sent them to subdue and possess the country . . . . They then came to us in the reeds, and the very first salute I had from them was a violent blow on the head with the fore part of a gun, and at the same time a grasp around the neck. I then had a rope put about my neck, as all the women in the thicket with me, and were immediately led to my father who was likewise pinioned and haltered for leading.

### Chapter II Containing an account of his life from the time of his leaving Africa to that of his becoming free

After all the business was ended on the coast of Africa, the ship sailed from thence to Barbadoes. After an ordinary passage, except great mortality by the small pox, which broke out on board, we arrived at the island of Barbadoes; but when we reached it, there were found, out of the two hundred and sixty that sailed from Africa, not more than two hundred alive. These were all sold, except myself and three more, to the planters there.

The vessel then sailed for Rhode Island, and arrived there after a comfortable passage. Here my master sent me to live with one of his sisters until he could carry me to Fisher's Island, the place of his residence. I had then completed my eighth year. After staying with his sister some time, I was taken to my master's place to live . . . . The first of the time of living at my master's own place, I was pretty much employed in the house, carding wool and other household business. In this situation I continued for some years, after which my master put me to work out of doors . . . .

[Venture describes his years in slavery and his attempts at gaining freedom until] Being thirty-six years old, I left Colonel Smith once more for all. I had already been sold three different times, made considerable money with seemingly nothing to derive it from, had been cheated out of a large sum of money, lost much by misfortunes, and paid an enormous sum for my freedom.

### Chapter III Containing an account of his life from the time of purchasing his freedom to the present day

The full text of Document 1.8.2 is available on the CD-ROM.

# The Slave Labor System — Where and Why?

Most often we think of slavery as a rural phenomena found mainly in the South on tobacco, rice, and cotton plantations. Although there is some truth to that picture, historians such as Ira Berlin now describe American slavery as a continually changing institution that differed from town to country, from region to region, and over time. Michael Guasco, in his review of Ira Berlin's book, *Many Thousand Gone*, wrote that slavery was "not simply a saga of labor and physical domination [but] a thoroughly human tale of the emergence of an African-American people and culture characterized by self-assertion, social consciousness, and political activism."

Slavery in this country was not strictly synonymous with race until the late 1600s. Before that time, some blacks and many whites came to British North America as indentured servants, earned their freedom, and became landowners. Perhaps one of the most well-known examples of this is Anthony Johnson, an African who arrived in Virginia in 1621 and who, by the end of his life, owned and farmed more than two hundred acres. For a short time, there was fluidity in social and economic relationships between black and white people, but by the 1660s, the ideal of Africans being confined to lifelong unpaid labor had become established in the minds of white colonists. Succeeding economically in this environment required cheap or unpaid labor. Land produced wealth, but only with labor force to improve and cultivate it. White colonists looked to the models of social organization in the nearby slave colonies of the West Indies.

As the historian William Pierson remarked, "the unexamined price for adopting a slave labor system without first developing a political rationalization was [by the 18th century] an insidious incompatibility between the new economic and social realities of colonial slavery and the basic political ideology of British North America."

The stereotype of slaves as ignorant, lazy, and content is challenged dramatically by primary sources that reveal people demonstrating "self assertion and political activism" and possessing a wide range of skills that was crucial to the economic success of an emerging nation. This lesson offers students an opportunity to read and consider these ideas and issues for themselves.

## Organizing Idea

Africans in early America were much more than field hands. In the early colonial period, some Africans and African Americans lived as free people, owning and farming land. As servitude hardened into racial slavery, the skills and labor of enslaved peoples provided the means by which colonial families functioned, communities developed, and the economic foundation for a new nation was built. In discovering evidence for this history, students look at primary documents that reveal who these Africans were, what kinds of work they were doing, and what skills they brought with them and/or developed as they labored.

## Student Objectives

Students will:

* use primary sources to investigate the range of work performed and skills possessed by black people in early America
* consider the implications of the use of enslaved labor in the development of this country
* consider the individuality and agency of enslaved people in the eighteenth century
* understand that the institution of slavery changed over time and had regional variations

## Key Questions

* What do we know about the skills and work accomplishments of enslaved Africans in early America?
* How can we use primary documents to discover the kinds of work that was done by men and by women?
* What do we learn from reading ads for runaways and ads for sales of businesses and estates?
* Why is it so important to study the lives and work of African Americans in early America?

## Primary Source Materials

DOCUMENT 1.9.1: "Tasks Identified by Age and Gender," based upon information from George Washington's diary, 1786–1787

DOCUMENT 1.9.2: *Virginia Gazette* newspaper advertisements for the sale or hire of slaves

DOCUMENT 1.9.3: "A Scheme of a Lottery" published in the *Virginia Gazette*, 14 April, 1768

DOCUMENT 1.9.4: Hunter Iron Works described by Ebenezer Hazard in *The Journal of Ebenezer Hazard*, June 1777

DOCUMENT 1.9.5: Runaway slave advertisement from the *Boston Gazette*, April 2, 1765

DOCUMENT 1.9.6: Broadside advertising a cargo of slaves for sale, Charleston, North Carolina, July 24, 1769

DOCUMENT 1.9.7: Newspaper advertisements from the 1700s for runaways, from the *Pennsylvania Gazette* and the *Virginia Gazette* (on the CD-ROM only)

## Supplies

Large sheets of butcher or chart paper

## Vocabulary

| | | | |
|---|---|---|---|
| chaferyman | finery | hostler | Poythress |
| collier | Flowerdew | lottery | |
| finer | Hundred | pig iron | |

## Student Activities

Activity 1

### Analysis of Washington's Diary

Students each receive and read a copy of "Tasks Identified by Age and Gender," based upon information from George Washington's diary, 1786–1787 (1.9.1), copies of the advertisements for sale or hire of slaves (1.9.2), and a copy of "A Scheme of a Lottery" (1.9.3). What kinds of information can we learn from these documents? Reading carefully, students identify and list particular skills possessed by black people in the eighteenth century. Why was skilled work important to colonial families and communities?

**Note:** In the eighteenth century, a lottery was a method by which some members of the gentry tried to raise money to pay off their debts. Individuals bought chances for various "lots" of another individual's personal property, sometimes including the slaves they owned.

Activity 2

### Creative Extensions: An Eighteenth-Century Industrial Village

Students receive the one-page description of the Hunter Iron Works (1.9.4) by Ebenezer Hazard, an early historian and postmaster general. The second line of this document reads: "A little above Falmouth are Mr. Hunter's Works which, with the Dwelling houses for the Workmen, form a small village." After reading the document carefully, students work in small groups to recreate this small village on large chart paper, carefully including all the industries, the terrain, the canal, and the houses. One historical source tells us that the Hunter Iron Works contributed to the war effort. What war would this have been? How would these workers, many of whom were slaves, have helped to win the war?

## Writing to Extend: A Poem for Two Voices

*Activity 3*

In a lesson plan centered around poems for two voices on the American Memory website of the Library of Congress (www.memory.loc.gov/ammem/), Gail Desler, a teacher in Elk Grove, California, describes a poem for two voices: a "two-column format allows writers to juxtapose two contrasting ideas, concepts, or perspectives. Alternating lines indicate opposing viewpoints and are read by an individual voice. Adjacent lines represent agreement or compromise and are therefore read in unison." Before beginning this activity, teachers and/or students find examples of poems for two voices online or in books. Poems should be read aloud.

Students receive copies of newspaper advertisements for runaways and slaves for sale from Massachusetts, North Carolina, Pennsylvania, and Virginia (1.9.5, 1.9.6, 1.9.7). Drawing from these ads and remembering previous readings describing slaves' work and skills, students take on the persona of a runaway, either one particular person or a composite. What were these people like? What skills did they have? What were they running away from? What did they hope for? Students should also imagine a slaveholder, highly dependent on enslaved people to support his or her way of life. What would that person be doing and thinking after losing skilled, valuable "property"? Using the style of a poem for two voices, students write a poem through which we can hear these two voices, with their very different dreams and goals.

## Research and Storywriting

*Activity 4*

Students research information on Anthony Johnson from the PBS website *Africans in America* (*www.pbs.org/wgbh/aia/*) and write a story about his life, contrasting it with the life of black people after the 1660s.

## Writing to Extend—What If?

*Activity 5*

Incorporating what they have learned from these lessons, students write an essay on how this country might be different today if the labor of black people in the eighteenth century had been paid labor instead of forced labor under the institution of slavery.

# Further Student and Teacher Resources

Berlin, Ira. *Many Thousand Gone: The First Two Centuries of Slavery in North America*. Cambridge, MA: Harvard University Press, 2000.

Piersen, William. *From Africa to America*. New York: Twayne Publishers, 1996.

# Contemporary Connection

⸻※⸻

## Anti-Slavery International

Anti-Slavery International (ASI) estimates that currently there are more than twenty-seven million slaves in the world. Throughout Asia, Africa, and even Latin America, men, women, and children are being enslaved. This modern slave trade includes such practices as forced labor, servile marriage, debt bondage, child labor, and forced prostitution. In his article "Slavery: Worldwide Evil," Charles Jacobs writes: "Modern slaves can be concubines, camel jockeys, or cane cutters. They might weave carpets, build roads, or clear forests." Although slaves in the twenty-first century are no longer sold at public auction and put in shackles, the lives they lead are just as dangerous and tragic as those of people who were enslaved in the past. Research the current status of slavery and efforts to abolish it on *www.iAbolish.com*.

Charles Jacobs is president of the American Anti-Slavery Group, based in Boston, Massachusetts. His article initially appeared in the April 1996 edition of *World & I*.

## Websites

http://gwpapers.virginia.edu/diaries/list/index.html
*Additional diary entries made by George Washington, including a list of slaves with their jobs on various parts of his plantation*

www.afrigeneas.com/slavedata

www.artmetal.com/project/Features/Africa/page1.htm
*Information about enslaved West African ironworkers who brought their skills across the Atlantic*

# Primary Source Materials for Lesson 9

### 1.9.1

"Tasks Identified by Age and Gender," based upon information from George Washington's Diary, 1786–1787

*Men's Skills*

| | | |
|---|---|---|
| Overseer | Miller | House servant |
| Shoemaker | Cooper | Ferryman |
| Sawyer | Blacksmith | Carter/wagonner |
| Carpentry | Gardener | Bake and lay brick |

A complete list of tasks done by Washington's slaves (1.9.1) is available on the CD-ROM.

### 1.9.2

*Virginia Gazette* newspaper advertisements for the sale or hire of slaves

**April 1769**

To be sold on Wednesday the 3rd of May, before Mr. Anthony Hay's door, in Williamsburg, for ready money. Twenty likely Virginia born Slaves, . . . among them a good shoemaker, gardener, and hostler, several men used to the house and field business, and several boys and girls fit for service.

**November 1773**

To be SOLD . . . Share in the Town Point Company . . ., likewise a very valuable Negro Fellow, who has worked at the Smith's Business some time, and still continues at the principal shop in Town, sundry Smith's tools, several exceeding good house wenches with their children, and some very fine Negro girls, all to be sold at private sale.

## June 1777

For sale, for ready money, or 12 months credit, an exceeding good plantation BLACKSMITH, who is very well acquainted with many other kinds of work in that branch of business, such as nail making, tiring wheels, etc. The terms may be known by applying to Joshua Poythress, sen. At Flower de Hundred, in Prince George county, or to William Poythress at York garrison.

**The full list of ads (Document 1.9.2) is available on the CD-ROM.**

### 1.9.3

## "A Scheme of a Lottery" published in the *Virginia Gazette*, 14 April 1768

### A SCHEME of a LOTTERY

**For disposing of certain LANDS, SLAVES, and STOCKS, belonging to the subscriber.**

[—excerpts—]

| VALUE. | CONTENTS of PRIZES. |
|---|---|
| 1750 | To consist of a forge and geared grist-mill, both well fixed, and situate on a plentiful and constant stream, with 1800 acres of good land, in *King* and *Queen* county, near *Todd's Bridge*; which cost 6000 £. |
| 1375 | To consist of 550 acres of very good land, adjoining and below the said tract lying on the *Pamunkey* river, called *Gooch's*, part of 1686 acres, purchased of *William Claiborne*, deceased; the line to extend from said river to the back line across towards *Mattapony*. |
| 1925 | To consist of 550 acres of very good land, adjoining and below the said tract lying on *Pamunkey* river, whereon is a good dwelling-house, 70 feet long and 20 feet wide, with three rooms below and three above; also all other good and convenient out-houses; 1000 fine peach trees thereon, with many apple trees and other sorts of fruit, a fine high and pleasant situation, and the plantation in exceeding good order for cropping; the line to extend from said river to the back line towards *Mattapony*. |

| | |
|---|---|
| 1750 | To consist of 586 acres, below the aforesaid two tracts; whereon is a fine peach orchard, and many fine apples trees; the plantation is in exceeding good order for cropping, and very fine for corn and tobacco, and abounds with a great quantity of white oak, which will afford, it's thought, a thousand pounds worth of plank and staves. |
| 3250 | To consist of 6500 acres of good land, in *Caroline* county; to be laid off in lots of 100 acres each. |
| 280 | A Negro man named *Billy*, about 22 years old, an exceeding trusty good forgeman, as well at the finery as under the hammer, and understands putting up his fire: Also his wife named *Lucy*, a young wench, who works exceeding well both in the house and field. |
| 200 | A Negro man named *Mingo*, about 24 years old, a very trusty good finer, and hammerman, and understands putting up his fire. |
| 250 | A Negro man named *Sam*, about 26 years old, a fine chaseryman; also his wife *Daphne*, a very good hand at the hoe, or in the house. |
| 200 | A Negro man named *Abraham*, about 26 years old, an exceeding good forge carpenter, cooper, and clapboard carpenter. |
| 120 | A Negro man named *Peter*, about 18 years old, an exceeding trusty good waggoner. |
| 110 | A Negro woman named *Rachel*, about 32 years old, and her children *Daniel* and *Thompson*, both very fine. |
| 70 | A Negro woman named *Hannah*, about 16 years old. |
| 75 | A Negro man named *Ben*, about 25 years old, a good house servant, and a good carter, &c. |
| 120 | A Negro man, *Robin*, a good sawyer, and *Bella*, his wife. |
| 70 | A Negro girl named *Sukey*, about 12 years old, and another named *Betty*, about 7 years old; children of *Robin* and *Bella*. |
| 80 | A Negro woman named *Kate*, and a young child, *Judy*. |
| 60 | A Negro girl, *Aggy*, and boy, *Nat*; children of *Kate*. |
| 110 | A fine breeding woman named *Pat*, lame of one side, with child, and her three children, *Laet*, *Milley*, and *Charlotte*. |
| 60 | A fine boy, *Phill*, son of *Patty*, about 14 years old. |
| 280 | A Negro man named *Caesar* about 30 years old, a very good blacksmith, and his wife named *Nanny*, with two children, *Tab* and *Jane*. |
| 100 | A team of exceeding fine horses, consisting of four, and their gear; also a good waggon. |
| 80 | A team of four horses, and their gear, with two coal waggons. |
| 200 | To consist of 100 head of cattle, to be laid off in 10 lots. |

**The complete original of Document 1.9.3 is available on the CD-ROM.**

## 1.9.4

### The Hunter Iron Works, described by Ebenezer Hazard in
### *The Journal of Ebenezer Hazard,* June 1777

At present he makes (from Pig Iron) Bar Iron, Anchors, all kinds of common Blacksmith's Work, Small Arms, Pistols, Swords, Files, Fuller's Shears, & Nails. He has a Grist Mill & Saw Mill, a Cooper's Shop, a Saddler's Shop, a Shoemaker's Shop's, a Brass Founder's Shop, & a Wheel-Wright's Shop. All these, except the Grist Mill are constantly employed in his own Business, & not to supply Wants of other people. Besides all these Mr. Hunter has erected Works for making Steel, (this Business he is just beginning upon) & raises large quantities of Wheat, Corn, Oats, Hay, &c: in short he is a great Farmer. He informs me that his different Works, & the Negroes he employs cost him £40,000 Virginia Currency.

**The full text of Document 1.9.4 is available on the CD-ROM.**

## 1.9.5

### Runaway slave advertisement from the *Boston Gazette,*
### April 2, 1765

RUN away from *Jacob Fowle,* Efq; the Twenty-ninth ult. a Negro Boy, about Eighteen Years old, was born in *Hopkington,* and brought up by the Rev. Mr. *Barret;* his Name is *Ishmael,* he has been a Soldier at the Lake, is thick fett, has thick Lips, and goes limping by Reafon of the great Toe of his right Foot being froze and not quite well. He had on when he went away, a ftriped Jacket, leather Breeches, chequered woolen Shirt, blue under Jacket, light coloured Stockings, brafs Buckles in his Shoes, and an old mill'd Cap. He is an artful Fellow, and is fuppofed will endeavour to pafs for a Soldier, as he carried off with him a Firelock and Blanket.—Whoever fhall take up the faid Negro and bring him to his Mafter, or confine him in any of his Majefty's Goals fo that his Mafter may have him again, fhall have FOUR DOLLARS Reward, and all Charges paid.
*Marblehead, April* 2. 1765.    JACOB FOWLE.

American Antiquarian Society

1.9.6

Broadside advertising a cargo of slaves for sale, Charleston, North Carolina, July 24, 1769

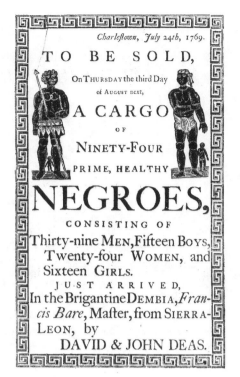

American Antiquarian Society

# Africans in Colonial Louisiana

The Senegambia region of West Africa was a main source of people for the transatlantic slave trade until 1640. After that, the region's role in the slave trade was greatly reduced—except for its trade with Louisiana. Senegal and Louisiana were connected by an exclusive trade monopoly through the Company of the Indies, a private company licensed and controlled by the king of France. Slave ships conveyed information back and forth between Senegal and Louisiana, ensuring close and current communication and control of the trade, and influencing events taking place in the French North American colony. Because so many Louisiana slaves originated from the Senegambia region, the roots of Afro-Creole culture can be traced back to this region of West Africa. The slave trade ended there in 1743.

Key to understanding the African presence and influence in colonial Louisiana is the process of creolization. In her book *Africans in Colonial Louisiana*, Gwendolyn Midlo Hall explains that the word *creole* comes from the Portuguese word *crioulo*, meaning a slave of African descent born in the New World. In eighteenth-century Louisiana, the term *creole* referred to locally born people, both enslaved and free, with at least some African heritage. When *creole* was used in slave inventories, it distinguished American-born slaves from those born in Africa.

Creolization, the cultural and racial mixing of peoples, was more common in Louisiana than in the British North American colonies. This process was facilitated by a number of factors. Hall describes French Louisiana as a "weak military outpost" before the founding of New Orleans in 1718 (p. 159). In 1719, the French began to import slaves from Africa, specifically from the Senegambia region. Because these enslaved peoples had lived in similar environments and shared many cultural elements, they developed cohesion and self-confidence, especially as the white population declined and the numbers of people of African descent increased. Africans brought crucial skills to the ailing and poorly governed colony. They also interacted with the sizable Native American population. Enslaved Africans and Creoles were able to escape along the many waterways lacing lower Louisiana.

Early French colonists were sent to live with indigenous people who taught them about local flora and fauna, thus ensuring their survival. French traders, soldiers, and sailors married Native American women, consolidating personal and business relationships. The French forged trading agreements and alliances with certain Native American nations such as the Choctaw to protect them from the English slave-raiders from the east (Hall pp. 14, 15).

Also important to understanding the history of Africans in Louisiana is learning about the history, process of production, and uses for indigo, a source of blue dye. According to Hall:

> Indigo grew wild along the rivers of Senegambia, where it was processed into a vivid, blue dye with which cotton cloth was colored. Indigo grew wild in Louisiana as well. In 1712, a settler noted the existence of wild indigo in Louisiana but stated that neither the few Frenchmen settled there nor the Indians understood its preparation . . . . Experiments in processing wild indigo began in 1721, two years after the arrival of the first slave ships from Africa. It is reasonable to conclude that African slaves with long experience in processing indigo in Africa first introduced and applied this technology in Louisiana. It was not the cultivation but the processing of indigo that required knowledge and skill. The plant grew two and a half feet high and was harvested twice a year. It was cut and brought to a twenty-foot-high, open shed and was processed through three vats arranged to allow water to run from one to the other. Water and indigo leaves were allowed to rot in the highest vat, which was frequently inspected, and the indigo maker had to choose the precise time to open the spout and let the water run into the second vat. If it remained too long in the first vat, the water would turn black. The indigo was beaten in the second vat until the indigo maker, through long experience, knew when to stop. The water was then allowed to settle, and the indigo formed a sediment at the bottom of the vat. As the liquid became clear, it was run off in gradual stages through spouts placed one beneath the other. The indigo was then removed from the vat and placed in cloth sacks. The remaining liquid seeped through the cloth, which was then dried on boards and cut into little squares, packed into barrels, and shipped to the French islands and thence to France . . . (pp. 125–26).

Indigo was one of the few export staples of eighteenth-century Louisiana. One of the skills regularly listed on slave inventories was that of indigo maker (*indigotier*).

## Organizing Idea

The French colonized Louisiana and began importing enslaved Africans from the Senegambia region in the early eighteenth century to work in the sugar, indigo, and rice industries. The mix of Native American, African, and French cultures created features unique to the colony. The development of creole culture is reflected in the language, foods, music, oral traditions, and history of Louisiana.

## Student Objectives

Students will:

❖ develop an understanding of the geography and wide variety of African-influenced lifeways in colonial Louisiana

❖ understand how the changing demographics of Louisiana during the eighteenth century laid the basis for the deep cultural influence of African people

❖ use visual images and oral histories to analyze the working conditions of enslaved peoples and their recorded responses to those conditions

## Key Questions

❖ How does close and frequent contact between people from a variety of cultures affect the development of a region?

❖ How did enslaved peoples use their music and oral literary traditions from Africa to express their sentiments regarding the master-slave, oppressor-resistor relationship?

❖ What was the nature of work in semitropical Louisiana?

## Primary Source Materials

DOCUMENT 1.10.1: Image of a seventeenth-century *indigoterie* in the French West Indies

DOCUMENT 1.10.2: Lyrics to creole folk songs

DOCUMENT 1.10.3: Creole sayings

## Supplementary Materials

ITEM 1.10.A: Map of Louisiana

ITEM 1.10.B: Map of the Senegambia region

ITEM 1.10.C: Chart of the slave and free population of French Louisiana, 1721–1763

ITEM 1.10.D: Chart of slaves landed in Louisiana by French slave trade: numbers and origins

ITEM 1.10.E: Translation of legend for *indigoterie*

## Supplies needed

❖ Transparency acetate for copy machine

❖ Large sheets of chart or butcher paper

## Vocabulary

| creole | *indigoterie* | Senegambia |

## Student Activities

### Mapping of Senegambia and Louisiana regions

Activity 1

Using blackline masters, students create large-scale maps of both the Senegambia region of Africa and the Louisiana region of North America (Items 1.10.A, 1.10.B), labeling physical features and geopolitical places. Refer to Lesson 1, Activity 1 for complete instructions.

### Analysis of Charts

Activity 2

Students study and compare the two demographic charts (Items 1.10.C and 1.10.D) of the enslaved population of Louisiana to understand growth and change over time in the region. Discussion questions include:

❖ How did climate and the nature of the labor being performed affect population growth?

❖ What is the nature of a trade monopoly, and how are its effects evident in the charts?

❖ How did the ratio between free and enslaved people change over time?

❖ What factors could explain the information the charts convey?

### Research, Analysis, and Writing on *Indigoteries*

Activity 3

Students conduct further research, study document 1.10.1 and the translation of the legend (Item 1.10.E), and then write a description of the kinds of work being performed in the *indigoterie*. Students consider questions such as the following:

❖ Who would have done this engraving and for what purposes?

❖ How accurate is this? In other words, what do students think might be missing from this scene?

### Songs and Sayings—Discussion and Creative Extension

Activity 4

Students read, discuss, and dramatize the folk sayings and songs of resistance (1.10.2, 1.10.3). Are there sayings in their own communities that are similar to those given here? Students write their own, or bring in examples of songs and poems of resistance from many cultures and in a variety of genres.

## Further Student and Teacher Resources

Hall, Gwendolyn Midlo. *Africans in Colonial Louisiana: The Development of Afro-Creole Culture in the Eighteenth Century*. Baton Rouge: Louisiana State University Press, 1992.

## Websites

**www.adire.clara.net/indigointroduction.htm**
*History of indigo production in Africa*

**www.nps.gov/cari/forest/index.html**
*National Park Service website describing the region's Afro-creole history*

**http://vic.nsula.edu/creole/index.htm**
*Website addressing creole history and culture*

---

### Contemporary Connection

✠

### Identities Restored

In July 2000, the *New York Times* ran the headline, "Identity Restored to 100,000 Louisiana Slaves." The article states that many black families have lacked the resources to do the extensive detective work required to identify their ancestors and that many white people did not want to know about their family's past involvement with slavery. After fifteen years of research in courthouses and archives focusing on the detailed records kept by French and Spanish proprietors of Louisiana, the New Orleans–born scholar Gwendolyn Midlo Hall has developed an extensive database of slave transactions in Louisiana, which details this history in terms of specific people and stories. Consider exploring your own genealogy.

# Primary Source Materials
## for Lesson 10

### 1.10.1

Image of a seventeenth-century *indigoterie* in the French West Indies

*Gwendolyn Hall explains that this* indigoterie *in the French West Indies shows the indigo-making process that was also used in Louisiana.*

I. Figuier d'Inde ou Raquette. 119    2. Genipa. 195.    3. Rocou, et les Negres qui le pillent. 143.    4. Cierge Espineux 130.    5. Bois de Trompette.    INDIGOTERIE.    6. Bassin.    7. la Trempoire.    8. La Batterie.    9. le Repofoir    10. Chauffe ou Segoute l'Indigo.    12. Plante d'Indigo.    13. Negres portant l'Indigo aux caissons pour le sécher.    14 Negres coupants e. portants l'Indigo. 107.

La Société d'Histoire de la Guadeloupe

107

## 1.10.2

## Lyrics to Creole Folk Songs

Two little birds were sitting,
Two little birds were sitting on the fence,
Two little birds were chattering.
What they were saying, I do not know.

A chicken hawk came along the road,
Pounced on them and ate them up
No one hears them chattering anymore
The two little birds on the fence.

Moulron! He! Moulron! He!
It's not today I'm in the world.
If you treat me well, I'll stay.
If you treat me bad, I'll escape.

**The full text of Document 1.10.2 is available on the CD-ROM.**

## 1.10.3

## Creole Sayings

"It isn't one time only that the ox needs his tail to drive the flies away."

"It isn't the fine head-dress that makes the fine negress."

"A good dog never gets a good bone."

"Idleness leaves the frogs without buttocks."

"What you push away from you to-day with your foot, you will pick up to-morrow with your hand."

"He who kills his own body, works for the worms."

"When the goat drinks, they say the sheep is drunk."

**The full text of Document 1.10.3 is available on the CD-ROM.**

# Runaway Slaves in Eighteenth-Century Virginia

Enslaved men, women, and children resisted the institution of slavery in a variety of ways in colonial Virginia. Slaves might negotiate with their master or mistress, pretend to be sick, work slowly, break tools, or run away. Those who decided to escape from their owner's plantation or house in one of the colony's towns took a risk when they "stole themselves." If captured, a runaway African or African American servant or slave faced punishment greater than that administered to a white indentured servant, as John Punch discovered in 1640. In July of that year, the members of Virginia's General Court determined the penalty for three runaway servants. Victor, a Dutch man, and James Gregory, a Scot, had to serve their master one additional year after the end of their indentures. John Punch, an African man, received a sentence of lifetime servitude. This decision was handed down twenty-two years before the institution of slavery was legalized in Virginia.

After Bacon's Rebellion (1676), Virginia's legislators decided to restrict the movement of slaves and to strip black people, both free and enslaved, of the few rights they had. A law passed in 1680 required slaves to have a pass if they left their master's plantation. It also became legal for a white Virginian to kill a runaway slave who resisted capture. In 1691, county sheriffs gained the authority to gather a posse of men to apprehend runaway slaves. A slaveowner would receive financial compensation if an "outlying" slave—a slave who had absconded and was hiding nearby—was killed by a man who tried to capture him or her. Virginia's lawmakers included these laws concerning runaway slaves in the 1705 slave code. The restrictions on slaves became harsher in the eighteenth century as Virginians struggled to control the increasing number of slaves in the colony, especially the men and women imported directly from Africa.

Slaveowners found that enslaved persons ran away in spite of the laws designed to limit their movement. Once a master found that a slave had left his plantation or household, he could alert his neighbors. He could also attend a meeting of the county court, inform other people about the absent slave, and offer a reward for the person who captured the runaway. After 1736, slave owners could place a notice in the colony's newspaper, the *Virginia Gazette*, about the missing slave. Although masters wrote these advertisements in order to regain possession of their enslaved laborers, these announcements include details about the lives of slaves in eighteenth-century Virginia, listing their skills, describing their families, and suggesting possible reasons that they decided to run and take control of their lives. The notices reveal that more men than women ran away. This difference reflects the fact that enslaved men who worked as carters, watermen, or waiting men were expected to travel as part of their jobs and might not be questioned by a white man who saw them away from their homes. Most slave women did not journey far from their homes. The advertisements indicate that masters needed to get their slaves back because the loss of a slave reduced the productivity of a plantation, disrupted the operation of a household, and threatened the authority of a master or mistress.

Virginians became especially concerned about the activities of slaves in the years before the Revolution. A law passed in 1755 gave the residents of Williamsburg the right to appoint individuals to serve as a slave patrol, a group of men who could visit any location within the city limits where they suspected that slaves might be gathering. However, the citizens of Williamsburg did not establish a slave patrol until 1772, an indication that they were not deeply concerned about slave unrest until that date. Tensions rose again in November 1775 after Lord Dunmore, the last royal governor of Virginia, offered freedom to all indentured servants and slaves who would join him and fight against those masters who supported separation from Great Britain. Some enslaved men, women, and children decided to join Dunmore and seize their freedom; others chose to run away during the Revolution because they hoped that the turmoil caused by the fighting would make it easier to avoid capture.

## Organizing Idea

Individual slaves and small groups of enslaved persons who lived in eighteenth-century Virginia decided to run away in spite of the punishment they would receive if captured. Advertisements placed in the *Virginia Gazette* by masters provide information about the variety of experiences of eighteenth-century slaves and clues about the reasons that some of the colony's enslaved men and women chose to run away from their masters.

## Student Objectives

Students will:

- ❖ analyze the reasons that slaves decided to run away in eighteenth-century Virginia
- ❖ interpret advertisements for runaway slaves in the *Virginia Gazette* as a source of information about the lives of enslaved men, women, and children who lived in eighteenth-century Virginia
- ❖ assess the variety of skills possessed by Virginia's enslaved men and women

## Key Questions

- ❖ Why did slaves run away? Did they plan their escapes or run away on the spur of the moment?
- ❖ Where did a slave go when he or she ran away? Was it relatively easy for a runaway slave to avoid capture?
- ❖ What did slaves take with them and why?
- ❖ Why did a runaway slave need help from other slaves or free people of color to be successful?
- ❖ Why did masters advertise for runaway slaves?
- ❖ What skills did Virginia slaves have?

## Primary Source Materials

DOCUMENT 1.11.1: Advertisements for runaway slaves in the *Virginia Gazette*

DOCUMENT 1.11.2: Additional advertisements for runaway slaves from the *Virginia Gazette* (on CD-ROM only)

DOCUMENT 1.11.3: "A map of the most inhabited part of Virginia containing the whole province of Maryland with part of Pennsylvania, New Jersey and North Carolina" drawn by Joshua Fry & Peter Jefferson in 1751

DOCUMENT 1.11.4: "A new and accurate map of Virginia wherein most of the counties are laid down from actual surveys. With a concise account of the number of inhabitants, the trade, soil, and produce of that Province" by John Henry, 1770

## Supplementary Materials

ITEM 1.11.A: A list of vocabulary, with definitions, related to clothing

## Vocabulary

| | | | |
|---|---|---|---|
| "bred to the house" | Governor's pardon | "Newlight preacher" | waterman, or one who |
| "bright mulatto wench" | hire | outlawed | "followed the water" |
| clinch work | hostler | pass | whitlow |
| cooper | "Marks of his Country" | "Pock-fretten" | "yellow complexion" |
| driver | mulatto | pound (£) | |
| flat | "new Negro" | sawyer | |
| | | waiting man | |

## Student Activities

Activity 1  **Mapping Escape Routes**

Using the early maps of Virginia (1.11.3, 1.11.4), have students read the runaway advertisements (1.11.1, 1.11.2) and map the locations mentioned in the selected documents to follow the path that a master believed a runaway slave took after he or she escaped from a plantation or house. How did slaves make their escape—on foot? In a vessel? On horseback?

Activity 2  **Drawing Conclusions Based on Clothing Runaways Wore**

Using descriptions in the advertisements (1.11.1 and 1.11.2 and Item 1.11.A) of the work runaways did and clothing they wore, discuss the differences between life on a plantation and life in a house in Williamsburg and between the work performed by men and by women.

Activity 3  **Analysis—Who Ran Away?**

Read the advertisements and tally the number of men and the number of women who escaped. Who ran away more often, males or females? Why? At what ages were slaves most likely to run away?

Activity 4  **Detecting Bias**

Have each student read the advertisements in order to find the biases of masters in their descriptions of slaves.

Activity 5  **Discussion—Why Run Away?**

Most runaway slave advertisements contain details about the reasons that enslaved men and women decided to escape. Have students discuss the main reason that Virginia's slaves "stole themselves"—to seize their freedom or see their families and friends?

Activity 6  **Research—The Risks, The Destinations**

Many runaway slaves depended on other slaves and/or free people of color to assist them. How could another slave or a free person of color help a runaway slave? What were the risks to people who aided runaways? Where could slaves go to gain their freedom before the American Revolution? Where could slaves run to seize freedom during the American Revolution?

## Further Student and Teacher Resources

Baumgarten, Linda. "'Clothes for the People': Slave Clothing in Early Virginia." *Journal of Early Southern Decorative Arts*, 14:2 (1988): 26–70.

*Contemporary Connection*

✠

**Twentieth-Century Runaway Slave**

The May 23, 2002, *Wall Street Journal* featured a story about Francis Bok, an escaped slave from Sudan. After being kidnapped at the age of 7, he was sold for about $35 to a master who forced him to tend cows. He endured beatings, was given only one meal a day, and was forced to sleep with the animals until he ran away at the age of 17. With the aid of a refugee office in Cairo and an uncle in Virginia, Francis Bok made it to the United States.

In 1999 Bok was relocated to Fargo, North Dakota, by Lutheran Social Services, and a year later he was working in a meat-packing plant in Iowa. It was here that a representative from the Boston-based American Anti-Slavery Group offered Bok the opportunity to become a spokesperson for the organization. The American Anti-Slavery Group (AASG) combats slavery around the world and has helped free more than 45,000 slaves to date. Bok now works for the organization, speaking regularly for this new abolitionist movement. As this example shows, escaping slavery is a contemporary issue. For more information on Francis Bok or the AASG, visit *www.iabolish.com*.

Frey, Sylvia. *Water from the Rock: Black Resistance in a Revolutionary Age*. Princeton: Princeton University Press, 1991.

Hodges, Graham Russell, and Alan Edward Brown, eds. *"Pretends to Be Free": Runaway Slave Advertisements from Colonial and Revolutionary New York and New Jersey*. New York: Garland Publishing, 1994.

Mullin, Gerald R. *Flight and Rebellion: Slave Resistance in Eighteenth-Century Virginia*. New York: Oxford University Press, 1972.

Smith, Billy G., and Richard Wojtowicz, eds. *Blacks Who Stole Themselves: Advertisements for Runaways in the Pennsylvania Gazette, 1728–1790*. Philadelphia: University of Pennsylvania Press, 1989.

Waldstreicher, David. "Reading the Runaways: Self-Fashioning, Print Culture, and Confidence in Slavery in the Eighteenth-Century Mid-Atlantic." *William and Mary Quarterly*, 3rd ser., 56 (1999):243–72.

Windley, Lathan A. *A Profile of Runaway Slaves in Virginia and South Carolina from 1730 through 1787*. New York: Garland Publishing, 1995.

Windley, Lathan A. *Runaway Slave Advertisements: A Documentary History from the 1730s to 1790*. 4 vols. Westport, CT: Greenwood Press, 1983.

## Websites

www.uvawise.edu/history/runaways/

http://memory.loc.gov/ammem/amhome.html
*Extensive information about slavery in Virginia*

# Primary Source Materials for Lesson 11

### 1.11.1

Advertisements for runaway slaves in the *Virginia Gazette*

RUN away from the subscriber in *Chesterfield*, about the end of *August* last, a middle sized Negro man named WILL, about 30 years old, of a yellowish complexion, very much marked on his face, arms, and breast, his country fashion, speaks very broken, and can hardly tell his master's name; had on when he went away a new osnabrugs shirt, *Virginia* linen short trousers, old cotton jacket, and felt hat, with part of the brim burnt off. He has made three attempts, as he said, to get to his country, but was apprehended. All masters of vessels are hereby forewarned from carrying the said slave out of the colony. Whoever apprehends him, and brings him to me, shall have 20 s. reward, besides what the law allows. JORDAN ANDERSON.

## THREE POUNDS REWARD.

RAN away from the Subscriber, on the 1st of *January*, a middling dark Mulatto named STEPHEN, about 21 Years of Age, and thick made; had on, when he went off, a Negro Cotton Waistcoat and Breeches, an Osnabrug Shirt, and Negro made Shoes, with Pegs drove in the Soals; his Hair is cut off the Top of his Head, and but little remains at the Sides. He carried with him a white Mulatto Woman Slave named PHEBE, whose Hair is long, straight, and black; she had on a blue Waistcoat and Petticoat, and took with her two new Osnabrug Shirts, and a Suit of striped *Virginia* Cloth; she is about 21 Years of Age. They also carried off two Osnabrug Shirts, 6 or 7 Ells of Rolls, a new *Dutch* Blanket, and one about Half worn. It is imagined they will make for *Carolina*, and endeavour to pass for free People. All Persons are forewarned from harbouring them, at their Peril. Whoever brings them to me, or secures them in any Gaol, so that I may get them again, shall have the above Reward.
HENRY HARDAWAY.

Colonial Williamsburg Foundation

## 1.11.2

Additional advertisements for runaway slaves from the *Virginia Gazette* (on CD-ROM only)

## 1.11.3

"A map of the most inhabited part of Virginia containing the whole province of Maryland with part of Pennsylvania, New Jersey and North Carolina" drawn by Joshua Fry & Peter Jefferson in 1751

Library of Congress

## 1.11.4

"A new and accurate map of Virginia, wherein most of the counties are laid down from actual surveys. With a concise account of the number of inhabitants, the trade, soil, and produce of that Province" by John Henry, 1770

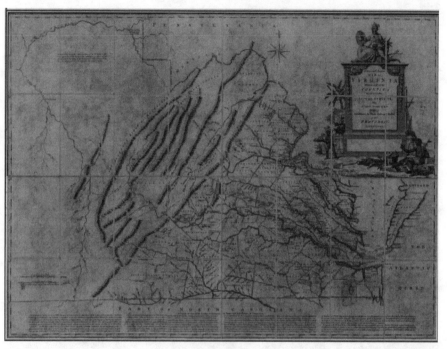

Library of Congress

# Riverine Watercraft—Bringing the Skills Over

Africans brought many skills to British North America, including the art and craft of making canoes. A number of historians believe that canoes surviving from the colonial period exhibit a mix of designs that indicates early contact among Native American, African, and European peoples, because all three groups had strong maritime cultures and long histories of canoe making before they met in the colonies. Canoes were used in both Africa and the Carolinas for coastal transportation as well as defense.

Canoes were a sensible mode of transportation in the North American colonies, particularly in the Carolinas. That region had a vast network of streams and rivers at its eastern ends, and in South Carolina water-intensive rice cultivation was well established. Early documents record the use of boats for fishing and hauling cargo, such as rice and tar, along waterways, which was easier than carting cargo along the few existing paths and bridges.

A significant number of enslaved Africans were from areas with rivers, streams, and delta waters. Plantation owners employed some African slaves as boat captains, or patroons. These slaves were often kept away from field hands and house slaves, because they were trusted with relative freedom of movement up and down the rivers and through surrounding areas.

W. Jeffrey Bolster's 1997 book, *Black Jacks, African American Seamen in the Age of Sail*, explores African influences on colonial American watercraft. According to Bolster, Africans rarely if ever voyaged in deep sea waters, instead staying close to the African coast or navigating the many rivers that laced West Africa. In describing the experiences of West African boatmen, he quotes the historian John Thornton: "Not only did the Niger-Senegal-Gambia [river] complex unite a considerable portion of West Africa, but the Niger provided a corridor that ultimately added the Hausa kingdoms, the Yoruba states, and the Nupe, Iglala and Benin kingdoms to a hydrographic system that was ultimately connected to the Atlantic" (p. 47).

Bolster describes African canoes as being able to handle surf better than the craft of the Europeans. He quotes the Portuguese explorer Alvise da Mosto, who described African canoes in 1455 of "a great size, one was almost as long as one of our vessels, but not so high, and in it were thirty Negroes." Another Portuguese explorer, Fernandez, in 1506 told of a canoe on the Sierra Leone River carrying 120 warriors.

Canoes were a common mode of transport in Africa, varying in design and ranging in size from quite small to very large. In contrast to ships, canoes depended on human rather than wind power. Their shallow draft also allowed them to be navigated up narrow and shallow rivers and streams and along riverbeds whose bottoms shifted continually with tides and storms. They could carry great weights of people and cargo. Terrain and occupation provided ample opportunity for West Africans to develop strong navigation and canoeing skills, which later would be used by West African and European traders.

In addition to canoes, other boats combining African and European styles were constructed in colonial North America and used extensively in the Chesapeake Bay and along the southeastern coast and estuaries. Bolster describes this combination of styles as being of both hollowed-out log canoe of African design and pettiaugers with masts and sails of European and Middle Eastern origin.

Historian Peter Wood defines pettiaugers as larger canoes constructed from two or more hollowed-out logs, often of cypress wood, and paddled or poled along waterways. Such vessels could transport many barrels of tar or rice. Wood points to the probable use of such vessels as means of escape, referring to an act passed in South Carolina in 1696. This law, based on already existing laws in the West Indies, threatened any slave who "takes away or lets loose with any boat or canoe" with thirty-nine lashes for the first offense and loss of an ear for repetition (p. 125).

**Note:** The website of the South Carolina Institute of Archaeology and Anthropology at the University of South Carolina (*www.cla.sc.edu/sciaa/staff/amerc/canoe.html*) is especially well done and conveys the skills Africans brought with them, as well as interactions among Native American, African, and European peoples during that time period. It includes text and photographs of riverine watercraft constructed and sailed along rivers and canals in the Low Country of southeastern colonial North America. Information is also provided on guides written for early travelers, early trade with Native Americans, fishing boats, plantation canoes, boat building, and ethnicity. Teachers might want to use this website as background for themselves and students before beginning the activities.

## Organizing Idea

Canoes as artifacts reveal a wealth of information about how Africans carried skills from Africa to the North American colonies, interacted with Native Americans and Europeans, and employed their knowledge in the work they performed in America.

## Student Objectives

Students will:

❖ use the perspective and skills of archaeology to describe and identify rivercraft such as canoes

❖ consider the important roles of rivercraft in both Africa and the colonies

❖ develop an understanding of how archaeologists and historians use artifacts to investigate and learn about the past

## Key Questions

❖ How do cultural transmissions show up in artifacts?

❖ How do the attributes of an artifact—design, materials, location, position—tell a story about people of African descent and their interactions with others in a given time and place?

❖ Which questions can we easily answer, and which require more research or have a number of possible responses?

## Primary Source Materials

DOCUMENT 1.12.1: Image: "Negro's cannoes, carrying Slaves, on Board of Ships att Manfroe," engraving by J. Kip, ca. 1700.

DOCUMENT 1.12.2: Image of canoes on the Kongo River, late sixteenth century

## Vocabulary

| | | | |
|---|---|---|---|
| canoe | log boat | narrow-beamed | patroon |
| draft, shallow | maritime | navigation | |

## Student Activities

### Analysis of Physical Features of Canoes

Activity 1

Using Documents 1.121 and 1.12.2, students analyze the canoe as an artifact. This includes:

❖ where the canoe was found

❖ physical description of the canoe: material(s), shape, size, length, width, moving parts, and any noticeable designs, motifs, or identifying marks

❖ how the canoe might have been constructed: tools, the amount of time it might have taken without electricity

❖ who might have made it, used it, for what purposes and where

❖ what details students would like to see but can't

### Compare and Contrast Images of Canoes

Activity 2

Students compare and contrast the images of African canoes (1.12.1 and 1.12.2) with recreational canoes as we know them today. Discuss the design of canoes,

## Contemporary Connection

※

### Ignoring African Contributions

In the summer of 2000, as two dozen tall ships sailed into Casco Bay, Maine, a crowd of people gathered in the parking lot of the Green Memorial A.M.E Zion Church of Portland to help work on two traditional West African ocean-going dugout canoes. The day was festive, with handicraft displays and music from traditional African instruments and voices of the Sudanese Women's Choir. But the message was a serious one: that in none of Operation Sail's promotional literature was mention made of Africans' contributions to the Atlantic traditions of navigation and transportation. Nor was there any description of the vital contribution of the slave trade to the prosperity of the Atlantic economy. One of the collaborators in this educational effort was the Museum of African Tribal Art located in Portland. This museum continues its educational outreach to students and the general public. For more information, check out the website *www.africantribalartmuseum.org*.

such as the ones shown in the images: shallow draft, generally low sides, pointed at both ends, maneuverable but challenging to steer in tight spaces such as canals, streams, and rivers, and designed to be paddled or poled along a shoreline. What comparable modes of transportation do we use today? Explain your answers.

**Activity 3**

### Creative Extensions—Cultural Mixing

A number of enslaved Africans brought over canoe-making and rice-growing skills from specific regions in West Africa where they had performed similar labors. They may have exchanged boat-making and canoe-carving techniques and designs with Native Americans in the region, resulting in a mix of designs. Think of things that you consider a mix of different ethnic styles, such as food, fashion, or languages. Describe how you think designs mix and blend, or create a hybrid. When and why might a design or style stay separate and not become a hybrid? Brainstorm and create posters with examples of both blended and unmixed designs.

## Further Student and Teacher Resources

Bolster, W. Jeffrey. *Black Jacks: African American Seamen in the Age of Sail*. Cambridge, MA: Harvard University Press, 1997.

Smith, Robert. "The Canoe in West African History." *Journal of African History*. 11:4 (1970): 515–33, London, UK.

Wood, Peter H. *Black Majority: Negroes in Colonial South Carolina from 1670 through the Stono Rebellion*. New York: W. W. Norton & Company, 1974.

## Websites

**www.cla.sc.edu/sciaa/staff/amerc/riverine.html**
**www.cla.sc.edu/sciaa/staff/amerc/canoe.html**
*Photos of canoes as well as articles and historical information*

**www.dnr.state.state.md.us/irc/boc.html**
*An informative website explaining the history of black people in the Chesapeake Bay region maintained by Historian Vincent O. Leggett, working with Maryland's Department of Natural Resources*

# Primary Source Materials
# for Lesson 12

1.12.1

Image: "Negro's cannoes, carrying Slaves, on Board of Ships att
Manfroe," engraving by J. Kip, ca. 1700

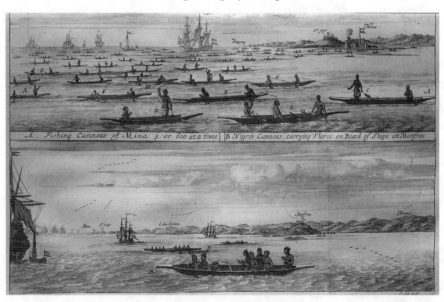

Boston Athenaeum

## 1.12.2

## Image of canoes on the Kongo River, late sixteenth century

*An engraving of the Kongo River (present-day Zaire River) in the kingdom of Kongo shows the variation of the canoes used in that era.*

American Heritage Picture Collection

# Cultural Memory and Transfer— Rice and Baskets

White planters often purchased West Africans from particular regions because they brought valuable agricultural skills and experience to North America, especially rice growing and basket making. Rice was domesticated along West Africa's middle Niger River about 3,500 years ago. By the seventeenth and eighteenth centuries, West Africans grew and sold rice to slave traders to provision their ships. A European explorer in the Congo-Angola region noted that rice was so plentiful that it could be purchased very cheaply. The first two slave ships that arrived in French Louisiana in 1719 brought several barrels of rice seed and skilled enslaved Africans who knew how to cultivate it. In the colony of South Carolina, rice production took permanent hold in 1695; the enslaved African population grew in proportion to the increase in rice production.

The plantations that gave rise to the Gullah (or Geechee) communities of the isolated coastal Sea Islands were established around this time. Many of the Africans who worked on these plantations were from regions in West Africa with rivers and fertile deltas, places such as Sierra Leone and locations along the Niger and Gambia rivers where rice was and remains today an important agricultural product. The most prominent rice-growing region was along what Europeans called the Grain Coast, upwind or westward of present-day Ghana, where, according to written accounts, rice was the staple of the local diet.

A number of scholars describe the process of rice planting, tending, and harvesting in North America as very similar to the routines used on the African continent. Peter Wood writes in *Black Majority*: "New World slaves planted rice in the spring by pressing a hole with the heel and covering the seeds with the foot, the motion used was demonstrably similar to that employed in West Africa. In summer when Carolina blacks moved through the rice fields in a row, hoeing in unison to work songs, the pattern of cultivation was not one imposed by European owners, but rather one retained from West African forebears. And in October when the threshed grain was fanned in the wind, the wide, flat winnowing baskets were made by black hands after an African design." In addition, the mortar-and-pestle grinding technique, used in Africa to husk and whiten rice grains, was also used by enslaved Africans in South Carolina.

Baskets woven from a variety of materials, including raffia and sweetgrass, were an essential tool in harvesting rice. Raffia, indigenous to Africa and other parts of the world, comes from the raffia palm, a large and heavy tree that can reach up to 25 meters or more than 80 feet. Its leave, or "feathers," are coated with wax and are processed to yield raffia fibers. These fibers are woven into baskets and other objects.

Sweetgrass, whose name comes from its fresh, sweet-smelling scent, is a tough grass that grows along the coasts of rivers and in marshes in many parts of North America. Sweetgrass has been used for centuries by Native Americans and people of African and European descent to weave baskets and other items. In a website describing the African origins of sweetgrass baskets, Dennis Adams of the Beaufort, South Carolina, Public Library writes:

> *The Encyclopedia of Africa South of the Sahara* describes two basic methods of basketry and mat making used on the continent of Africa well before slaves came to America. The first of the Old-World methods is plaiting, where braids of wood strips, reeds, grasses or roots are twined or twilled into many different patterns. But it is from the second method that our local sweetgrass baskets descend. [In the encyclopedia, Margaret Casey explains that] "sewn basketry, often called coil-sewn, involves a thin continuous foundation, usually of grass, which is sewn spirally on itself, using split palm leaf, raffia, or similar fiber. Some baskets are so tightly sewn that they can be used for containers of liquid, being watertight when the fibers have swelled. Other sewn basketry may have the foundation elements plaited or lying in parallel rows, sewn together and then sewn to the rest of the basket." In Africa, a basket can be more than just a basket. Other daily uses include roof and wall framework, fish and animal traps, beer strainers, flour sifters, clothing and hats (including ceremonial headdresses and crowns), and dance masks *(www.co.beaufort.sc.us/bftlib)*.

A number of rice recipes were brought by African cooks across the Atlantic. Author Karen Hess describes one, Hoppin' John, as the African American rice and bean dish of South Carolina, a dish that contains a variety of peas, such as cow peas, red peas, small black peas, field peas, black-eyed peas, crowder peas, and whipporwill peas.

## Organizing Idea

The cultivation of rice and the design and skills of basket making by people of African descent in North America provide interrelated subjects for study. Each reveals a wealth of information about ways that Africans and people of African descent carried skills from Africa to the North American colonies and utilized this knowledge in colonial America.

## Student Objectives

Students will:

❖ learn about the crop cycle of rice cultivation

❖ understand the connection between rice farming and wild-fiber basket making in West Africa and the Low Country of the Carolinas in North America

❖ understand that Africans with experience in rice cultivation were critical to the growth of the South Carolina plantation system and economy

❖ understand ways that culture can survive despite forced migration

## Key Questions

❖ What are the geographic and cultural origins of rice and baskets in West Africa?

❖ Why do some traditional baskets have a flat and wide shape? How do various basket shapes reveal their uses?

❖ How can the transmission of culture be revealed through artifacts?

❖ How can the attributes of a culture, such as rice cultivation and basket design and production, tell a story of African peoples in a given time and place?

## Primary Source Materials

DOCUMENT 1.13.1: Excerpt from Captain Samuel Gamble's journal, 1793

DOCUMENT 1.13.2: Engraving of rice hoeing, 1878

DOCUMENT 1.13.3: Photograph of Gullah women pounding rice using African-derived techniques and tools, late nineteenth century

DOCUMENT 1.13.4: African raffia baskets

DOCUMENT 1.13.5: Photograph of twentieth-century handcrafted sweetgrass-woven baskets from South Carolina

## Supplementary Materials

ITEM 1.13.A: Words for the song "Peas and Rice"

## Vocabulary

| | | | |
|---|---|---|---|
| coil-sewn | mortar and | raffia | winnowing |
| cultivation | pestle | sweetgrass | |
| delta | plait | threshing | |

## Student Activities

Activity 1 | **Flowchart for the Process of Rice Cultivation**

Teachers and students can access detailed information on rice growing in encyclopedias or online (*www.riceweb.org*). Together, students read the information on rice cultivation and the early account by Samuel Gamble (1.13.1). Show students where the Windward Coast is located on a map of Africa as well as the area of Upper Gambia where Captain Gamble traveled. As the class reads, ask them to write down all references to the stages of growing rice as they find them. List them on the board. Ask each student to create a poster or flowchart listing the tasks involved in this work and indicating how long it takes for one crop cycle to be ready for harvest.

## Map Analysis—Rice Growing

*Activity 2*

Looking at a large map of the world, ask, "What did the rice-growing areas in West Africa have in common with rice-growing areas in the Americas?" Use classroom resource books to identify and then compare the geography of (1) the countries along the Upper Guinea Coast, stretching from present-day Senegal to Liberia and encompassing three slave-trading regions, Senegambia, the Windward Coast, and Sierra Leone and (2) those parts of the Americas traditionally associated with rice crops, especially the Low Country of the Carolinas. Look at their environmental pictures, such as rainfall, temperatures, land drainage, types of vegetation, etc. Draw regional maps that clearly identify the following areas that are best for rice production: tidal floodplain, mangrove swamp, inland swamp, and rain-fed swamp. Give students this hypothesis: Records show that many Africans who were bought and selected for work in the Carolinas were originally from West Africa's Grain Coast. Can you suggest what advantages this might have offered to the plantation owner?

## Writing to Extend—Enslaved Africans at Work

*Activity 3*

Distribute the images of rice farming and baskets (1.13.2, 1.13.3, and 1.13.4). As students think back on information and insights they gathered from Activities 1 and 2, have them create a piece of writing—an essay, a story, a poem, a diary entry—describing what they observe in the pictures, what questions they have, and something about what the experience of cultivating, harvesting, and processing rice must have been for the Africans engaged in this work. Students may choose to write from the point of view of the working man or woman in the first person.

## Comparison and Contrast of Wild-Fiber Baskets

*Activity 4*

Ask students to look at the basket images (1.13.4, 1.13.5) and describe what they see. What kinds of shapes, colors, and materials are used? Are there patterns noticeable in the design? How have the baskets been put together? What might each of these particular baskets be used for? What does their shape say about their purpose? Is it possible to tell which ones are from West Africa and which ones were made in the United States? Students can use the websites listed to research grass basket making.

## Music Connection

⟶⟩⟨⟵

On southern tobacco, rice, and cotton plantations, "singing accompanied all kinds of work," writes Eileen Southern in *The Music of Black Americans*. For slaves, singing lessened to some degree the monotony of the labor and gave them a sense of communion. Plantation owners and slave drivers encouraged the singing because it increased productivity. Work songs were characterized by repetition and steady rhythm. They often incorporated the African call and response tradition in which one individual sings and everyone else comes in on the refrain.

Listen to the call and response song "Peas and Rice" on the CD-ROM and read the words (Item 1.13.A). (Students can also explore the websites listed under Further Resources.) Provide students with wild rice and any kind of container with a lid in which to place the rice. If possible, locate flat, wide-rimmed baskets. Ask students to sing the song while one group enacts the rocking motion of the winnowing and the rest of the class provides the sound of the rice being shaken and thrown up in the air. Students can then create and perform their own call and response work song using what they've learned about rice farming or repetitive tasks from their own life experiences.

**Activity 5**

### Using Food to Learn About a Culture

Looking at the Contemporary Connection with this lesson, students cook Hoppin' John for a shared classroom meal. Students should be encouraged to bring in other favorite rice recipes from home and discuss the origins of these dishes.

**Activity 6**

### Further Research—Rice-Growing Today

Students research rice-growing in Africa and in the United States today. They may focus on such topics as technological advances made in production; reasons for rice's labor-intensive cultivation; the crop's need for water and relatively long growing period; areas in the world where rice is a food staple.

## Further Student and Teacher Resources

Carney, Judith A. *Black Rice: The African Origins of Rice Cultivation in the Americas*. Cambridge, MA: Harvard University Press, 2001

"Growing Rice." *Faces*, published by Cobblestone Publications, Gullah Issue, February, 1998: 14–15.

Hall, Gwendolyn Midlo. *Africans in Colonial Louisiana, The Development of Afro-Creole Culture in the Eighteenth Century*. Baton Rouge: University of Louisiana Press, 1992.

Hess, Karen. *The Carolina Rice Kitchen: The African Connection*. Columbia: University of South Carolina Press, 1992.

## Contemporary Connection 1

✠

### Contemporary Basket Making

"Though the traditions are ancient, sweetgrass baskets are a recent development in our Sea Islander communities . . . Coiled, handmade baskets of sweetgrass (sewn with longleaf pine needles and strips of palmetto leaf) command good prices at roadside stands or on the City Market and streets of Charleston. Slaves had been making coiled baskets (an African technique different from the European weave) since the late 1600s, and the Sea Island baskets are related to those of Angola, Senegambia, and the Congo . . ." Dennis Adams, Library Services Coordinator of the Beaufort County, South Carolina Public Library, 1990s. Can anyone in the class locate a sweetgrass basket for students to examine?

Mouser, Bruce L., ed. *A Slaving Voyage to Africa and Jamaica*: *The Log of the Sandown, 1793–1794—'A journal of an intended voyage, by God's permission' . . . by me Samuel Gamble Commander*. Bloomington : Indiana University Press, 2002.

Rosengarten, Dale. *Row Upon Row: Sea Grass Baskets of the South Carolina Low Country*. Columbia: University of South Carolina Press, reprinted 1993.

Wood, Peter H. *Black Majority: Negroes in Colonial South Carolina from 1670 through the Stono Rebellion*. New York: W. W. Norton & Company, 1974.

### Websites

www.pbs.org/wgbh/aia/part1/1h305.html

www.kingtisdell.org/gullah.htm

www.sierra-leone.org/calendar.html

www.historycooperative.org/journals/wm/59.3/br_8.html

www.sierra-leone.org/culture.html

*For Information About Gullah Communities*

www.gullahgourmet.com/history.htm

www.gullahcelebration.com/

*For Baskets*

www.africantreasures.net/baskets/baskets.asp

*For Songs*

www.folkways.si.edu/45030.htm
*Ella Jenkins children's songs, including sound clips*

www.northbysouth.org/1998/music/rhythm/rhythm.htm
*Syncopation, call and response, and timbre, including sound clips*

www.americaslibrary.gov/sh/kidsongs/sh_kidsongs_callresp_1.html
*Three 1930 sound clips from the Library of Congress*

www.gacoast.com/navigator/quimbys.html

www.uwm.edu/Course/660-309/ClassTwo.html

www.tulane.edu/~mrbc/2001/music/roots_of_the_blues.htm

*About Rice*

www.riceweb.org

www.ricefarming.com/home/main.html

---

## Contemporary Connection 2
✠

## Hoppin' John Recipe

Hoppin' John is a dish that was brought to the United States by Africans. It is traditionally dish served by people throughout the South, particularly in South Carolina, on New Year's Day because it is said to bring good luck.

### Traditional Hoppin' John

#### Yield: 10 Servings

| | |
|---|---|
| 4 | Bacon strips |
| 1/4 c | Onion, diced |
| 1/2 c | Green bell pepper, diced |
| 1/2 c | Red bell pepper, diced |
| 2 c | *Fresh* Blackeyed peas (precooked) |
| | -or purple hull peas (precooked) |
| | -or 2 pk (10 oz) frozen blackeyed peas |
| 1/2 c | Uncooked white rice |
| 2 c | Water |
| | Salt & pepper, to taste |
| | Louisiana Hot Sauce |

Dice bacon. Brown in Dutch oven with onion and peppers until bacon is crisp and vegetables are soft. Add peas and rice, then water. Cover and simmer over very low heat about 20 minutes, until the rice is tender. Salt & pepper to taste. Add a dash of hot sauce (to taste).
www.northbysouth.org/1999/food/neh/backtoafrica.htm

# Primary Source Materials for Lesson 13

## 1.13.1

### Excerpt from Captain Samuel Gamble's Journal, 1793

The Bagos are very expert in Cultivating rice and in quite a Different manner to any of the Nations on the Windward Coast. The country they inhabit is chiefly loam and swampy. The rice they first sew on their dunghills and rising spots about their town; when 8 or 10 Inches high [they] transplant it into Lugars made for that purpose which are flat low swamps, at one side . . . they have a reservoir that they can let in what water they please, [on the] other side . . . is a drain out so they can let off what they please. The Instrument they use much resembles a Turf spade with which they turn the grass under in ridges just above the water which by being confined Stagnates and nourishes the roof of the plant. Women and Girls transplant the rice and are so dexterous as to plant fifty roots singly in one minute. When the rice is ready for cutting, they turn the water off till their Harvest is over then they let the Water and let it stand three or four seasons it being so impoverished. The time of planting is in September.

## 1.13.2

Engraving of rice hoeing, 1878

South Carolina Department of Archives and History Picture Collection,
Box 6, Folder 23 (P900051)

## 1.13.3

Photograph of Gullah women pounding rice using African-derived techniques and tools, late nineteenth century

Courtesy of the Georgia Division of Archives and History, Office of Secretary of State

## 1.13.4

## African raffia baskets

*West Africans made their raffia baskets from the processed leaves of raffia palms. The baskets had many uses: large ones for winnowing rice; others to store grain, seafood, other foods, and clothing.*

Photograph by Renée Covalucci;
Baskets courtesy of Hamill Gallery of African Art, Boston, MA

<u>1.13.5</u>

## Photograph of twentieth-century handcrafted sweetgrass-woven baskets from South Carolina

*A sweet-smelling grass grows in marshes and swamps in many parts of North America. Slaves from West Africa brought with them their skills in basket weaving and handed down the tradition from generation to generation.*

Photograph by Renée Covalucci

# Cultural Memory and Transfer — Textiles and Quilts

Africans who were brought to the American colonies as slaves retained their languages, belief systems, and other cultural memories despite horrific experiences during the Middle Passage, the journey across the Atlantic from West Africa to European colonies in the West Indies and mainland North America. They did so even though relatives and covillagers were deliberately separated, either on the African coast or in American ports, to limit communication and avert possible uprisings. Africans and people of African descent were typically prohibited from speaking their own languages, practicing their religious and spiritual beliefs, and using distinctly African objects such as drums.

Until the 1960s, most U.S. historians felt comfortable asserting that African slaves had effectively lost their culture when they were transported to the New World. This was certainly not the case, and research over the past several decades has provided ample documentation that many African cultural lifeways persisted throughout the colonial period. Examples include the material evidence for religious, civil, and naming ceremonies; textile and agricultural production; pot cooking and cooking with rice; and design motifs such as West African Akan *Adinkra* symbols, strip weaving, and geometric patterns.

In contrast to traditional European American quilting techniques, art historian Maude Southwell Wahlman points out that African American quilts in particular were characterized by African-inspired "strips, bold colors, large designs, asymmetry, multiple patterns, and improvisation," which can still be seen in southern quilting today.

## Organizing Idea

Many textiles made by Africans and people of African descent in colonial North America express distinctively African designs and execution, despite the influences of European and Native American cultures. These artifacts serve as evidence that Africans practiced skills from Africa in North American colonies and integrated this knowledge into lives in colonial America.

## Student Objectives

Students will:

❖ use perspective-taking and analytical skills to describe and identify a number of designs of African origin and influence found in selected textiles

❖ consider the importance of cultural transmission as an essential strategy for individuals and groups coping with a new and oppressive situation

## Key Questions

❖ What designs did Africans bring from Africa to the American colonies?

❖ How do cultural transmissions show up in artifacts such as quilts and textiles?

❖ How do these cultural features tell a story of people of African descent in a given time and place?

## Primary Source Materials

DOCUMENT 1.14.1: Appliqué quilt from Benin

DOCUMENT 1.14.2: Quilt made by Harriet Powers, 1896–1898

DOCUMENT 1.14.3: *Adire* cloth made by Yoruba people of Ibadan, Nigeria.

DOCUMENT 1.14.4: *Korhogo* cloth from Ivory Coast

DOCUMENT 1.14.5: Samples of strip weaving from Ghana

DOCUMENT 1.14.6: Akan *Adinkra* symbols

DOCUMENT 1.14.7: *Adinkra* cloth designer at work

DOCUMENT 1.14.8: "Twenty-five Patch," quilt made by Rachel Carey George, 1935

DOCUMENT 1.14.9: "Basket Weave," quilt made by Nettie Jane Kennedy, 1973

DOCUMENT 1.14.10: "Pinwheel," quilt made by Essie Bendolph Pettway, 2000

## Vocabulary

| *Adinkra* symbols | Akan | motif | strip weaving |
|---|---|---|---|

## Student Activities

**Activity 1**

### Comparison and Contrast—African American and African Textiles

Students look carefully at the images of the quilt from Ghana (1.14.1) and the Harriet Powers pictorial quilt (1.14.2) and take notes as to what they notice. What colors and materials are used? Are the styles similar?  How? How do the students *feel* when they see the quilts? Now ask students to study the examples of African textiles (1.14.3, 1.14.4, and 1.14.5) and record their responses to the same questions. What kinds of information do these textiles convey about the people who made them? Why did Africans who were brought to North America continue to use their native designs? Compare the African designs to the images in the Powers quilt. Notice the strip-weaving technique, which is carried over into quilting.

## Analyzing Akan *Adinkra* Symbols

Activity 2

Students look at the Akan *Adinkra* symbols (1.14.6), and the image of textile production in West Africa (1.14.7). What do they notice? What strikes them about each of these images? Ask them to write a brief response. Discuss the concept of using symbols in a design. What do they see? Why might African Americans have passed down some of the symbols from one generation to the next?

## Comparison and Contrast—*Adinkra* Symbols and Quilt Patterns

Activity 3

Distribute the images of quilts made by African American women in Alabama in the twentieth century (1.14.8, 1.14.9, 1.14.10). Students identify all possible points of comparison between these and the *Adinkra* symbols from West Africa.

## Creative Extensions

Activity 4

Students create a set of their own symbols to represent wisdom, equality, and strength. Then they design a quilt in which they incorporate these symbols. Alternatively, students may identify and research significant symbols from their own cultural heritage and design a quilt using those symbols.

## Role Playing and Writing

Activity 5

Artifacts lend themselves to perspective-taking activities that help students develop a more in-depth understanding of that artifact: its creator, owner(s), journey through time and place, identity, etc.

* Students imagine that one of the quilts came with a letter explaining its creation and write such a letter in prose or poetry form.

* Students create a dialogue between Africans who remained on that continent and Africans who were taken to America that addresses what Africans left behind in Africa, and what they miss, as well as what they brought with them.

* For additional drama-based activities see Carla Blank and Jody Roberts' *Live on Stage, Performing Arts for the Middle School*, a useful, adaptable resource for older students (high school and beyond).

*Activity 6*   **Research and Discussion—In Whose Safekeeping?**

Students research how we can preserve fragile objects such as antique quilts to ensure their survival for future generations. Who can best preserve them? Contact a local museum to learn how textiles are preserved.

## Further Student and Teacher Resources

Arthur, George Kojo, and Robert Rowe. *Cloth as Metaphor: The Akan Cultural Symbols Project.* Beltsville, MD: CEFIKS Publications, 1998

Beardsley, John., et al. *Gee's Bend—The Women and Their Quilts. Atlanta,* GA: Tinwood Books, 2002.

Blank, Carla, and Jody Roberts. *Live On Stage, Performing Arts for the Middle School, Teacher Resource Book.* Palo Alto, CA: Dale Seymour Publications, 1997.

Clarke, Duncan. *The Art of African Textiles.* London: Grange Books, 1997.

Deetz, James. *Flowerdew Hundred: The Archaeology of Virginia Plantation, 1619–1864.* Charlottesville: University Press of Virginia, 1993.

Fry, Gladys-Marie. *Stitched from the Soul.* New York: Dutton Studio Book, 1990.

Hall, Robert "Religious Symbolism of the Iron Pot: The Plausibility of a Congo-Angola Origin." *Western Journal of Black Studies* 13:3 (1989).

Lyons, Mary E., *Stitching Stars: The Story Quilts of Harriet Powers.* New York: Simon and Schuster—Aladdin Paperbacks, 1997.

Tobin, Jacqueline L, and Raymond G. Dobard, *Hidden in Plain View: A Secret Story of Quilts and the Underground Railroad.* New York: Doubleday, 1999.

Wahlman, Maude Southwell. *Signs and Symbols: African Images in African-American Quilts.* New York: Studio Books, 1993.

Walsh, Lorena. *From Calabar to Carter's Grove: The History of a Virginia Slave Community.* Charlottesville: University Press of Virginia, 1997.

Yentsch, Anne Elizabeth. *A Chesapeake Family and Their Slaves.* Cambridge, U.K.: Cambridge University Press, 1994.

### Websites

*African Images on the Internet*

**www.du.edu/duma/africloth/** and

**http://students.clarku.edu/~jborgatt/african_textiles.htm**
*Textiles and looms*

**http://xavier.xula.edu/~jrotondo/Kingdoms/Gallery/gallDaily.html**
*Images of daily life and weaving*

**www.adire.clara.net/afgallery.htm**
*Adire African Textiles Gallery*

www.marshall.edu/akanart/

www.marshall.edu/akanart/lessonplans.htm
*Akan Cultural Symbols Project*

*Quilting*

http://xroads.virginia.edu/~UG97/quilt/intro.html

www.du.edu/duma/africloth/study.html
*Ways of looking at cloth*

www.quiltethnic.com/historical.html

www.quiltethnic.com/textiles.html

www.si.edu/revealingthings/data/content/O-194/index.html
*Image and sound clip describing a quilt made by enslaved girls (Smithsonian online exhibit about material culture)*

www.uwrf.edu/history/prints/women/africanquilts.html
*Three mid-nineteenth-century African American quilts (attributed to enslaved women)*

---

## Contemporary Connection 1

### Seven Sisters' Quilt Show

A Stitch In Time Performers calling themselves "Seven Quilts for Seven Sisters" are originally of the Williams family of Clayton, New Jersey. Their quilt show explores the South in slavery days in a performance featuring song, dance, history, stories, skits, and quilts. Their lively performance depicts the joys of sisterhood and the trials of slave life and shows how quilting helped women cope. With their combined knowledge of African American slave history and the practical craft of quilting, their program is dedicated to the idea of educating the public with entertainment. Contact one of the Seven Sisters, Phyllis Walker, at 856-478-6811 or via email at cornyw@aol.com for questions about the Seven Sisters' show availability.

---

## Contemporary Connection 2

### National Museum of African Art

The National Museum of African Art is one of sixteen museums and galleries that make up the Smithsonian Institution in Washington, D.C. The website for this museum states that "African art embodies one of humanity's greatest achievements—fusing visual imagery with spiritual beliefs and social purpose." The museum's collection includes many forms of artistic expression including textiles, tools, masks, and musical instruments. The work of living artists is also represented in the collection. The museum's website is informative and visually interesting, including permanent and traveling exhibits as well as slides and videotapes available for loan (*www.nmafa.si.edu/pubaccess/index.htm*).

# Primary Source Materials
# for Lesson 14

## 1.14.1

### Appliqué quilt from Benin

*The tradition of appliqued textiles has been practiced extensively by the Fon people of West Africa.*

Photograph by Renée Covalucci

<u>1.14.2</u>

## Quilt made by Harriet Powers, 1896–1898

*Harriet Powers' pictorial quilt shows biblical scenes and ones of local history and natural phenomena, for example, the Leonid meteor shower of 1833. Harriet Powers, born a slave in Georgia in 1837, died in 1911.*

Photograph ©2003 Museum of Fine Arts, Boston

<u>1.14.3</u>

## *Adire* cloth made by Yoruba people of Ibadan, Nigeria

*A combination of natural and synthetic indigo is used in the dyeing process. Designs are inspired by nature and include the unique image of pillars alternating with spoons. The pillars represent those of Mapo Hall, the town hall in Ibadan.*

Photograph by Renée Covalucci

## 1.14.4

### *Korhogo* cloth from Ivory Coast

*Figures are applied, using blackish-brown dye, onto coarsely woven, naturally colored fabric.*

Photograph by Renée Covalucci

<u>1.14.5</u>

## Samples of strip weaving from Ghana

*The narrow-strip textile, rich in color, is seen by some scholars as a visual mirror of African and African American music.*

Photograph by Renée Covalucci

## 1.14.6

## Akan *Adinkra* symbols

*Each symbol holds meaning. Moving across the top row from left to right:*

1. Knowledge comes from ongoing study
2. Purity and chastity
3. Wisdom comes with age
4. Knowledge comes with thoughtful examination
5. Security and prosperity

   *Bottom row, left to right:*

6. Unity with diversity
7. Strength and authority
8. Wisdom uses the past as a guide
9. Uniqueness in each individual's growth
10. Knowledge requires attentive listening

## 1.14.7

*Adinkra* cloth designer at work

G. F. Kojo Arthur and CEFIKS Publications

1.14.8

"Twenty-five Patch," quilt made by Rachel Carey George, 1935

<u>1.14.9</u>

"Basket Weave," quilt made by Nettie Jane Kennedy, 1973

## 1.14.10

"Pinwheel," quilt made by Essie Bendolph Pettway, 2000

# The Gullah

Gullah (locally called Geechee) is a distinctive culture created by people of African descent living on the coastal islands and nearby mainland inlets of South Carolina and Georgia in the southeastern United States. The terms Gullah and Geechee have African origins. Gullah and Geechee probably derive from the names of peoples who were living along the rice coast of West Africa in what is now Sierra Leone and Liberia, both areas from which large numbers of Africans were brought to the Sea Islands.

Until after World War II, the Sea Islands were inhabited almost entirely by African Americans whose forebears were brought as slaves from Barbados and Africa as early as the 1680s. New Africans continued to arrive on the islands even after Britain declared the transatlantic slave trade illegal in 1807, and the importation of slaves to the United States officially ended in 1808. Almost 15,000 new arrivals from the Congo and Angola landed on the Sea Islands during the first decade of the 1800s.

In these mosquito-infested lowlands, Africans provided both the knowledge and the labor needed for the cultivation of rice and indigo, and they manufactured the baskets, mortars, and other tools needed for processing these staple crops. Later, they labored on cotton plantations. Because of the climate of the Sea Islands, few white people lived there year-round. With little white influence, the Gullah merged several African as well as European traditions into a lively body of folkways expressed through religion, music, dance, oral traditions, and philosophy. Historian Ira Berlin in *Many Thousands Gone* describes blacks in the Low Country of South Carolina and Georgia as "physically separated and psychologically estranged from the European-American world, and culturally closer to Africa than any other black people in continental North America" (p. 143).

In November 1861, Federal troops occupied the Sea Islands and white landowners fled inland. More than 30,000 former slaves remained on the islands, and the islands physical and cultural isolation continued well into the twentieth century. It was not until the late 1940s that bridges began to be built, and then only to the larger islands. This isolation enabled the Gullah to preserve aspects of African languages, songs, legends, burial traditions, crafts, foods, and folk medicine into the twentieth and twenty-first centuries. Homes are often grouped into family compounds, with modern houses placed in a semicircle of extended family that mirrors African traditions.

Because of their long period of isolation, the Gullah are an exceedingly rich source for linguistic studies, and have bridged the Atlantic with a new dialogue between Sierra Leoneans and African Americans. A 1979 survey by the Summer Institute of Linguistics found 100,000 Gullah speakers in Georgia and South Carolina. Ten percent of the Gullah speakers spoke no English. The *Cambridge Encyclopedia of Language* cites Gullah as one of six English-derived Atlantic creoles, languages evolved from the mixing of African languages, regional dialects of English, and creoles spoken in the Caribbean, particularly Barbados. Gullah is not "broken English"; rather, it is a language in its own right. The syntax and grammar of Gullah are closer to African languages than to English. In Joel Chandler Harris' Brer Rabbit tales, Uncle Remus speaks Gullah.

## Organizing Idea

Gullah culture provides a living model of the development and evolution of traditions by African slaves and their descendants living as a majority population in relative isolation in coastal South Carolina and Georgia. Through examination of the Gullah people, students will learn how language may be used to trace cultural roots and to establish historical connections. Additionally, students can discover how some slaves were able to give meaning to their lives by reestablishing important religious, social, and philosophical elements from their African worldviews.

## Student Objectives

Students will:

❖ develop an understanding of some of the many components that comprise a culture, specifically the Gullah, including language, social institutions, shared histories, myths, oral traditions, culinary arts, music, dance, and moral codes

❖ gain insights into the influence of such factors as demographic mix, typography, social organization, and economic structures on cultural retention

❖ identify aspects of Gullah culture that have entered other cultures in the United States, such as cooking, storytelling, music, religion, and vocabulary

## Key Questions

❖ What does Gullah culture teach us about the nature and legacy of enslavement in the Sea Islands?

❖ How was Gullah culture shaped by the climate and isolation of the Sea Islands?

❖ How were the Gullah people able to consolidate and express an understanding of the world in which they found themselves, and how did that understanding empower them?

❖ Why has language been so important in the study of the Gullah?

❖ How does a multidisciplinary approach to the study of Gullah culture enhance our understanding?

## Primary Source Materials

DOCUMENT 1.15.1: "Carrying a Song Back Home, North Carolina, *News & Observer*, May 12, 1997.

DOCUMENT 1.15.2: Extract from "Brother Rabbit & Brother Bull-Frog," an Uncle Remus tale by Joel Chandler Harris, 1903

## Supplementary Materials

Item 1.15.A:  Lyrics to "Amelia's Song"

## Vocabulary

| | | | |
|---|---|---|---|
| archaic | ditty | impingement | sovereignty |
| chaff | ethnomusicologist | purge | |

## Student Activities

### Reading, Discussion, and Research on Origins of Songs

*Activity 1*

Mary Moran, a resident of Harris Neck on the mainland of coastal Georgia, sang a song passed down by generations of women in her family.  She knew it was in an African language but could not translate it. With the help of anthropologists and linguists, Moran traced the origins of the song to the village of Senehun Ngola in Sierra Leone, where the song is still sung.

Read the newspaper article "Carrying a Song Back Home" (1.15.1) and lyrics to the song (Item 1.15.A); then have students discuss the story of Mary Moran. If possible, obtain a copy of *The Language You Cry In*, a 1998 video that tells the story of Mary Moran and her song. Why is music such a powerful tool for retaining and evoking memory? Do students' families have any special songs that are passed down through the generations and sung at special times? These can be lullabies, birthday songs, or songs with religious themes, for example. Have students research the origins of these special songs and write one-page papers on their history and meaning.

### Reading and Discussion of Uncle Remus Tales

*Activity 2*

Although Joel Chandler Harris was not himself from the Gullah culture, his Uncle Remus tales are among the best-known folk tales from the Low Country. Read both Harris' original telling of the stories (1.15.2) and borrow a more recent retelling from a library, such as a version by Julius Lester. Harris' use of dialect makes very challenging reading for students. They may want to read it aloud, paraphrasing as they progress through the story. Alternatively, teachers may want to have students simply compare the original to the retold versions. Discuss the meaning behind these tales. Why have they endured for so long?

## Activity 3     Research the Origins

Students research the various theories regarding the origins of the Uncle Remus Brer Rabbit tales and write a paper summarizing their findings.

## Activity 4     Creative Extensions

Ambrose E. Gonzales is another writer who collected and published Gullah folklore, including *The Black Border: Gullah Stories of the Carolina Coast*. Other Gullah folk tales can be found through an Internet search. After reading these and the Uncle Remus stories, student responses might include a dramatization, video, mural, movement piece, original book and or recreation.

## Activity 5     Origins of Words

Students work with a partner and choose one or two words from the list below. Using a dictionary or the Merriam Webster's online dictionary (*www.m-w.com*), students look up the origin of their assigned words, determine the meaning of the words, and examine how they tie in with Africa. Each partner group then presents this information to the class. Are there any obvious categories these words can be grouped into? In what ways have African languages influenced American English today?

Words from African languages used in American English today include:

| | |
|---|---|
| banana (via Portuguese) | juke(box) |
| banjo | juju |
| boogie-woogie | mumbo-jumbo |
| chigger | okra |
| goober | tote |
| gorilla | voodoo |
| gumbo | yam |
| jazz | zebra |
| jitterbug | zombie |
| jitters | |

This word list is from *www.wordorigins.org/loanword.htm#African*. Additional information on the history of the English language is given in *www.wordorigins. org/histeng.htm*.

*Music Connection*

⋈

Both these songs, recorded at the Sea Island Folk Festival on Johns Island, South Carolina, were sung by the Moving Star Hall Singers and Alan Lomax. Both are examples of some of the oldest African American songs in the United States that are stongly connected to African music elements. As you listen to "See God's Ark A'Moving," a religious song, and "Somebody Stole My Henhouse Key," a children's game song (on the CD-ROM), identify all the elements you heard in the samples of West African music in earlier lessons. Students should note the call and response style, hand-clapping rhythmic patters used to recreate the sound of drums, and improvisational elements.

## Creative Extensions: A Gullah Celebration

*Activity 6*

After researching Gullah history and culture, students create a Gullah celebration, including projects such as cooking, song, and storytelling/drama. Traditional Gullah foods, with roots in African cooking, include Hoppin' John, a mixture of cowpeas (field peas) and rice; okra soup; greens; sweet potato pie and pone; and benne candy made with sesame seeds.

## Additional Activities

**Note:** Materials are not provided.

*Daughters of the Dust* is a 1991 feature film set in August 1902 on the Sea Islands. Although there are many flashbacks to the past, the action takes place on a single day when a woman, now a Baptist missionary, arrives to take her extended family to the mainland and on to the North. Nana Peazant, the family matriarch, will not be making the move. The film deals with leaving home, the influence of heritage and roots, and changing values. Themes are adult, including a pregnancy resulting from a rape and the return to the island from Cuba of a "ruint" woman.

Older students should view the movie or read the script and then discuss the movie. What question does the film present about the relationship of blacks to Native Americans, Islam, traditional African ideas about ancestors, the role of education, and the inevitability of change?

Julie Dash, who wrote the script and directed the film, developed a companion book, *Daughters of the Dust: The Making of an African American Woman's Film*. She has also written a historical novel, *Daughters of the Dust*. The novel is a sequel to the movie, although it provides sufficient background and detail that a reader does not have to have seen the film before reading the book.

Younger students can watch and discuss the video *God's Gonna Trouble the Water—Leaving Slavery Behind: Music and Other Sources of Strength of the Gullah Culture*, available from South Carolina Educational Television (SCETV) or public libraries. Narrated by Ruby Dee, the video discusses the history and contemporary culture of the Gullah. Working in small groups, students should identify and debate key issues raised in the video regarding challenges faced by Gullah people and the endurance they need to face them.

*Family Across The Sea*, another SCETV video for all ages, tells the story of the recent visits between Sea Islanders and residents of Sierra Leone and their discovery of shared language and culture.

## Further Student and Teacher Resources

Berlin, Ira. *Many Thousands Gone: The First Two Centuries of Slavery in North America*. Cambridge, MA: Harvard University Press, 2000.

Branch, Muriel Miller. *The Water Brought Us: The Story of Gullah-Speaking People*. New York: Cobblehill Books/Dutton, 1995.

Daise, Ronald. *Reminiscences of Sea Island Heritage: Legacy of Freedmen on St. Helena Island*. Orangeburg, SC: Sandlapper Publishing, Inc., 1986.

Dash, Julie. *Daughters of the Dust: The Making of an African American Woman's Film*. New York: New Press, 1992.

Gullah issue, *Faces*. Published by Cobblestone Publications.

Ferguson, Leland. *Uncommon Ground: Archaeology and Early African America, 1650–1800*. Washington: Smithsonian Institution Press, 1992.

Gonzales, Ambrose E. *The Black Border: Gullah Stories of the Carolina Coast*. Gretna, LA: Pelican Publishing Co., 1999.

Goodwine, Marquetta L., ed. *The Legacy of Ibo Landing: Gullah Roots of African-American Culture*. Atlanta, GA: Clarity Press, Inc., 1998.

Harris, Joel Chandler. *Told By Uncle Remus*. New York: Grosset & Dunlap, 1903.

Lester, Julius. Retelling *The Tales of Uncle Remus: The Adventures of Brer Rabbit*. New York: Dial Books, 1987.

### Websites

**www.gcrc.musc.edu/sugar/Gullah.htm**
*An excellent website on the Gullah people created by Project Sugar at the Division of Endocrinology at the Medical University of South Carolina*

**www.co.beaufort.sc.us/bftlib/gullah.htm**
*Another superb website about Gullah history and traditions created by staff at the Beaufort County, South Carolina, Public Library*

**www.pbs.org**
*Information about a video called* The Story of English *that has a segment on the Gullah language*

*Contemporary Connection*

✵

**The Penn Center**

Descendants of Africans brought to St. Helena Island, South Carolina, centuries ago still live on the island and value old traditions that have endured. The Penn Center on St. Helena Island, now a historical landmark, was founded by abolitionist Quakers in 1862 to educate ex-slaves for self-sufficiency. It remained a school until the 1940s. In the 1950s and 1960s, Penn Center was one of only two places in the South where blacks and whites could meet together safely to plan actions during the Civil Rights Movement.

The Penn Center now serves the community through a series of community-based projects. Each year in the second week of November, a Heritage Celebration is held to keep Gullah culture alive and to inform the public about a rich tradition that few people know about. Find out about recent Heritage Celebration events. What events in your region celebrate residents' heritages?

## Videos

*The Language You Cry In*, a 1998 video (52 minutes) from California Newsreel, 149 Ninth Street, San Francisco CA 94103; 415-621-6196;  Fax: 415-621-6522; *www.newsreel.org/films/*

*Daughters of the Dust* is a 1991 feature film (113 minutes), written and directed by Julie Dash, released by Keno Video. Available for rental in video stores.

*God's Gonna Trouble the Water—Leaving Slavery Behind: Music and other Sources of Strength of the Gullah Culture*, a 60-minute video available from South Carolina Educational Television (SCETV); 1-800-553-7752.

*Family Across The Sea—Leaving Slavery Behind: Music and Other Sources of Strength of the Gullah Culture*, another SCETV video (60 minutes); 1-800-553-7752.

# Primary Source Materials
# for Lesson 15

## 1.15.1

### "Carrying a Song Back Home," Raleigh, North Carolina,
*News & Observer*, May 12, 1997

Tune is a living link to Africa . . . .

Mary Moran knew her song was special, even if she never understood the words. While her husband trapped crabs in the inlets and estuaries surrounding the Sea Islands of Georgia, she sang the songs as she took care of their 13 children.

More than 4,000 miles across the ocean, a woman named Baindu Jabati was also singing the song—the same words, same language—as she raised her own children. The two had never met . . . .

Through remarkable luck, and perseverance—and research begun by a North Carolina linguist 65 years ago—the song has become the most substantial musical link between Africa and the 33 million black Americans whose ancestors were brought here in chains . . . .

**The full text of Document 1.15.1 is available on the CD-ROM.**

## 1.15.2

### Extract from "Brother Rabbit & Brother Bull-Frog," an Uncle Remus
tale by Joel Chandler Harris, 1903

In dem times—de times what all deze tales tells you 'bout—Brer Bull-Frog stayed in an' aroun' still water des like he do now. De bad col' dat he had in dem days, he's got it yit—de same pop-eyes, an' de same bal' head. Den, ez now, dey wa' n't a bunch er ha'r on it dat you could pull out wid a pa'r er tweezers. Ez he bellers now, des dat a-way he bellered den, mo' speshually at night. An' talk 'bout setting' up late—why, ol' Brer Bull-Frog could beat dem what fust got in de habits er etting' up late . . . .

**The full text of Document 1.15.2 is available on the CD-ROM.**

# African Religious Legacies

In his book *Slave Religion: The Invisible Institution in the Antebellum South*, Albert J. Raboteau writes: "In the New World slave control was based on the eradication of all forms of African culture because of their power to unify the slaves and thus enable them to resist or rebel . . . . One of the most durable and adaptable constituents of the slave's culture, linking African past with American present, was his religion . . . . African styles of worship, forms of ritual, systems of belief, and fundamental perspectives have remained vital on this side of the Atlantic, not because they were preserved in a 'pure' orthodoxy, but because they were transformed" (p. 4).

In the fifteenth through the nineteenth centuries, Africans practiced a variety of religions, including Christianity, Islam, Judaism, Buddhism, and Hinduism, as well as indigenous traditions such as those of the Yoruba or Bakongo peoples. Thus, enslaved Africans brought many different religious traditions with them to the Americas. Islam and the indigenous traditions are the most clearly documented, and indigenous religions have had the greatest influence on how African Americans transformed Christianity, the faith to which they were converted.

Despite their many differences, indigenous African religions had several broad communalities, including a monotheism with a creator god to whom no shrines were kept; a community of spiritual intermediaries who could negatively or positively affect daily life; and a prime place for ancestors who were regarded as vitally related to the living. Additionally, these traditions viewed nature and ordinary daily life as infused with spirituality, called *anima* (soul-power). Many traditions valued the notion of spiritual possession and acknowledged the role of priests and priestesses who, through apprenticeships and initiations, became guardians of special knowledge. Closely related to the overall health, organization, and well-being of the community and often expressed though music, dance, and masquerades, these traditional belief systems embodied a worldview with ethical and philosophical as well as practical implications.

Africans in colonial and revolutionary-era America encountered serious difficulties in preserving their religious traditions. Depending on the region, those difficulties included isolation into groupings too small to sustain religious practice, separation from others who spoke the same language, the absence of religious specialists, the suppression of beliefs as superstition, and the impossibility of reinstitutionalizing belief systems under conditions of enslavement.

Because part of the justification of slavery was that it offered a means of saving the souls of Africans, it is not surprising that many colonists encouraged slaves to adopt Christianity, often allowing them to attend religious services where they sat in segregated sections. Considerable numbers of Africans converted, undergoing a baptism similar to the water rites that many knew from their traditional religions. Africans who adopted Christianity interpreted it, contrary to their white sponsors' intentions, as a force for liberation, a balm for their suffering, rather than internalizing it as a rationale for their permanent slave status. In time, Christianity, like indigenous African religions, became strongly associated with revolts, including the Stono rebellion, Denmark Vesey's uprising, and conspiracies to win freedom. (*Note*: Additional information on resistance and rebellions can be found in the context essays and in Lesson 18 of this Sourcebook.)

## Organizing Idea

Africans came to the American colonies with religious beliefs of their own. Many were Muslim, especially those from the Senegambia region and areas that were part of the kingdoms of Mali and Songhay. Other African people brought indigenous belief systems that placed high value on the role of ancestors, spiritual intermediaries, and special priests, healers, and diviners. Still others were already acquainted with Christianity through contacts with Europeans along the Atlantic coast or through the early establishment of Christian kingdoms (for example, in Ethiopia) in the Horn of Africa. Africans in America were generally unable to sustain their traditional beliefs except as fragmented practices greatly frowned upon by the colonists or by merging their beliefs with Christianity.

## Student Objectives

Students will:

- ❖ understand that enslaved Africans arrived in the American colonies with their own religious and spiritual beliefs
- ❖ learn about the origins and sources of Islamic and indigenous belief systems brought by Africans
- ❖ gain an appreciation of the complex factors that affected the survival of religious ideas brought by the Africans
- ❖ understand how material artifacts can be interpreted in different ways and how ordinary objects might have been used for religious purposes by enslaved Africans

## Key Questions

- ❖ How were religious beliefs of enslaved Africans expressed in colonial America?

- ❖ Why do we not know more about the beliefs brought to the colonies by Africans?

- ❖ When did the large-scale conversion of Africans began, and why?

- ❖ In what ways were the beliefs of the Africans different from those of the European colonists?

- ❖ What are some evidences of African religious or spiritual belief retained by some Africans and African Americans?

## Primary Source Materials

DOCUMENT 1.16.1: Excerpts from the autobiography of Olaudah Equiano, *The Interesting Narrative of the Life of Olaudah Equiano or Gustavus Vassa*, 1789

DOCUMENT 1.16.2: Excerpt from *The Autobiography of Omar Ibn Said, Slave in North Carolina*, 1831

DOCUMENT 1.16.3: Portrait of Yarrow Mamout by Charles Wilson Peale, 1819

DOCUMENT 1.16.4: Excerpt from the autobiography of Charles Ball, *Slavery in the United States: A Narrative of the Life and Adventures of Charles Ball, A Black Man*, 1837

DOCUMENT 1.16.5: Excerpt from *Breaking Ground, Breaking Silence: The Story of New York's African Burial Ground* by Joyce Hansen and Gary McGowan, 1998

DOCUMENT 1.16.6: Excerpt on burial customs of the Gullah from the Beaufort County, South Carolina, Public Library website

## Vocabulary

| | | | |
|---|---|---|---|
| amber | girded | oblations | transmigration |
| cowrie shells | infidel | parched meal | vessel |
| doctrine | inter | pilgrimage | |
| ethnological | muslin | realm | |
| fancier | numismatic | sheikh | |

## Student Activities

### Comparison and Contrast in Religious Practices

*Activity 1*

Students should read the excerpt from Equiano's autobiography (1.16.1) on the religious beliefs and practices of his people and then discuss how these beliefs and practices are similar to or different from the religions with which they are familiar.

*Activity 2*          **Reading and Discussion**

CHANGING PERCEPTIONS

After students have read the excerpt from the autobiography of Omar Ibn Said (1.16.2), ask them how learning about the story and writings of this particular man has changed their perceptions of the enslaved people brought to this country from Africa. Students can search the Internet and find out more about Omar Ibn Said.

ORIGIN OF NAMES

Muslim names can also be a springboard for a number of discussions, including the origins of names. Students can discuss the origins and meaning of their own names and how names identify us and shape and reinforce our identities. What impact did losing their African names and being given European or Biblical names—especially demeaning ones—have on enslaved people?

*Activity 3*          **Portrait Analysis**

Have students study the portrait of Yarrow Mamout (1.16.3) by Charles Wilson Peale (1819). Mamout was brought to the colonies in the 1730s and was more than 100 years old when Peale did his portrait. Have students name what they see in the portrait. How is Mamout dressed? What does he look like? Are there clues in the portrait that tell the viewer Mamout was a Muslim? Check *www.pbs.org/ wgbh/aia/part/2h16.html* for additional information about the painting of the portrait.

*Activity 4*          **Mapping Muslim Populations**

On a map of the Atlantic world (Item 1.5.B on the CD-ROM), students should locate areas of West Africa with large Muslim populations (Senegambia, Sierra Leone, the empires of Mali and Songhay) and the portions of the southeastern American coast (South Carolina and Georgia) and Louisiana where many Muslims were sold during slavery.

*Activity 5*          **Research on Islam; Ancient African Kingdoms**

Students can research Islam to gain a deeper understanding of the religion: its tenets, practices, sacred objects, and burial practices. They can also study West African kings such as Mansa Musa (Mali), Khagan Maga (Ghana), Askia Muhammad, and Sunni Ali Ber (Songhay), whose kingdoms encompassed indigenous African belief systems as well as Muslim beliefs. Mansa Musa and Idris Alooma, Sultan of Bornu, had themselves made the *haaj* (pilgrimage) to Mecca. How did these kings reconcile the coexistence of various religious systems in their kingdoms?

## Analysis of Burial Practices

Activity 6

Divide students into small groups and give each group one of the following documents to read: an excerpt from the autobiography of Charles Ball (1.16.4); an excerpt from *Breaking Ground, Breaking Silence: The Story of New York's African Burial Ground* (1.16.5), or an excerpt on burial customs of the Gullah from the Beaufort County, South Carolina, Public Library website (1.16.6).

What objects did Africans consider important for burials or for religious rituals after a death? What significance did these objects have? Taking care to avoid prejudice, ask students to compare these African practices with the burial practices of their own religious, spiritual, and family cultures. What is similar, and what is different?

## The Use of Everyday Objects

Activity 7

In a winter 1994 article for the *Newsletter of the African-American Archaeology Network*, Patricia Samford points out: "No longer having access to the same commodities once at their disposal, West African slaves and their descendants lived in a material world populated largely with goods of English or European manufacture. It is likely that the enslaved thought about and used some objects differently than their creators had originally intended, adapting these new forms of material culture for use within African American cultural systems." Samford describes how slaves reshaped fragments of English earthernware pottery into playing pieces for an African game; engraved religious symbols on everyday knives, forks, and spoons; and filled bottles and cloth sugar and tobacco bags with objects of religious significance. Have students compile a list of everyday objects that they use differently than their creators intended. Two hundred years from now, would an archaeologist digging up these things know how they were used—or what they meant—to Americans in the twenty-first century?

## Further Student and Teacher Resources

Austin, Allen. *African Muslims in Antebellum America: Transalantic Stories and Spiritual Struggles.* New York: Routledge, 1997.

Gomez, Michael. *Exchanging Our Country Marks: The Transformation of African Identities in the Colonial and Antebellum South.* Chapel Hill: University of North Carolina Press, 1998.

Gomez, Michael. "Muslims in Early America." *Journal of Southern History*, 60: 1994, 671–710.

Hansen, Joyce, and Gary McGowan. *Breaking Ground, Breaking Silence: The Story of New York's African Burial Ground.* New York: Henry Holt and Company, 1998.

Roboteau, Albert J. *Slave Religion: The Invisible Institution in the Antebellum South.* New York Oxford University Press, 1980.

*Contemporary Connection*

❈

**African American Religious Experiences**

In 1903, W. E. B. Du Bois, in *Souls of Black Folk*, wrote that he intended "to sketch, in vague, uncertain outline, the spiritual world in which ten thousand thousand Americans live and strive." Before that time, little had been written about black religious experience. Over the next seventy-five years, interest in the subject gained momentum, and by the last quarter of the twentieth century the religious experiences of African Americans had attracted great interest among scholars. This trend was stimulated and supported by the Civil Rights Movement of the 1960s and 1970s and was part of the heightened interest in African American history in general. More information on current scholarship may be found in *African-American Religion, Interpretive Essays in History and Culture*, edited by Timothy Fulop and Albert Raboteau. Topics in the book include the relationship between slavery and Christianity, the role of black churches after emancipation, the place of Africa in African American religious consciousness, the emergence of new religious movements, and the resurgence of traditional African religions.

———. *African American Religion (Religion in American Life)*. New York: Oxford University Press, 1999.

Wright, Roberta Hughes, and Wilbur B. Hughes III. *Lay Down Body: Living History of African American Cemeteries*. Canton, MI: Visible Ink Press, 1995.

**Website**

www.co.beaufort.sc.us/bftlib/gullah2.htm#Burial

# Primary Source Materials for Lesson 16

## 1.16.1

Excerpts from the autobiography of Olaudah Equiano, *The Interesting Narrative of the Life of Olaudah Equiano, or Gustavus Vassa*, 1789

As to religion, the natives believe that there is one Creator of all things, and that he lives in the sun, and is girded round with a belt, that he may never eat or drink; but according to some, he smokes a pipe, which is our own favorite luxury. They believe he governs events, especially our deaths or captivity; but, as for the doctrine of eternity, I do not remember to have ever heard of it: some however believe in the transmigration of souls in a certain degree. Those spirits, which are not transmigrated, such as their dear friends or relations, they believe always attend them, and guard them from the bad spirits of their foes. For this reason, they always, before eating, as I have observed, put some small portion of the meat, and pour some of their drink, on the ground for them; and they often make oblations of the blood of beasts or fowls at their graves . . . .

**The full text of Document 1.16.1 is available on the CD-ROM.**

## 1.16.2

Excerpt from *The Autobiography of Omar Ibn Said, Slave in North Carolina*, 1831

My name is Omar ibn Said. My birthplace was Fut Tur, between the two rivers. I sought knowledge under the instruction of a Sheikh called Mohammed Seid, my own brother, and Sheikh Soleiman Kembah, and Sheikh Gabriel Abdal. I continued my studies twenty-five years, and then returned to my home where I remained six years. Then there came to our place a large army, who killed many men, and took me, and brought me to the great sea, and sold me into the hands of the Christians, who bound me and sent me on board a great ship and we sailed upon the great sea a month and a half, when we came to a place called Charleston in the Christian language. There they sold me to a small, weak, and wicked man, called Johnson, a complete infidel, who had no fear of God at all . . . .

Before I came to the Christian country, my religion was the religion of "Mohammed, the Apostle of God—may God have mercy upon him and give him peace." I walked to the mosque before day-break, washed my face and head and hands and feet. I prayed at noon, prayed in the afternoon, prayed at sunset, prayed in the evening. I gave him alms every year, gold, silver, seeds, cattle, sheep, goats, rice, wheat, and barley . . . .

**The full text of document 1.16.2 is available on the CD-ROM.**

## 1.16.3

### Portrait of Yarrow Mamout by Charles Wilson Peale, 1819

*This portrait, done in 1819 by Charles Wilson Peale, was painted when Mamout was more than one hundred years old.*

Courtesy of The Historical Society of Pennsylvania Collection, Atwater Kent Museum of Philadelphia

## 1.16.4

### Excerpt from the autobiography of Charles Ball, *Slavery in the United States: A Narrative of the Life and Adventures of Charles Ball, Black Man*, 1837

*In this section Ball describes an enslaved couple burying their infant:*

I assisted her and her husband to inter their infant . . . and its father buried with it a small bow and several arrows; a little bag of parched meal; a miniature canoe, about a foot long, and a little paddle (with which he said it would cross the ocean to his own country); a small stick, with an iron nail, sharpened and fastened into one end of it; and a piece of white muslin, with several curious and strange figures painted on it in blue and red, by which, he said, his relations and countrymen would know the infant to be his son, and would receive it accordingly, on its arrival amongst them . . . He cut a lock of hair from his head, threw it upon the dead infant, and closed the grave with his own hands. He then told us the God of his country was looking at him, and was pleased with what he had done.

## 1.16.5

### Excerpt from *Breaking Ground, Breaking Silence: The Story of New York's African Burial Ground* by Joyce Hansen and Gary McGowan, 1998

On a spring day in 1992, the archaeologists were still in the process of excavating burials. In the midst of their work, the crew spotted a large burial pit, its dirt disturbed, like the other burials, by the recent construction . . . .

Burial # 340 was one of the most significant discoveries since the excavations had begun. A strand of about 111 waist beads lay around her hips. No burial had ever been found in North America with beads used in this way; however, waist beads have been worn in Africa for centuries. Some of the beads were cowrie shells, most of them were made of glass, and one bead was amber. Small blue and white beads also found near her remains had probably been wrapped around her wrists.

Beads were and still are important and powerful symbols in many West African cultures and in other cultures around the world. They have been used for exchange (as money) and to denote the important passages of life such as birth, marriage, and death. They were also used to keep the wearer from harm in life and to help the individual make the journey into the afterlife.

**The full text of Document 1.16.5 is available on the CD-ROM.**

## 1.16.6

### Excerpt on burial customs of the Gullah from the Beaufort County, South Carolina, Public library website

A number of Sea Island burial customs are West- and Central African in origin. John Michael Vlach in *The Afro-American Tradition in Decorative Arts* (Cleveland Museum of Art, 1978) compared the same east-west alignment to the Central African custom of laying the coffin with the face of the deceased looking eastward.

"The continuity here is obvious," he added, "and it results from a shared concept of the cosmos—that the world is oriented east to west following the sun." Vlach wrote that African-American "graves are often indistinguishable from African graves . . . because the religious systems which shape the attitude toward death, and therefore the way death is treated, are not very different."

**The full text of document 1.16.6 is available on the CD-ROM.**

# Lucy Terry Prince

The concept of freedom is important to Americans. As a nation and as individuals, we quote the inspiring words from the Declaration of Independence to define who we are and what we believe in. Yet the translation of freedom into equality for all has often been incomplete, revealing contradictions between ideology and reality—none so glaring as the legal maintenance of slavery.

Slavery was a national institution. Although slave labor was employed on a much grander scale in the South and for a longer period of time, "the peculiar institution," as it was called, existed in the North as well. We are able to learn about the nature of northern slavery through stories of individual lives using the records left behind.

Lucy, or Luce as she was called, was a slave in New England, freed sometime between 1756 and the American Revolution (the records are ambiguous). She was literate, a woman of faith and of courage. Lucy lived as a child and young adult in Deerfield, Massachusetts. At about age 22, in 1746, she witnessed an Indian attack on Deerfield and composed a vivid account of the ordeal. The poem, "The Bars Fight," is recognized as the first poetry by an African American.

In 1756, Lucy married Abijah Prince, a freeman twenty years her senior. They lived for some years in Deerfield, then moved to Vermont, acquired land, and became the parents of several children. Two of their sons fought in the Revolutionary War.

Lucy Terry Prince died in 1821 at the age of 97. Her obituary was unusually long for a woman at that time and gives us insight into the remarkable woman she was. Her funeral oration was delivered by Reverend Lemuel Hayes, a well known black minister. He used the occasion to make a statement about slavery: "How long must Ethiopia's murder'd race be doomed by men to bondage and disgrace? And hear such taunting insolence from those 'we have fairer skin and sharper nose'? Their sable mother took her rapt'rous flight, high orb'd amidst the realms of endless light."

## Organizing Idea

Learning about one eighteenth-century woman, Lucy Terry Prince, enables us to see how some African Americans claimed freedom for themselves and their families and, against the odds, became respected members of their communities.

## Student Objectives

Students will:

- ❖ gain some understanding of Prince's ability, even as a young woman, to tell a vivid and compelling story through study of "The Bars Fight"

- ❖ learn about Prince's life and accomplishments and consider the kind of person she must have been through study of her obituary

## Key Questions

- ❖ What do we need to know about slavery in New England to understand the story of Lucy Terry Prince?

- ❖ What can we learn about the conflict between the colonists and the Abenaki Indians who attacked Deerfield, and about whom Lucy wrote the poem?

- ❖ What is an obituary? Who writes them? Why are they significant? Does everyone get an obituary? Why or why not?

- ❖ What questions are we left with about Lucy Terry Prince's life and character?

## Primary Source Materials

DOCUMENT 1.17.1: "The Bars Fight" by Lucy Terry, 1746

DOCUMENT 1.17.2: Obituary for Lucy Terry Prince, August 21, 1821

## Student Activities

Activity 1        **Discussion of Poem**

Students may first need to define words such as ambush, rods, and valiant. Then students read and discuss "The Bars Fight" (1.17.1), Lucy Terry's poem about the 1746 Native American attack on Deerfield. What is Terry's perspective?

Activity 2        **Writing a Narrative Version of the Attack**

Students write a prose version of the story. Students can consider what might have happened before and after this brief scene. (*Note:* The Bars, near Deerfield, was the name given to a field shared by several families. It seems to have got that name because of a barway in the common field fence. Thus the title denotes the place where the attack occurred.)

Activity 3        **Analysis of Obituary**

After defining assemblage, volubility, fluency, destitute, and deference, students read the obituary (1.17.2). Where did the author find information about Lucy Terry's early life story? What qualities was she being praised for? Consider why the obituary remarks that these qualities were "rarely to be found among her sex." Ask students to choose one quality that especially interests them, describe it in a sentence, and illustrate it; then, as a group, they assemble a bulletin board to celebrate the life of Lucy Terry Prince.

## Further Research and Creative Extensions

*Activity 4*

During the nineteenth and twentieth centuries, several researchers and historians discovered numerous other pieces of information about Lucy and her husband, Abijah. These were found in land records, birth registry actions, court and census records, documentation of consumer transactions, and recorded oral histories. Some of these original records cannot now be found, but the stories and legends left by earlier historians are no doubt based on fact and make a fascinating story. Using Proper's *Lucy Terry Prince, Singer of History*, a well-footnoted book published by Historic Deerfield, interested students can create a fictionalized biography of this remarkable woman.

## Further Student and Teacher Resources

"Deerfield." *Cobblestone*. Peterborough, NH. September 1995.

Green, Lorenzo. *The Negro in Colonial New England*. New York: Columbia University Press, 1942.

Katz, Bernard. *Black Woman: A Fictionalized Biography of Lucy Terry Prince*. New York: Pantheon Books, 1973. (This book is out of print but is available in some libraries.)

Proper, David R. *Lucy Terry Prince, Singer of History*. Deerfield, Massachusetts: Pocumtuck Valley Memorial Association and Historic Deerfield, Inc., 1997.

Sheldon, George. *A History of Deerfield*, Mass. Vol 1. Greenfield, MA: E. M. Hall, 1895. (This work is in print and may be ordered from *www.historic-deerfield.org*. It may also be available in libraries.)

Stetson, Erlene. *Black Sister: Poetry of Black American Women*, 1746–1980. Bloomingdale: Indiana University Press, 1981.

Wright, Martha R. "Bijah's Luce of Guilford." *Negro History Bulletin* 27, 152–53, 159, 1965. Published by the Association for the Study of African American Life and History, Silver Spring, MD. (Back issues are available.)

## Website

www.pbs.org/wgbh/aia/part2/2p15.html
*Africans in America*

## Contemporary Connection

✣

### Online Poetry Classroom

In 1999, the Academy of American Poets, responding to requests from teachers, initiated the Online Poetry Classroom (*www.onlinepoetryclassroom.org*). The purpose of the website is to assist teachers as they foster in students the critical skills necessary to understand and appreciate poetry. This free teacher resource includes curriculum units and lesson plans, poems to teach, a time line, critical essays, and teacher discussion forums. As students learn about the poem of America's first black poet, Lucy Terry Prince can be presented as part of a long and ongoing tradition.

# Primary Source Materials for Lesson 17

"The Bars Fight" by Lucy Terry, 1746

August, 'twas the twenty-fifth,
Seventeen hundred forty-six,
The Indians did in ambush lay,
Some very valient men to slay,
The names of whom I'll not leave out.
Samuel Allen like a hero fout,
And though he was so brave and bold,
His face no more shall we behold.
Eleazer Hawks was killed outright,
Before he had time to fight,—
Before he did the Indians see,
Was shot and killed immediately.
Oliver Amsden he was slain,
Which caused his friends much grief and pain.
Simeon Amsden they found dead,
Not many rods distant from his head.
Adonijah Gillett, we do hear
Did lose his life which was so dear.
John Sadler fled across the water,
And thus escaped the dreadful slaughter.
Eunice Allen see the Indians coming
And hopes to save herself by running,
And had not her petticoats stopped her,
The awful creatures had not catched her,
Nor tommy hawked her on the head,
And left her on the ground for dead.
Young Samuel Allen, Oh lack-a-day!
Was taken and carried to Canada.

<u>1.17.2</u>

## Obituary for Lucy Terry Prince, August 21, 1821

At Sunderland, Vt., July 11th, Mrs. Lucy Prince, a woman of colour. —From the church and town records where she formerly resided, we learn that she was brought from Bristol, Rhode Island, to Deerfield, Mass. when she was four years old, by Mr. Ebenezer Wells; that she was 97 years of age—that she was early devoted to God in Baptism; that she united with the church in Deerfield in 1744—Was married to Abijah Prince, May 17th, 1756, by Elijah Williams, Esq. and that she had been the mother of seven children. In this remarkable woman there was an assemblage of qualities rarely to be found among her sex. Her volubility was exceeded by none, and in general the fluency of her speech was not destitute of instruction and education. She was much respected among her acquaintance, who treated her with a degree of deference. Vt. Gaz.

# Resistance and Rebellions

A more complete history of the transatlantic slave trade must include information about the resistance to enslavement by African people in Africa as well as by enslaved Africans and people of African descent in America. Throughout the entire period of slavery, people resisted in any number of ways: enslaved Africans jumped off the ships carrying them to America; some women refused to bear children; there were work slowdowns, equipment tampering, self-injury, or escape. Black people filed lawsuits and written appeals, as well as engaging in outright—and sometimes armed—rebellion and resistance. The primary sources included in this lesson reveal a range of efforts by enslaved people—in northern and southern colonies and on board ship along the Triangle Trade route—to throw off the yoke of slavery.

This lesson provides primary sources that document three acts of resistance and rebellion. The first, recorded by James Barbot, Jr., a sailor, describes the actions taken by enslaved Africans aboard the English slave ship *Don Carlos*. The second document is a list of black people condemned at the trial following the New York City slave revolts of 1741. This list, compiled by Daniel Horsmanden, the prosecuting justice, also includes the fates of those convicted. The third event, the Stono Rebellion in South Carolina in 1739, continued to cause unrest among white slaveowners both in the South and further north. The Stono Rebellion is recounted in a letter from South Carolina Lieutenant Governor William Bull to Britain's Board of Trade that describes what he saw. An additional related document is a set of laws passed that underscored the increasing unease whites felt as blacks continued to resist enslavement in any form. This document also shows how attempts were made to pit Native Americans against African Americans. (These attempts were generally unsuccessful; more often, Indians harbored black fugitives.)

**Note:** Students and teachers alike may respond to these documents with very strong emotions—sadness, anger, outrage, disbelief, desire for revenge. Teachers should provide a forum for students to discuss these responses in an honest and safe manner, with clearly stated guidelines for supporting this important work. Many students will see a connection with racism, sexism, and other forms of discrimination that exist in our society today.

## Organizing Idea

Africans and people of African descent resisted enslavement by Europeans both in Africa and in the American colonies. Little of this resistance has been included in history textbooks. The documents in this lesson help to tell a more empowering, inclusive, and therefore complete story of the transatlantic slave trade and colonial America. Whenever and wherever enslavement was imposed, there were courageous attempts to resist and rebel.

## Student Objectives

Students will:

- ❖ learn that resistance and rebellion occurred in Africa, en route, and in the American colonies, in both rural and urban settings

- ❖ understand that slavery was a legal institution; owners had all the rights, and lifelong intimidation and threat of bodily harm were often effective methods used to try to control enslaved people

- ❖ understand that enslaved people felt continued frustration regarding their slim chances for obtaining freedom from their masters

- ❖ examine original records to learn how to interpret their contents, purposes, and effects on the historical record

## Key Questions

- ❖ What characteristics did people need in order to defy, rebel, and revolt (e.g., courage, despair, anger, determination)?

- ❖ How do we know when, where, and how enslaved people resisted? What kinds of documents are available, who created them, and what do they tell us about the recorders of history?

- ❖ What information does each document leave out and why might that be so?

- ❖ "Indeed I tremble for my country when I reflect that God is just, that his justice cannot sleep forever . . . ." (Thomas Jefferson, *Notes on Virginia. Query xviii. Manners* 1803). How does this statement and how do the primary source documents included here inform us about social and economic tensions in colonial America?

- ❖ What were some consequences and ramifications of the rebellions?

## Primary Source Documents

DOCUMENT 1.18.1: Description of a slave uprising on a vessel, by James Barbot, Jr., 1732

DOCUMENT 1.18.2: "A List of Negroes Committed on Account of the Conspiracy" in the New York City slave revolts, 1741, from the journal of Daniel Horsmanden, prosecuting justice

DOCUMENT 1.18.3: William Bull's letter, October 5, 1739, describing the Stono Rebellion

DOCUMENT 1.18.4: "A Commons House of Assembly Committee Report, in a Message to the Governor's Council, November 29, 1739" regarding Stono Rebellion slave-catchers

## Supplementary materials

Item 1.18.A: Map of thirteen British colonies

Item 1.18.B: Additional vocabulary lists

## Vocabulary

| | | | |
|---|---|---|---|
| arraignment | inquiry | *mustee* | province |
| conspiracy | militia | mutiny | shackles |
| desertion | | | |

## Student Activities

### Document Analysis

Activity 1

Working in teams with each team responsible for one document, students study Documents 1.18.1–1.18.4 and answer the following questions: How is the rebellion described? From whose point of view is the document written? What information might be missing? What are the similarities and differences among these actions? Responses can be given in writing or in oral presentations.

### Research on Rebellions

Activity 2

Using additional materials from listed websites, students investigate the rebellions in more detail in an effort to learn what led up to each uprising and why these attempts to secure freedom failed. Working in teams, students discuss the motivations for and outcomes of each rebellion. Were the rebellions just? What other options did the participants have to remedy the wrongs they were protesting? Each team then reports to the class on the conclusions reached in their discussions.

### Writing—Creative Extensions

Activity 3

Taking the perspective of a participant in one of the revolts, students individually create a letter, journal, or chart that might have been written and left behind as a record. Ask students to explain why they chose to write about a particular revolt.

Activity 4     **Creative Extensions—A Time Line**

Students design and create a large-scale illustrated time line of the rebellions and important events leading up to and following from them. The class can be divided into teams, with each team responsible for documenting a particular rebellion and adding critical events related to that rebellion to the time line.

Activity 5     **Mapping and Illustrating Sites of Rebellions**

Using a Big Map of colonial America (Item 1.18.A), students locate and illustrate each of the rebellion sites. Students can use a diagram of a slave ship to depict the uprising on board the *Don Carlos* en route from Africa to America. (*Note*: See Lesson 1 in this Sourcebook for details on the creation and use of Big Maps.)

## Further Student and Teacher Resources

Franklin, John Hope and Loren Schweninger. *Runaway Slaves: Rebels on the Plantation*. New York: Oxford University Press, 1999.

Katz, William Loren. *Breaking the Chains: Afro-American Slave Resistance*. New York: Atheneum, 1990.

McKissack, Patricia C. and Frederick L. *Rebels Against Slavery*. New York: Scholastic, 1996.

### Websites

*James Barbot's Account*

http://vi.uh.edu/pages/mintz/5.htm

*Stono Rebellion*

http://web-cr05.pbs.org/wgbh/aia/part1/1h312.html

http://lcweb2.loc.gov/ammem/today/sep09.html

*Library of Congress*

www.pbs.org/wgbh/aia/part1/1p284.html

*Second Stono Rebellion*

www.pbs.org/wgbh/aia/part1/1h312t.html

*New York City Slave Revolts of 1712 and 1741*

http://r2.gsa.gov/afrburgro/history.htm
www.csmonitor.com/durable/1999/06/17/fp16s1-csm.shtml
http://r2.gsa.gov/afrburgro/pressR200-008ABGIC.htm1.18.1

## Contemporary Connection

⇥⧓⇤

### Free the Slaves

Slavery still exists for twenty-seven million people in the world today, and there are abolitionists such as the group Free the Slaves fighting to eradicate this institution. "Founded by Americans who did not want to live in a world with slavery," Free the Slaves provides information on contemporary situations of slavery around the world, offers social action opportunities, supports grassroots antislavery organizations, and provides an educational guide for teachers. In addition to these resources, the online library provides news and document archives as well as links to other antislavery organizations. For more information, visit the website at *www.freetheslaves.net*. This important antislavery work begun hundreds of years ago continues today.

# Primary Source Materials
## for Lesson 18

### 1.18.1

Description of a slave uprising on a vessel, by James Barbot, Jr., 1732

*James Barbot, Jr., a sailor aboard the English slaver* Don Carlos, *describes a slave uprising that took place aboard the vessel:*

"Premeditated A Revolt"
About one in the afternoon, after dinner, we, according to custom caused them, one by one, to go down between decks, to have each his pint of water; most of them were yet above deck, many of them provided with knives, which we had indiscreetly given them two or three days before, as not suspecting the least attempt of this nature from them; others had pieces of iron they had torn off our forecastle door, as having premeditated a revolt, and seeing all the ship's company, at best but weak and many quite sick, they had also broken off the shackles from several of their companions' feet, which served them, as well as billets they had provided themselves with, and all other things they could lay hands on, which they imagin'd might be of use for this enterprize. Thus arm'd, they fell in crouds and parcels on our men, upon the deck unawares, and stabb'd one of the stoutest of us all, who receiv'd fourteen or fifteen wounds of their knives, and so expir'd . . . .

The full text of Document 1.18.1 is available on the CD-ROM.

1.18.2

## "A List of Negroes Committed on Account of the Conspiracy" in the New York City slave revolts, 1741, from the journal of Daniel Horsmanden, prosecuting justice

### A List of Negroes Committed on Account of the Conspiracy

| Negroes | Masters or Owners | Committed | Arraigned | Convicted | Confessed | Burnt | Hanged | Transported to |
|---|---|---|---|---|---|---|---|---|
| Bill alias Will | C. Ten Eyck | June 12 | July 3 | | June 30 | | | Madeira |
| Bridgewater | A. Van Horne | June 22 | July 3 | | June 27 | | | Hispaniola |
| Billy | Mrs. Ellison | June 25 | July 1 | | | | | |
| Braveboy | Mrs. Kierstede | June 27 | July 10 | | June 30 | | | Madeira |
| Burlington | Joseph Haines | July 3 | | | | | | |
| Caesar | Vaarck | March 1 | April 24 | May 1 * | | | May 11 | |
| Cuffee | A. Philipse, esq. | April 6 | May 28 | May 29 | | May 30 | | |
| Cuba, a wench | Mrs. C. Lynch | April 4 | | | | | | |
| Curacoa Dick | Cornelius Tiebout | May 9 | June 8 | June 10 | | June 12 | | |
| Cato | Alderman Moore | May 9 | July 15 | | June 22 | | | |
| Caesar | Do. Pintard | May 9 | July 3 | | June 22 | | | Madeira |
| Cuffee | Lewis Gomez | May 24 | June 6 | June 8 | | June 9 | | |
| Caesar | Benjamin Peck | May 25 | June 6 | June 8 | | June 9 | | |
| Cato | Joseph Cowley | May 25 | June 12 | June 13 | | | June 16 | |
| Cook | Gerardus Comfort | May 26 | June 6 | June 8 | | June 9 | | |
| Cambridge | C. Codwise | May 30 | July 10 | | June 30 | | | Cape Francois |
| Caesar | Israel Horsefield | May 30 | June 26 | | June 27 | | | St. Thomas |
| Cato | John Shurmur | June 9 | June 16 | June 19 | June 27 | | July 3 | |

* Convicted of a robbery but appears to have been a principal negro conspirator.

**A full chart (Document 1.18.2) is available on the CD-ROM.**

## 1.18.3

## William Bull's letter, October 5, 1739, describing the Stono Rebellion

*William Bull as Lieutenant Governor of South Carolina wrote a letter to Britain's Board of Trade informing the Lords about the Stono Rebellion. He had personally spread the alarm to whites during the uprising and suggested that Native Americans be used to intercept and capture the escaped slaves.*

My Lords,

I beg leave to lay before your Lordships an account of our Affairs, first in regard to the Desertion of our Negroes . . . . On the 9th of September last at Night a great Number of Negroes Arose in Rebellion, broke open a Store where they got arms, killed twenty one White Persons, and were marching the next morning in a Daring manner out of the Province, killing all they met and burning several Houses as they passed along the Road. I was returning from Granville County with four Gentlemen and met these Rebels at eleven o'clock in the forenoon and fortunately deserned the approaching danger time enough to avoid it, and to give notice to the Militia who on the Occasion behaved with so much expedition and bravery, as by four a' Clock the same day to come up with them and killed and took so many as put a stop to any further mischief at that time, forty four of them have been killed and Executed; some few yet remain concealed in the Woods expecting the same fate, seem desperate . . . .

It was the Opinion of His Majesty's Council with several other Gentlemen that one of the most effectual means that could be used at present to prevent such desertion of our Negroes is to encourage some Indians by a suitable reward to pursue and if possible to bring back the Deserters, and while the Indians are thus employed they would be in the way ready to intercept others that might attempt to follow and I have sent for the Chiefs of the Chickasaws living at New Windsor and the Catawbaw Indians for that purpose . . . .

My Lords,

Your Lordships Most Obedient and Most Humble Servant

Wm Bull

<u>1.18.4</u>

## "A Commons House of Assembly Committee Report, in a Message to the Governor's Council, November 29, 1739" regarding Stono Rebellion slave-catchers

5.   That upon Inquiry your Committee find that a negro man named July belonging to Mr. Thomas Elliott was very early and chiefly instrumental in saving his Master and his Family from being destroyed by the Rebellious Negroes and that the Negro man July had at several times bravely fought against the Rebels and killed one of them. Your Committee therefore recommends that the [said] Negro July (as a reward for his faithful Services and for an Encouragement to other Slaves to follow his Example in case of the like Nature) shall have his Freedom and a Present of a Suit of Cloaths, Shirt, Hat, a pair of stockings and a pair of Shoes . . . .

**The full text of Document 1.18.4 is available on the CD-ROM.**

# Amos Fortune

Reading historical fiction is a legitimate way to engage students in the study of another time and place. Stories can illuminate a time period, enrich a history lesson, and help teachers and students integrate learning. "A well written historical novel can provide its readers with a sense of historical understanding and realism that otherwise would be denied to all but the professional scholar," writes Leonard Irwin in *Guide to Historical Fiction*.

The story of Amos Fortune can be told with documentation only from his late middle age until his death at age 91. It is, however, a story worth telling, even though the early years are reconstructed from fragments of information, research into the history of the period, and an author's imagination. Beginning with manumission papers, which officially freed Fortune from slavery, documents exist to give some information about Fortune's life, and it is clear that he was skillful, hardworking, patient, and successful. The people of his community of Jaffrey, New Hampshire, considered him to be a man of substance.

Amos Fortune was born in Africa, most probably on the Guinea coast, in 1710. He was a youth, certainly not over 20, when he was captured and enslaved. His first owners may have been a Quaker family in Massachusetts who taught him to read and write. His second and final owner, Ichabod Richardson, was a tanner in Woburn, Massachusetts; it is from this man that Amos Fortune learned his trade.

Papers for his manumission were first drawn up in 1763, but he was required to buy his freedom, and his final liberation did not occur until 1769, when Amos Fortune was 59 years old.

In 1779, Amos purchased the freedom of Violet, his wife. Some years later, Fortune moved to Jaffrey, New Hampshire, where he spent the remainder of his life working and contributing to his community. The extant records of his life are to be found in this community.

## Organizing Idea

Through the story of Amos Fortune, we meet a colonial man who, although he remained enslaved until late middle age, nevertheless secured his freedom and flourished in his later years through his intelligence, skill, hard work, and perseverance. Combining the reading of historical fiction with the study of extant primary sources, students discover that there are many ways to learn about and present the past.

## Student Objectives

Students will:

❖ learn that in uncovering the contributions made by African Americans to our early history, it is often necessary to work from fragments of evidence; it can actually be easier to learn about slaves, as compared to poor whites, because enslaved men, women, and children appeared in wills, deeds, and inventories since they were considered to be property

❖ understand that historical fiction is constructed through research in primary sources, and through an author's imagination, together with an understanding of the historical period

❖ understand, through working with the same primary sources, how information from these sources shaped the story

❖ compare and contrast how two authors interpret the material and fill in the missing pieces through reading historical fiction

## Key Questions

❖ How do historians and writers use historic documents to understand the life of someone who lived long ago?

❖ When much information is unknown, how do writers construct and present an interesting story? What kinds of further research do they need to do?

❖ What are the advantages and disadvantages of learning history through historical fiction?

❖ Why is it important to uncover the stories of African Americans as we look toward a fuller understanding of our country's history?

## Vocabulary

| | | | |
|---|---|---|---|
| bequeath | extant | indemnify | traffick (as used |
| covenant | husbandry | manumission | in this period) |
| estate | improvement (as | testator | |
| executor | used in wills) | | |

## Primary Source Materials

DOCUMENT 1.19.1: Selections from Manumission Papers for Amos Fortune, 1763 and 1770

DOCUMENT 1.19.2: Excerpts from an Account of Amos Fortune's Estate, 1801

DOCUMENT 1.19.3: Bill of Sale for Vilot (Violet), 1779

DOCUMENT 1.19.4: Amos Fortune's will, 1801

## Student Activities

Activity 1      **Reading and Discussion of *Amos Fortune, Free Man***

Arrange for student copies of *Amos Fortune, Free Man* by Elizabeth Yates or read the story aloud to the whole class. Discuss each chapter for understanding. For Chapters 1 and 2, the author had little direct documentation. Students may want to discuss what kinds of sources she could have used to create this part of the story. As documents appear in the text, there should be vocabulary work as part of the study. For a few of the words, students and or the teacher may need to look in the Oxford English Dictionary.

Activity 2      **Creating a Time Line**

Students create a class time line tracing the life of Amos Fortune; include events in American history that would certainly have influenced and affected his life.

Activity 3      **Analysis of Manumission Papers**

As a class, read through the selections from the manumission papers (1.19.1) and discuss their meaning. Ask students to write a version of the documents in their own words. What do these documents tell us about the economy of eighteenth-century New England, the ways of providing for the indigent, and the uses of legal language? Do you think a lawyer drew up the papers?

Activity 4      **Drawing Conclusions—Slavery in New England**

Students read copies of the bill of sale for Vilot (1.19.3). Discussion questions: What does this document, together with the manumission papers (1.19.1), tell us about slavery in the North? Do we learn anything about whether the white owners cared about gaining or losing money? Because these papers do not include any evidence of antislavery views, how can we find out who might have been opposed to slavery at that time?

Activity 5      **Writing to Extend**

Students read through Fortune's will (1.19.4) together or in small groups. Students create a class list of the objects and animals mentioned in the will. Then, students read the inventory of items sold at public auction after his death (1.19.2) and add these items to the list. Ask students to write a poem, a story, or a diary entry describing the ways Amos Fortune and his wife might have used these objects in their daily lives.

## Writing to Extend

Activity 6

At the end of the will, students will note that money Amos Fortune dedicated to education in 1801 is still in use in the community of Jaffrey, New Hampshire. Using the ideas and information about Amos Fortune gained from the novel and from the primary sources, each student writes and delivers a speech honoring Amos Fortune for his generosity and community spirit, indeed for his life.

## Extension Activity

Older students may want to read, for comparison, selections from another version of the Amos Fortune story written several years later than the Yates book. In *Amos Fortune's Choice*, author Alexander Magoun envisions a somewhat different beginning, and throughout the book the existing evidence is interpreted in ways that differ from the Yates book. Students develop a chart comparing the two books and document at least five ways in which the books differ.

## Further Student and Teacher Resources

*Amos Fortune, Free Man.* Newbery Award Records, Inc. New York: Random House, 1986. (Book-based video recording, color, 45 minutes.)

Galt, Margot Fortunato. *The Story in History, Writing Your Way into the American Experience.* New York: Teachers and Writers Collaborative, 1992. (Many wonderful exercises for helping students "get into" history.)

Magoun, F. Alexander. *Amos Fortune's Choice.* Freeport, Maine: Bond Wheelwright Company, 1964. (Out of print; available in some local libraries.)

Nadeau, Frances A. "Fiction as a Springboard to U.S. History Research Projects." *The Social Studies.* Sept–Oct., 1944: 222–24.

Pelttari, Carol. *Amos Fortune, Free Man Study Guide.* Eau Claire, WI: Progeny Press, 1996.

Yates, Elizabeth. *Amos Fortune: Free Man.* New York: Puffin Books, 1989.

## Website

**www.dohistory.org**
*DoHistory invites students to explore the process of piecing together the lives of ordinary people in the past.*

## Contemporary Connection

✠

### The Amos Fortune Forum Series

In the 1930s, Jaffrey's schools were consolidated, and money willed to a local school by Amos Fortune was moved by the town to a fund that underwrites another of Amos Fortune's interests, rhetoric. These community-sponsored discussions, now called the Amos Fortune Forum Series, still run every summer in Jaffrey.

In January 2001, the town launched a new forum series entitled *Jaffrey Celebrates Its Own*. Not surprisingly, the first program, which included lectures and exhibits, presented the story of Amos Fortune. The announcement for the event described it this way: "Amos Fortune, Jaffrey's pioneer settler, businessman and philanthropist will be honored at a Forum exploring the contributions to early New Hampshire life of black slaves, settlers and freemen." For more information about Amos Fortune and his continuing legacy, contact the Jaffrey Public Library, or write to *pbntrail@aol.com* for information on the history of black community life in New Hampshire.

# Primary Source Materials for Lesson 19

1.19.1

## Selections from Manumission Papers for Amos Fortune, 1763 and 1770

*Written in 1763 by Ichabod Richardson and unsigned*

Know all men by these presents that I, Ichabod Richardson of Woburn in the country of Middlesex and province of Massachusetts-bay in New England, Tanner, for diverse good reasons . . . have and by these presents do covenant promise, grant and agree to, and with my negro man, Amos, that at the end of four years next . . . (or at my decease if it should fall within that term) that he, the said Amos, shall then be discharged, freed, and set at liberty from my service, power and command forever, and have full liberty to trade, traffick and dispose of himself in all respects as he pleases, and have and enjoy and convert to his own use all the profit of his own labor and industry, equal to men that are freeborn, and that neither I, nor my heirs, nor any other person, or persons acting or claiming by or under me . . . shall claim any right to . . . his person, property or labors. . . . In witness whereof, the said Ichabod Richardson, have hereunto set my hand and seal the thirtieth day of December 1763 in the fourth year of His Majesty's reign . . . .

**The full text of Document 1.19.1 is available on the CD-ROM.**

1.19.2

## Excerpts from an Account of Amos Fortune's Estate, 1801

An account of the administration of the estate of Amos Fortune late of Jaffrey, where the executor Eleazer Spofford chargeth himself with the proceeds of the real estate as sold by order of the testator amounting to the sum of, exclusive of the tanning tools $554.16. Also with the personal effects of said deceased as sold at public auction.

> To Stephan Laws a shovle 18 cents
>
> To Jonathan Fox a horse collar 97 cents
>
> To David Adams a grindstone 5 cents
>
> To Nathan Cutter a 1/2 bushel mesure 34 cents
>
> Stephen Laws a peck mesure 30 cents
>
> To John Stone the old mare $3.17

**Note: A full text of Document 1.19.2 is available on the CD-ROM.**

## 1.19.3

## Bill of Sale for Vilot (Violet), 1779

This day received of Amos Fortune Fifty pounds in full for a Negro Woman named Vilot being now my property which I now convey to the afore said Amos and I do covenant with the said Amos that I have a just and lawful right to sell and convey the said Vilot in manner as afore said and I will Warrant and defend the said Vilot to him, the said Amos against the laws full claims and demands of all Persons whatever.

Dated Woburn 9th November 1779

Signed Sealed and Delivered
In presence of us
Samuel Willson
Mary Baldwin
James Baldwin

## 1.19.4

## Amos Fortune's will, 1801

*Amos Fortune wrote his will a few months before he died.*

In the name of God Amen, I, Amos Fortune of Jaffrey in the county of Cheshire and State of New Hampshire, Tanner

Being weak in body but of sound and perfect mind and memory, blessed be Almighty God for the same, do make and publish this my last will and testament in manner and form following:

(That is to say.)

First, I give and bequeath to Vilot my beloved wife all the improvement and profits of my real estate during her natural life to be ordered and disposed at the discretion of my executor whom I shall hereafter name.

Secondly, I order my executor to settle and discharge all the just debts and demands that lays against my estate at my decease at such time or times as shall appear to him to be necessary and to make up of my personal estate for that purpose as far as it will go toward paying the same. . . .

Seventhly, I further order my said executor that after my decease and the decease of the said Vilot that if there is any remainder of my estate, that he give a handsome present of the same to the Church of Christ in this town, and the remaining part if any their be, he give as a present for the support of the school in school house No. eight in this town.

**The full text of Document 1.19.4 is available on the CD-ROM.**

*Copies of all of the extant primary sources are available from the Jaffrey Public Library, 38 Main Street, Jaffrey, NH 03452-6144 (603-532-7301).*

# Seaman's Protection Certificates

Ships carried Africans in chains to North American shores, but they also offered many black men an opportunity to escape—temporarily or forever—the conditions of slavery they faced on shore. Many Africans brought over in slavery to the American colonies had strong connections to sailing and the sea back in their homeland. They were already experienced canoe and surfboat makers, river navigators, and coastal sailors and traders. Many were multilingual, having traded with Europeans along the African coast and with Arabic-speaking traders on the coast and along inland trade routes. A number of enslaved Africans had assisted in ferrying other Africans to slave ships anchored offshore. Water travel, as well as the contact it brought with others, was a familiar experience for many enslaved Africans in the Americas.

Black sailors faced challenges and enjoyed advantages that both united them with and divided them from their white fellow sailors. Whether free or enslaved, black sailors were involved in an occupation that was both romanticized and held in contempt by society. Many sailors were engaging storytellers, travelers to exotic places, collectors of strange souvenirs, transporters of news and culture. Sailors had to submit to and live by maritime law and culture, a tradition dating back to medieval codes that was designed to protect the property of ship owners and merchants, restrict and punish seamen, and maintain the rigid hierarchy that shaped life aboard ship. Sailors' wages were low, often equally so regardless of race. Only a crew position with higher status, such as mate, would pay higher wages to a seaman of any color. Within this prescribed world, where seamen's very lives depended on the skill and attention of the entire crew, sailors, white and of color, experienced a fundamental equality. Storms and doldrums were color-blind, and in an emergency all seamen were equally necessary. This situation shaped sailors' culture, so that an ordinary seaman's race made little difference to his fellows.

These maritime opportunities, however, did not eliminate racism. Although some black men attained high-status positions, such as captain, mate, and pilot, particularly on ships owned or commanded by men of color, many black seamen were confined to the jobs of steward, cook, sailor, and musician. Free black sailors always ran the risk of being captured and sold into slavery. White seamen's journals often referred to their black shipmates in racially derogatory terms; black sailors experienced physical assaults as well.

Most black sailors through the eighteenth century were enslaved, sent to sea by their owners as a way of earning money for their owners. For example, Briton Hammon of Marshfield, Massachusetts, was allowed by his owner to go to sea in December, off-season for New England agricultural tasks. Ironically, enslaved sailors could and often did assume command of a ship, especially on ships based in the Southern colonies. These black captains and navigators, with highly valued skills, had an enormous amount of unsupervised time away from the watchful eyes of their owners. Legal employment of slaves on New England vessels ended, officially if not in practice, after 1770, when a Nantucket court freed Prince Boston, instead of returning him to the Swain family, who claimed ownership of him.

For free black men, seafaring offered much-needed job opportunities and relatively steady employment, enabling them to financially support themselves, their families, and their dependents. Despite the abolition of slavery in New England states after the Revolution, black men were confined by persistent custom, stereotyping, and the law to certain maritime jobs, among them laborer, sailor, and related trades, such as caulker, cordwainer, and sailmaker. Certainly, other land-based occupations were available to blacks, as documented in city directories, government censuses, and account ledgers. These occupations included barber, tallow and soap maker, cooper, cook, brickmaker, butcher, and chimney sweep as well as more complex skilled crafts, such as furniture maker, tailor, watchmaker, and tanner.

The whaling industry, based in port cities such as New Bedford and Nantucket, acted as a magnet for free and escaped blacks. Whaling logbooks and journals document the presence and participation of men of color aboard whaling vessels from the early seventeenth through the early twentieth centuries. Crispus Attucks, a fugitive slave of mixed Native American and African descent from Framingham, Massachusetts, who later became the first casualty in the 1770 Boston Massacre, was a professional sailor who spent documented time aboard at least one whaling ship out of Nantucket. According to Lorenzo Greene's book *The Negro in Colonial New England*, black men comprised nearly half of all whaling crews. (See Sourcebook 2, Lesson 7.)

Paul Cuffe, born in 1759, son of an Aquinah Wampanoag mother and a formerly enslaved African father, joined a whaling crew when he was sixteen years old. Many black men became officers on Yankee whaling ships; opportunities were more plentiful on vessels where crews were all or predominately black.

During the seventeenth, eighteenth, and early nineteenth centuries, all sailors faced the threat of capture by pirates, privateers, and European naval ships intent on impressing them into naval service. Black sailors aboard whaling ships, merchant vessels, or naval ships also faced the additional risk of being "man-stolen" and sold into slavery. Before 1796, a mariner could obtain a document declaring his United States citizenship from a public notary or, with authentic proof of citizenship and 25 cents, from a customs official. In many situations, recognizing that sailors were often not in their home ports, only an authorized affidavit and a witness would be required to obtain papers.

In 1796 the federal government required each American sailor to carry a Seaman's Protection Certificate. This certificate was ordered on May 28, 1796, by "An Act for the Protection and Relief of American Seamen," as a way of protecting American sailors from impressment into foreign navies, particularly the British and French. To obtain one, a sailor had to apply at a customs house, where officials interviewed the applicant, recorded the necessary data in registers, and issued the certificate.

Local printers printed the protection certificates, so there is some variation in their design and appearance. Wording also varied until the language was standardized. Each certificate included the person's name, birthplace, approximate age, height, skin and eye color, any distinguishing marks such as scars or tattoos, and a serial number. Each document stated that the sailor was a citizen of the United States of America. The word "protection" may have also been included somewhere. In Massachusetts and New York, a separate protection certificate was issued for black seamen, stating that "the black man, mariner, is a free man of the United States of America and is to be respected accordingly."

The need to carry passes would not have been a new experience for black mariners who had experienced slavery, where a pass was often needed to move around. Eighteenth-century newspapers, the *Boston Gazette*, for example, frequently advertised for the capture and return of a runaway Negro slave carrying a forged or counterfeit pass. When Frederick Douglass escaped from slavery in 1838, he used a set of borrowed seaman's papers.

Seaman's Protection Certificates did not offer full-proof protection and were disregarded by the Royal Navy and privateers alike. Nevertheless, they were proudly displayed and carefully guarded whenever possible. These certificates were used as passports and proof of citizenship and were a powerful reminder for all of equality and inclusion—real citizenship—in the United States of America.

## Organizing Idea

Work on board a sailing vessel provided opportunities for African Americans to escape slavery by sailing to larger cities that provided an anonymity of sorts, as well as to the North and elsewhere in the Atlantic world. Although working on a merchant or whaling vessel brought its own dangers, many considered it superior to a life of enslavement or preferable to the constant fear of reenslavement. In addition, Seaman's Protection Certificates provided proof of U.S. citizenship for sailors, white and black, as a protection against impressment into foreign navies.

## Student Objectives

Students will:

- ❖ learn the obstacles and opportunities facing men of color seeking employment in the eighteenth century
- ❖ understand that working at sea presented risks as well as opportunities for black men to attain job advancement and mobility

❖ explain the purpose of Seaman's Protection Certificates and why they are important as primary sources

## Key Questions

❖ What opportunities for employment and mobility were open to men of color during the eighteenth century?

❖ What special opportunities did work as a seaman offer a man of color?

❖ Why did the Congress pass "An Act for the Protection and Relief of American Seamen" on May 28, 1796?

❖ How did Seaman's Protection Certificates affect the day-to-day life of black men working at sea?

## Primary Source Materials

DOCUMENT 1.20.1: Excerpts from *A Narrative of the Uncommon Sufferings and Surprising Deliverance of BRITON HAMMON, A NEGRO MAN*, 1760

DOCUMENT 1.20.2: Seaman's Protection Certificate for Edward Scare, issued in Virginia

DOCUMENT 1.20.3: Seaman's Protection Certificate for Charles Storey, issued in Gloucester, Massachusetts

DOCUMENT 1.20.4: Seaman's Protection Certificate for James Wilkerson of Virginia, issued by consular agent in Amsterdam, the Netherlands

DOCUMENT 1.20.5: Seaman's Protection Certificate for Samuel Fox of Philadelphia

## Supplementary Materials

Item 1.5.B: Map of the Atlantic world

## Vocabulary

| | | | |
|---|---|---|---|
| cast away | dungeon | leagues (a | press-gang |
| cutlass | gaol | measure of | provisions |
| doldrums | impressment | distance) | reef |

## Student Activities

### Mapping Hammon's Journeys

*Activity 1*

After reading selections from Briton Hammon's *Narrative* (1.20.1), students use a map of the Atlantic world (Item 1.5.B) to chart his journeys at sea during his thirteen years away from Massachusetts.

Activity 2    **Reading and Discussion of Hammon's *Narrative***

Following a careful reading of selections from the *Narrative of Briton Hammon*, students discuss the dangers any sailor faced at sea. They may want to speculate how Hammon's experiences may have differed from those of a white sailor. Discuss Hammon's reaction to discovering his owner on board Capt. Watt's vessel.

Activity 3    **Research and Discussion—Work at Sea**

Working in small groups, students examine several Seaman's Protection Certificates 1.20.2–1.20.5). (Words such as certify, citizen, collector, district, protection, pursuant, relief, seaman, and witness may need to be defined.) They then discuss the kinds of employment men of color had during the eighteenth century and the opportunities that work at sea offered black men. Students report back on their discussions to the entire class.

Activity 4    **Creative Extensions**

The Seaman's Protection Certificates offered men of color and their white counterparts proofs of there legal "citizenship." What do students possess that is as important to them as a protection certificate would have been to a black seaman? Students can write, dramatize, or create a visual in response to this question.

Activity 5    **Create a Protection Certificate**

Students design their own protection certificate. What information did the Seaman's Protection Certificates provide? What information would students include on their protection certificate and why?

Activity 6    **Compare and Contrast Travel Documents**

What does a modern-day passport look like? Students study a current U.S. passport and (if applicable) passports from other countries where classmates were born. What is the same and what is different from a Seaman's Protection Certificate? Why might these changes have taken place?

## Further Student and Teacher Resources

Bolster, W. Jeffrey. *Black Jacks: African American Seamen in the Age of Sail*. Cambridge, MA: Harvard University Press, 1997.

Diamond, Arthur. *Paul Cuffe: Merchant and Abolitionist*. New York: Chelsea House Publishers, 1989. (Part of the *Black Americans of Achievement* series, with an introduction by Coretta Scott King. Particularly good for middle school students.)

## Contemporary Connection 1

⟞⟊⟝

### Paul Cuffe's Legacy

Paul Cuffe, a very successful African American ship owner, trader, and navigator of the late eighteenth and early nineteenth centuries, is well remembered in southern Massachusetts, where he lived, and in neighboring Rhode Island. One of his accomplishments was to fund and build a school in his hometown of Westport, Massachusetts, that welcomed both black and white children. In September 2001, a new charter school in Providence, Rhode Island, was named for Paul Cuffe.

The school has a maritime theme and is open to children of all races and backgrounds. Its mission is "to increase the diversity of students pursuing scientific and technical careers through high quality academic and maritime training in a kindergarten through 12th grade program." As part of this program, children learn how to swim, paddle, row, and sail. They study maritime history, literature of the sea, navigation, ecology, and environmental issues. Older students have opportunities to learn boat building and restoration, commercial fishing, and scientific research done from boats. A possible research project for students would be the life of Paul Cuffe, especially his commitment to education.

Since 1989, Mystic Seaport in Connecticut has provided funds to researchers from universities, colleges, and museums through its Paul Cuffe Memorial Fellowship. The fellowship was expressly established for the study of minorities in American maritime history. Check *www.mysticseaport.org*

## Contemporary Connection 2

⟞⟊⟝

### Blacks on the Chesapeake Foundation

In 2003, the Speaker of the Maryland House of Delegates bestowed the title "Admiral of the Chesapeake" on Vincent O. Leggett. He joins a line of individuals honored in this way for service to the great bay. Leggett, a former public school teacher, has made his life work researching, documenting, and writing about the contributions of African Americans to the maritime and seafood industries of Chesapeake Bay.

In 1984, he founded the Blacks of Chesapeake Project, and in 1999 became the president of Blacks on the Chesapeake Foundation, a nonprofit historical, cultural, and environmental organization. In 2000, the foundation received the Local Legacy Award presented by the United States Congress and the Library of Congress. His most recent research project is "Chesapeake Underground: Charting a Course Toward Freedom." His two previous books are *Blacks of the Chesapeake: An Integral Part of Maritime History (1997)* and *The Chesapeake Bay Through Ebony Eyes* (1999).

Kaplan, Sidney, and Emma Nogrady Kaplan. *The Black Presence in the Era of the American Revolution*. Amherst: University of Massachusetts Press, 1989.

Malloy, Mary. *African Americans in the Maritime Trades: A Guide to Resources in New England*. Sharon, MA: Kendall Whaling Museum, 1990. (Malloy's book is available at the New Bedford Whaling Museum in Massachusetts.)

Westgate, Michael. *Captain Paul Cuffe (1759–1817), A One-Man Civil Rights Movement, 3 Vols*: Boston: Museum of the National Center for Afro-American Artists and Education and Resources Group (ERG), Pilot Edition, 1989.

# Primary Source Materials
## for Lesson 20

1.20.1

Excerpts from *"A Narrative of the Uncommon Sufferings, and Surprising Deliverance of* BRITON HAMMON, A NEGRO MAN," 1760

*"Hammon's* Narrative," *writes Jeffrey Bolster in* Black Jacks, *"the first voyage account published by a black American, indicates the extent to which enslaved sailors and nominally free men of African descent rode economic and military currents to every corner of the eighteenth-century Atlantic world."*

Containing

An account of the many hardships he underwent from the time he left his master's house, in the year 1747, to the time of his return to Boston.—How he was cast away in the capes of Florida,—The horrid Cruelty and inhuman Barbarity of the Indians in murdering the whole ship's crew,—the manner of his being carry'd by them into captivity. Also, an account of his being confined four years and seven months in a close dungeon,—And the remarkable manner in which he met with his good old master in London; who returned to New England, a passenger, in the same ship.

BOSTON, Printed and sold by Green & Russell,
in Queen-Street, 1760.

ON Monday, 25th day of *December,* 1747, with the leave of my master, I went from Marshfield, with an Intention to go a voyage to sea, and the next day, the 26th, got to Plymouth, where I immediately ship'd myself on board of a Sloop, Capt. John Howland, Master, bound to Jamaica and the Bay. We sailed from Plymouth in a short time, and after a pleasant passage of about 30 days, arrived at Jamaica; we was detain'd at Jamaica only 5 days, from whence we sailed for the Bay, where we arrived safe in 10 days. We loaded our vessel with longwood, and sailed from the Bay the 25th day of May following, and the 15th we were cast away on Cape Florida, about 5 leagues from the shore; being now destitute of every help, we knew not what to do or what course to take in this our sad condition . . . .

**The full text of Document 1.20.1 is available on the CD-ROM.**

## 1.20.2

## Seaman's Protection Certificate for Edward Scare, issued in Virginia

No. 313

### STATE OF VIRGINIA,
*DISTRICT OF NORFOLK AND PORTSMOUTH.*

I WILSON C. NICHOLAS, Collector of the District of Norfolk and Portsmouth, do hereby certify, that *Edward Score* an American Seaman, aged *Thirty Two* years, or thereabouts, of the height of *five* feet, *Seven* inches, of a *Dark* complexion, *Dark* hair *Hagle Eyes has a Scar on the back Was born in The Town of Boston in the State of Massachusetts*

Hath this day produced to me proof in the manner directed in the Act, entitled, " *An Act for the Relief and Protection of American Seamen ;*", and pursuant to the said Act, I do hereby certify that the said *Edward Score* is a Citizen of the United States of America.

IN WITNESS whereof, I have hereunto set my Hand and Seal of Office, this *Thirty first* day of *August* one thousand eight hundred and

*Wm Thomson D. coll*

4389

National Archives of the United States

## 1.20.3

## Seaman's Protection Certificate for Charles Storey, issued in Gloucester, Massachusetts

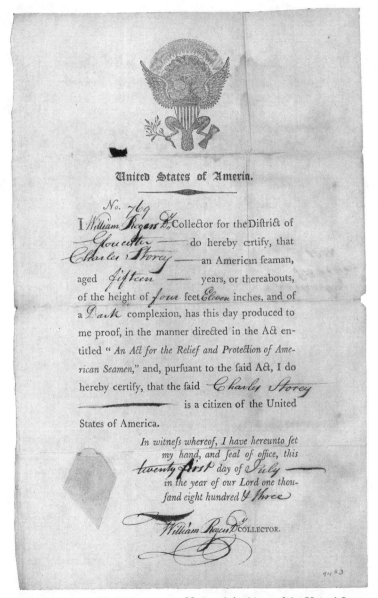

National Archives of the United States

## 1.20.4

## Seaman's Protection Certificate for James Wilkerson of Virginia, issued by consular agent in Amsterdam, The Netherlands

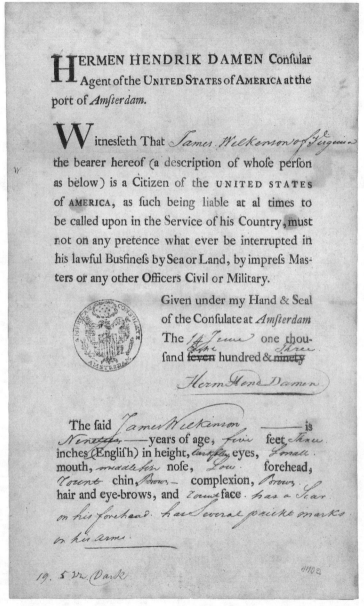

National Archives of the United States

1.20.5

## Seaman's Protection Certificate for Samuel Fox of Philadelphia

National Archives of the United States

Educators can contact National Archives for additional samples of Seaman's Protection Certificates for men of color.

# Glossary

*Adinkra:* type of cloth made by the Ashanti people of Ghana.

**Akan:** a cluster of ethnic groups living in southern Ghana and adjacent parts of the Ivory Coast and Togo.

**amber:** a hard translucent yellow, orange, or brownish-yellow fossil resin, used for making jewelry and other ornamental objects.

**American plantation:** large agricultural enterprises, employing twenty or more slaves producing cash crops such as sugar, rice, indigo, tobacco, and cotton for domestic and foreign markets.

**archaeology:** the systematic study of past human life and culture by the recovery and examination of remaining material evidence, such as graves, buildings, tools, and pottery.

**archaic:** of, relating to, or characteristic of a much earlier, historical period.

**arraignment:** calling an accused person before a court to answer the charge made against him or her by indictment, information, or complaint.

**artifact:** an object produced or shaped by human craft, especially a tool, weapon, or ornament of archaeological or historical interest—a product of human conception.

**artisan:** a skilled manual worker, or craftsperson, who practices some trade or handicraft.

**atlas:** a book or bound collection of maps, sometimes with supplementary illustrations and graphic analysis.

**benefactor:** one that gives aid, especially financial aid; one who confers a benefit or benefits.

**Benin:** a kingdom of western Africa, now part of Nigeria, that flourished from the fourteenth to the seventeenth centuries.

**bequeath:** to leave or give property by a will.

**Berber:** a member of a North African, primarily Muslim, people living in settled or nomadic groups from Morocco to Egypt; any Afro-Asiatic language of the Berbers.

**Bight of Benin:** a wide indentation of the Gulf of Guinea in West Africa.

**bile:** bitterness of temper, ill humor, irascibility, bitterness of feeling, choler, anger.

**Bondu:** French protectorate in West Africa dependent on Senegal lying between the Falene River and the upper course of the Gambia River.

**"bred to the house":** a term to describe a slave, male or female, who performed household work from the time he or she was old enough to work.

**"bright mulatto wench":** a young woman of mixed African and European descent, in her late teens or early twenties, who had light-colored skin.

**Broteer:** the original African name of Venture Smith.

**call and response:** a pattern of singing from West Africa in which a leader calls out the verses and a group joins in the refrain; found in African American religious music and work songs.

**Canary Islands:** a group of islands in the Atlantic Ocean off the northwest coast of Africa; the Canaries have been part of Spain since 1479.

**canoe:** a light, open, slender boat that has pointed ends and is propelled by men with paddles.

**canoe farming:** a method of farming rice plantations that required extensive irrigation systems and maintenance; navigating these waterways via canoes provided a useful way of cultivating this labor-intensive crop.

**Cape Verde Islands:**   a group of islands in the Atlantic Ocean off the coast of Senegal; formerly controlled by Portugal and now independent.

**caravel:**   any of several types of small, light sailing ships, especially one with two or three masts and lateen sails used by the Spanish and Portuguese in the fifteenth and sixteenth centuries.

**castaway:**   a neglected or discarded person.

**castle:**   heavily armed forts built along the West African coast, providing European captains with safe harbor and serving as a holding place for enslaved Africans awaiting shipment.

**chaferyman:**   man who works in a type of forge.

**chaff:**   the husks that are removed when grain is thrashed and winnowed; also straw used as bedding for animals or people.

**charter:**   a written grant from the sovereign power of a country conferring certain rights on a person, a corporation, or group of people.

**Christian:**   professing belief in Jesus Christ or following religions based on the life and teachings of Jesus.

**clinch work:**   a kind of hitch in which the end of the rope is fastened back by seizing.

**collier:**   coal miner.

**commerce:**   the buying and selling of goods, especially on a large scale, as between cities or nations.

**Congo River:**   a river of Central Africa flowing about 2,900 miles north, west, and southwest through the Democratic Republic of the Congo (formerly Zaire) into the south Atlantic.

**conspiracy:**   a group of people bonded together to perform an illegal or subversive act.

**conversion:**   a change in which one adopts a new religion, faith, or belief.

**cooper:**   one who makes or repairs casks, barrels, or tubs.

**copperas:**   cloth that has been dyed green.

**covenant:**   a binding agreement; a compact.

**cowrie shells:**   seashells used as form of currency in Benin.

**creole:**   a person of European descent born in the West Indies or Spanish America, or a person of mixed European and African descent born in Louisiana.

**cultivation:**   production of food by preparing the land and planting and tending crops.

**cultural exchange:**   a sharing of ideas, artifacts, skills, and customs between cultures.

**current:**   general tendency, movement, or course.

**cutlass:**   a short, heavy sword with a curved, single-edged blade, once used as a weapon by sailors.

**delta:**   triangular alluvial deposit at the mouth of a river.

**desert:**   a barren or desolate area.

**desertion:**   withdrawing support or help despite allegiance or responsibility; leaving naval or military service without permission.

**diplomacy:**   the art or practice of conducting international relations, as in negotiating alliances, treaties, and agreements; resolving international conflicts without conducting war.

**ditty:**   a simple song.

**doctrine:**   a principle or body of principles presented for acceptance or belief, as by a religious, political, scientific, or philosophical group.

**doldrums:**   a region of the ocean near the equator, characterized by calms, light winds, or squalls.

**draft:**   depth of a boat, or the depth of water in which it can navigate.

**driver:**   a person who supervises slaves working in the fields.

**dropsy:**   swelling from excessive accumulation of fluid in tissue.

**ducat:**   a piece of money; coin usually gold or silver.

**dungeon:**   a dark, often underground chamber or cell used to confine prisoners.

**Edo:**   ethnic group of Nigeria; ruled the kingdom of Benin between the fifteenth and nineteenth centuries.

**equator:**   imaginary great circle around the earth's surface dividing the earth into the Northern Hemisphere and the Southern Hemisphere.

**estate:**   the whole of one's possessions, especially all the property and debts left by one at death.

**ethnology:**   branch of anthropology that describes the characteristics of particular cultures based on observation and documentation.

**ethnomusicology:**   the comparative study of music of different cultures.

**evidence:**   information or objects used to draw a conclusion or arrive at a legal judgement.

**excavate:**   to expose or uncover by digging as in archaeology

**executor:**   person appointed by a testator to carry out the terms of the will.

**extant:**   still in existence; not destroyed, lost, or extinct.

**factory:**   also known as a fort or castle, the place where enslaved Africans awaited shipment.

**fancier:**   one who breeds a plant or animal for those features held to be desirable.

**finer:**   one who finishes items produced in a blacksmith shop.

**finery:**   hearth where cast iron is made malleable; show clothing

**flat:**   a flat-bottomed boat used to transport goods on a river.

**floodplain:**   a flat area bordering a river and subject to flooding.

**Flowerdew Hundred:**   the name of a Virginia plantation built in 1619.

**flux:**   mineral added to the metals in a furnace to promote fusing.

**fort:**   a fortified place or position stationed with troops; a place where slaves were held on the West African coast before transatlantic shipment.

**fossil:**   a remnant or trace of an organism of a past geologic age, such as a skeleton or leaf imprint embedded and preserved in the earth's crust.

**functionary:**   one who holds an office or a trust or performs a particular function.

**Futah Jallon:**   highland region of 30,000 square miles in central Guinea, West Africa; a stronghold of Islam since the eighteenth century.

**Gambia River:**   a river of western Africa flowing about 700 miles from northern Guinea through southeast Senegal and Gambia to the Atlantic Ocean at Banjul.

**gaol:**   jail.

**Genoa:**   seaport in northwestern Italy, provincial capital of Liguria.

**girded:**   fastened or secured with a belt or bond.

**Governor's pardon:**   a provincial or colonial governor could grant a pardon to anyone convicted of a crime, including those sentenced to death.

**Governour:**   head of a provincial or colonial government; also the superior official at a British outpost on the coast of West Africa.

**Gromettoes:**   free or enslaved black men employed in the Royal African Company's factories who could not be sold to transatlantic slave traders.

**Guinea:**   historical region of western and equatorial Africa extending along the coast from Gambia to Angola.

**Gulf of Guinea:**   broad inlet of the Atlantic Ocean formed by the great bend in the west-central coast of Africa.

**gum arabic:**   natural product that is exuded from the stems and branches of the acacia tree.

**hillocks:**   small hills.

**hiring out:**   the process by which a white person hired a slave owned by another white person to work for a day, a week, a month, or an entire year.

**hiring himself or herself out:**   the process by which a slave agreed to work for a white person and pay his or her master a set sum out of those earnings.

**hostler:**   one who takes care of horses, especially at an inn or tavern.

**House of Commons:**   the lower house of the British Parliament, with representatives elected by voters.

**husbandry:**   act or practice of cultivating crops and breeding and raising livestock; agriculture.

**Ibo/Eboe:**   one of the largest ethnic groups in modern Nigeria; members had a sense of cultural unity and were able to unite for political action.

**impingement:**   to collide, strike, encroach, or trespass.

**impressment:**   forcible enrollment of men for military duty; in this case, of merchant seamen into the navy.

**improvement (as used in wills during this period):**   an increase in value.

**indemnify:**   to make compensation for damage, loss, or injury suffered.

**indigenous:**   originating and living or occurring naturally in an area or environment.

**indigoterie:**   a factory that processed the indigo plant into blue dyestuff.

**infidel:**   an unbeliever with respect to a particular religion.

**inquiry:**   a close examination of a matter in a search for information or truth.

**inter:**   to place a dead body in a grave or tomb.

**"Interloper":**   an illegal slave trader, one without a license to trade granted by the government, for example, the Royal African Company.

**Islam:**   a monotheistic religion originating in the Middle East characterized by the recognition of Muhammad as the chief and last prophet of God.

**jollof:**   in Ghana, a traditional rice dish.

**jula (djoula):**   a Mandinka term for Moslem scholars who also traded; in some cases they constructed their own villages and held land, worked by their own slaves, who provided the merchants with provisions for their commercial expeditions.

**justification:**  something that shows an action to be reasonable or necessary.

**Kanem Bornu:**  an African Empire that practiced the Islamic faith; at the height of the empire, it controlled territory from Libya to Lake Chad to Hausaland.

**Kano (a major Hausa state):**  located in Nigeria, its history dates back to C.E. 949. It was a cultural, handicraft, and commercial center with wide trade contracts with western and northern Africa, and accepted Islam in the early sixteenth century.

**key:**  legend for a map.

**Kongo:**  a people living in west central Africa, along the lower Congo River.

**Koran:**  the sacred text of Islam, considered by Muslims to contain the revelations of God to Muhammad.

**league:**  a unit of distance equal to 3.0 statute miles.

**log boat:**  boat carved out of the trunk of a tree.

**lottery:**  (in the eighteenth century) a method by which some gentry tried to raise money to pay off debts; individuals bought chances for various lots of another individual's personal property, often including slaves.

**"lycence to trade":**  permission granted by a government to trade in a certain port or area.

**Madeira:**  island 350 miles off Morocco, occupied by Britain in the nineteenth century; sugar cane and wine are produced here.

*manilla:*  piece of copper or metal shaped like a horseshoe or ring used as money by some peoples of West Africa.

**Mansa Musa:**  King of Mali ruled from C.E. 1307 to 1332; Mali became the richest and largest realm in Africa during his reign; remembered for his pilgrimage to Mecca.

**manumission:**  setting a person free from slavery or bondage, done by slave owner.

**marabout:**  Muslim hermit or saint, especially in northern Africa.

**maritime:**  of, relating to, or adjacent to the sea, marine shipping, or navigation.

**"Marks of his Country" (also "country marks," "marked in the face," "long marks down each of his cheeks," and "some Scars on his Temples"):**  terms that refer to the ritual scarification that a number of the Africans had on their bodies when they were sold into slavery; the "country marks" helped to preserve aspects of the cultures that Africans brought with them to the American colonies during the eighteenth century.

**medicinal:**  a preparation or product having healing properties.

**medieval:**  relating to or belonging to the Middle Ages (ca. C.E. 1100–1350).

**melancholia:**  mental disorder characterized by severe depression, guilt, hopelessness, and withdrawal.

**merchant:**  one whose occupation is the wholesale purchase and retail sale of goods for profit.

**Middle Passage:**  journey of slave ships across the Atlantic Ocean between the west coast of Africa and the West Indies, the longest and most dangerous part of the journey made by slave ships.

**militia:**  an army composed of ordinary citizens rather than professional soldiers.

**monopoly:**  exclusive control by one group of the means of producing or selling a commodity or service.

**Moor:**  a member of a Muslim people of mixed Berber and Arab descent; now living chiefly in northwest Africa.

**mortar and pestle:**  a strong container in which substances are finely ground by a pestle, a small, handheld tool.

**motif:**  a recurrent thematic element in an artistic or literary work; a dominant theme or central idea.

**mulatto:**  a person with both African and European ancestry; in the eighteenth century; the term could also refer to a person of mixed Native American and African ancestry.

**Muslim:**  a believer in or adherent of Islam.

**muslin:**  sturdy cotton fabrics of plain weave.

**mustee:**  the Spanish term for a person of mixed Native American and African ancestry.

**mutiny:**  open rebellion against constituted authority, especially rebellion of sailors against superior officers aboard ship.

**narrow-beamed:**  referring to a boat that is narrow in width.

**nautical:**  of, relating to, or characteristic of ships, shipping, sailors, or navigation on a body of water.

**navigation:** theory and practice of charting a course for a ship; travel or traffic by vessels, especially commercial shipping.

**"new Negro":** a term used to describe an enslaved African who had recently been brought to America.

**"Newlight preacher":** a Baptist preacher.

**Niger River:** a river of western Africa rising in Guinea and flowing about 2,600 miles in a wide arc through Mali, Niger, and Nigeria to the Gulf of Guinea.

**nomadic pastoralists:** shepherds or herders with no fixed settlement, who move with the seasons from place to place in search of food, water, and grazing land.

**numismatic:** of or relating to coins or currency.

**Nzinga:** queen of the Mbundo in Angola, leading opponent of Portuguese colonialism.

**oasis:** fertile or green spot in a desert or wasteland, made so by the presence of water.

**oblation:** the act of offering something, such as worship or thanks, to a deity or ancestral spirits.

**"outlawed":** an escaped slave who could be killed by men trying to capture him without their incurring any legal penalty.

*padrao:* stone pillar (Portuguese).

**palliation:** to make an offense or crime less serious.

**parched meal:** slightly roasted ground grain, usually corn.

**pass:** written permission for a slave to be away from his or her master's plantation or house.

**patroon:** a landholder in New Netherland who, under Dutch colonial rule, was granted propriety and mayoral rights to a large tract of land in exchange for bringing 50 new colonists.

**perspective:** a person or group's characteristic way of understanding or interpreting situations or subjects; a point of view.

**petition:** formal written document requesting a right or benefit from a person or group in authority.

**pig iron:** crude iron cast in blocks.

**pilgrimage:** a journey to a sacred place or shrine, especially one with religious or moral significance.

**pinioned:** restrained or immobilized by binding the arms.

**"Pock-fretten":** a term used to describe a person whose face had scars from smallpox.

**polygamy:** condition or practice of a man having more than one wife at one time.

**pound sterling (£):** English legal tender; 20 shillings made up 1 pound.

**Poythress:** surname of an eighteenth-century Virginia family who lived at Flowerdew Hundred plantation in the eighteenth century.

**press-gang:** a group commissioned to force men into military service, particularly into the navy.

**privateer:** a ship privately owned and crewed but authorized by a government during wartime to attack and capture enemy vessels, including merchant ships, and take them as a "prize."

**province:** territory governed as an administrative or political unit within a country or empire.

**provisions:** stipulation or qualification, especially a clause in a document or agreement; or food and clothing supplied to seamen, slaves, and others unable to purchase these necessities for themselves.

**purge:** to remove impurities and other elements by or as if by cleansing.

**radio-carbon dating:** the determination of the approximate age of an ancient object, such as an archaeological specimen, by measuring the amount of carbon 14 it contains.

**raffia and raffia basket:** African palm tree having large leaves that yield a useful fiber; the leaf fibers of this plant are used for mats, blankets, and baskets.

**realm:** region, sphere, or domain.

**reef:** portion of a sail rolled and tied down to lessen the area exposed to the wind; strip or ridge of rocks, sand, or coral that rises to or near the surface of a body of water.

**rivalry:** act of competing, as for a profit or a prize.

**Royal African Company:** British monopoly on the slave trade; established in 1672; between 1680 and 1686, it transported 5,000 slaves a year.

**sahel:** semiarid region of north central Africa south of the Sahara Desert.

**saltcellar:** container for salt.

**Sao Tome:** island in the Gulf of Guinea; important trade center for slaves.

**saracen:** a member of a pre-Islamic nomadic people of the Syrian-Arabian deserts.

**savanna:** a flat grassland of tropical or subtropical regions.

**sawyer:** one who saws

**seasoned:** to render suitable or appropriate, to prepare; also refers to the process of adaptation enslaved

Africans and other colonists underwent during their initial years in the Americas.

**Senegal:**  republic in western Africa on the Atlantic coast.

**Senegal River:**  river of western Africa rising in western Mali and flowing about 1,000 miles generally northwest and west along the Mauritania.

**Senegambia:**  former federation incorporating both Senegal and Gambia.

**shackles:**  metal fastening used for encircling and confining the ankle or wrist of a prisoner, captive, or slave.

*sheikh:*  a religious official or leader of an Arab family or village.

**shilling:**  twenty shillings made up a pound sterling British currency.

**Sierra Leone River:**  now known as the Rokel River; Freetown, the capital of Sierra Leone, lies at its mouth.

**sovereignty:**  complete independence and self-government.

**strip weaving:**  made by men on narrow, double-heddle looms; several long, narrow bands of cloth are woven and then sewed together side by side to make one large piece of cloth.

**Sudan:**  a region of northern Africa south of the Sahara Desert and north of the equator; it extends across the continent from the Atlantic coast to the mountains of Ethiopia.

**sweetgrass:**  grass that grows from underground runners and rarely produces seeds, found along coastal waterways and used in  basket making.

**tell:**  a mound, especially in the Middle East, made up of the remains of a succession of previous settlements.

**testator:**  one who makes a legally valid will before death.

**thrashing:**  a severe beating.

**threshing:**  to separate grain or seeds from the husks.

**Timbuktu:**  city in central Mali near the Niger River, formerly famous for its gold trade.

**topography:**  detailed, precise description of the geography of a place or region.

**traffick:**  (as used in this context) importation of slaves.

**transmigration:**  the passing of the soul after death into another mortal body.

**transmission:**  act of sending a message or causing a message to be transmitted; also, the carrying of cultural elements from one place to another by migrants.

**tropical forest:**  warm, moist tropical lowlands having both a high temperature and plentiful rainfall.

**vessel:**  a craft, especially one larger than a rowboat, designed to navigate over water; a hollow utensil, such as a cup, vase, or pitcher, used as a container for liquids.

**victuals:**  food fit for human consumption, source of nourishment.

**waiting man:**  a personal servant, sometimes a slave, who tended to the daily needs of a gentleman.

**waterman, or one who "followed the water":**  a male slave who worked on the water; a waterman carried goods from one plantation to another on a flat-bottomed boat, caught fish, and transported people across creeks.

**whitlow:**  an inflamed sore or swelling in a finger or thumb, usually at a joint.

**winnowing:**  to separate the grain from the chaff, or the good from the bad.

**work-calls and response-calls:**  ways Africans (and others) could develop a rhythm among workers for such repetitive and strenuous work as farming, manufacturing, and sailing; using phrases, words, sounds, and gestures, a caller would establish a rhythmic, pace, as well as community, and workers could respond with a phrase, song, sound, and movement that would help the work move along. This mode of communication was brought over from Africa and, in the Americas, was used in many kinds of work.

**"yellow complexion":**  a light, or "bright," mulatto face.

✥

# Credits

Document 1.1.1: Used by permission of the National Geographic Society.

Documents 1.1.2 and 1.1.3: Used by permission of Dr. Roderick James McIntosh, Professor of Anthropology.

Document 1.2.1: Courtesy of the Bibliothèque Nationale de France.

Document 1.2.2: Reproduced by permission of The Huntington Library, San Marino, California.

Document 1.2.3: Carta Universal de Juan de la Cosa (1500) is used by permission of Museo Naval de Madrid.

Document 1.3.3: From *Servants of Allah: African Muslims Enslaved in the Americas* by Sylviane Diouf. New York: New York University Press, 1998, 82–83. Used by permission of New York University Press.

Documents 1.3.8 and 1.3.9: © Copyright The British Museum.

Document 1.3.10: Courtesy of The Metropolitan Museum of Art, Gift of Mr. and Mrs. Klaus G. Perls, 1991 (1991.17.13). Photograph, all rights reserved, The Metropolitan Museum of Art.

Documents 1.4.1, 1.4.2, 1.4.3, and 1.4.4: From *Documents Illustrative of the History of the Slave Trade to America* by Elizabeth Donnan. New York: Octagon Books, 1969. Used by permission of Hippocrene Books.

Document 1.4.6: Used by permission of the Rare Books Division, New York Public Library.

Document 1.4.7: Photograph by Roberta Logan.

Documents 1.5.1, 1.5.2, and 1.5.3: From *Sweetness and Power* by Sidney W. Mintz. Copyright © 1985 by Sidney W. Mintz. Used by permission of Viking Penguin, a division of Penguin Group (USA) Inc.

Documents 1.6.2, 1.9.5, and 1.9.6: Courtesy of the American Antiquarian Society.

Extract about indigo in the introduction of Lesson 10: *From Africans in Colonial Louisiana: The Development of Afro-Creole Culture in the Eighteenth Century* by Gwendolyn Midlo Hall. Copyright © 1992 by Louisiana State University Press. Reprinted by permission of Louisiana State University Press.

Document 1.10.1: Used by permission of La Société d'Histoire de la Guadeloupe.

Document 1.10.2: From *Africans in Colonial Louisiana: The Development of Afro-Creole Culture in the Eighteenth Century* by Gwendolyn Midlo Hall. Copyright © 1992 by Louisiana State University Press. Reprinted by permission of Louisiana State University Press.

Documents 1.11.1 and 1.11.2: Courtesy of Colonial Williamsburg Foundation.

Documents 1.11.3 and 1.11.4: Courtesy of the Library of Congress.

Document 1.12.1: Courtesy of the Boston Athenæum.

Document 1.12.2: From *The History of Africa*, edited by Alvin Josephy, Jr. American Heritage Publishing Company, 1971. Used by permission of American Heritage Picture Collection.

Document 1.13.2: Courtesy of the South Carolina Department of Archives and History Picture Collection, Box 6, Folder 23 (P900051).

Document 1.13.3: Courtesy of the Georgia Division of Archives and History, Office of Secretary of State.

Documents 1.14.1, 1.14.3, 1.14.4, and 1.14.5: Photographs by Renée Covalucci.

Document 1.14.2: Courtesy of the Museum of Fine Arts, Boston, Bequest of Maxim Karolik; 64.619. Photograph © 2003 Museum of Fine Arts, Boston.

Document 1.14.7: Used by permission of G. F. Kojo Arthur and CEFIKS Publications.

Documents 1.14.8, 1.14.9, and 1.14.10: Copyright © 2002 by Tinwood Books.

Document 1.15.1: Reprinted with permission of *The News & Observer* of Raleigh, North Carolina.

Document 1.16.3: Courtesy of The Historical Society of Pennsylvania Collection, Atwater Kent Museum of Philadelphia.

Document 1.16.5: *From Breaking Ground, Breaking Silence: The Story of New York's African Burial Ground* by Joyce Hansen and Gary McGowan. Copyright © 1998 by Joyce Hansen and Gary McGowan. Reprinted by permission of Henry Holt and Company, LLC.